Help (Not) Wanted

Help (Not) Wanted

Immigration Politics in Japan

MICHAEL STRAUSZ

SUNY
PRESS

Cover image (center): Gabriele Vogt. Image reprinted with permission.

Published by State University of New York Press, Albany

© 2019 State University of New York

For information, contact State University of New York Press, Albany, NY
www.sunypress.edu

Library of Congress Cataloging-in-Publication Data

Names: Strausz, Michael, author.
Title: Help (not) wanted : immigration politics in Japan / Michael Strausz.
Description: Albany : State University of New York Press, [2019] | Includes
  bibliographical references and index.
Identifiers: LCCN 2018040416 | ISBN 9781438475516 (hardcover) |
    ISBN 9781438475523 (pbk.) | ISBN 9781438475530 (ebook) Subjects: LCSH:
                    Japan—Emigration and immigration—Government policy. |
  Japan—Emigration and immigration—Social aspects. | Foreign workers—Japan.
Classification: LCC JV8723 .S87 2019 | DDC 325.52—dc23
LC record available at https://lccn.loc.gov/2018040416

10 9 8 7 6 5 4 3 2 1

Contents

List of Figures and Tables   vii

Preface   xi

Acknowledgments   xiii

Chapter 1
Foreign Laborers, Not Immigrants   1

Chapter 2
Help Wanted: Immigration Restriction in a World of Labor
Shortages, Aging Populations, and Refugee Crises   5

Chapter 3
Minority Rights and Minority Invisibility: Oldcomer Koreans
in Japan   29

Chapter 4
The Crow Is White: Foreign Labor and the Japanese State   61

Chapter 5
Asylum as Exception   93

Chapter 6
Is Another Japan Possible? Public Opinion and Immigration
Reformists   121

vi / Contents

Chapter 7
Japanese Immigration in the Age of Trump   143

Appendix: Description of Interview Subjects   157

Notes   161

References   169

Index   183

Figures and Tables

Figures

2.1 Percentage of firms having difficulty filling jobs in Organization for Economic Cooperation and Development (OECD) countries 6

2.2 Labor shortages and foreign residents in OECD countries 7

2.3 Aging populations and foreign residents in OECD countries 8

2.4 Models of immigration control policy among select countries 19

3.1 Map of South Korean Special Permanent Residents per thousand people in Japanese prefectures, 2017 35

4.1 Undocumented foreign residents in Japan 65

4.2 Japan's job-seeker ratio 68

4.3 Percentage employed in agriculture 69

4.4 Entertainer visas in postwar Japan 77

4.5 Nurses and caregivers admitted to Japan by Economic Partnership Agreements 79

4.6 Trainees and technical interns in Japan 82

4.7 Trainees and technical interns by industry, 2016 83

4.8 Trainees and technical interns and labor shortages in Japanese prefectures, 2017 85

4.9   Maps of labor shortages and trainees and technical
      interns in Japan, 2017   86–87

4.10 South Americans and trainees and technical interns in Japan   89

5.1   Asylum in Japan and the European Union   95

5.2   Asylum applicants and asylum approvals in Japan   96

5.3   Japan's annual admissions of and quota for Indochinese
      refugees   99

6.1   Diet members' (DM) views on whether Japan should
      promote the admission of foreign labor   135

6.2   DMs' views on whether Japan should promote the
      admission of foreign labor, by party   136

6.3   House of Representatives DMs' views and the public's views
      on whether Japan should promote the admission of foreign
      labor, by party   136

6.4   Public opinion and House of Representatives DMs' views on
      whether Japan should promote the admission of foreign
      labor, by prefecture, 2009   137

6.5   Public opinion and House of Representatives DMs' views
      on whether Japan should promote the admission of foreign
      labor, by prefecture, 2012   138

6.6   Public opinion and House of Representatives DMs' views
      on whether Japan should promote the admission of foreign
      labor, by prefecture, 2014   139

Tables

2.1   Percent foreign populations in Organization for Economic
      Cooperation and Development (OECD) countries, 2013   25

4.1   Foreign residents of Japan in 2017 by citizenship   63

4.2   Foreign residents of Japan in 2017 by visa type   64

5.1   Refugee populations in OECD countries, 2016   93

5.2   Japan's resettlement of Indochinese refugees compared with
       G7 countries, 1975–1994   103

6.1   Reaction to the statement "Japan should promote the
       admission of foreign labor" by Liberal Democratic Party
       House of Representatives candidates who were members
       of the Caucus for the Promotion of Foreign Human
       Resources   133

Preface

Today, Japanese people are having no more than two children per couple. If we continue like this, after 200 years there will be no Japanese people. You need not be worried about Japan.

—Prime Minister Kakuei Takana, answering a question about the resurgence of Japanese militarism from Chinese Premier Zhou Enlai in 1972 (Ishii et al. 2003: 65)

Toward the end of my field research for this book, I interviewed a Diet member (DM) from the Clean Government Party (CGP) who was particularly knowledgeable about economic issues and opposed to immigration. He stated that if firms want to solve labor shortages, they should just raise their wages. I asked him about the limitations of that strategy, given that Japan's declining population means that there are too few laborers overall, so even if one sector can solve its labor shortage with domestic labor by raising wages, laborers would have to leave another sector, thus intensifying the labor shortage there. In reply, he observed how Japanese companies in Mexico, for example, have Japanese managers and Mexican workers, and he said that he did not want foreign bosses to manage Japanese workers in Japan. Japan must focus on high-value products, he said. Otherwise Japanese will be hired as cheap laborers (interview 1123).[1]

This answer is telling because it reveals that, even among those extremely well versed in economic issues, immigration is much more than an economic issue; it is an issue of national identity. This DM has a vision of Japanese national identity that is primarily ethnic, and he sees the idea of ethnic Japanese, in Japan, working for foreign managers, as a challenge to something essential about Japan's national identity.

The title of this book, *Help (Not) Wanted*, refers to three different things. First, it refers to the specific problems stemming from *shōshikōreika*—Japan's dual problems of low birthrate and long life expectancy. In short, who will help care for Japan's elderly, given the small size of the working-age generation relative to the large size of the retired and retiring generation? This question is more vexing because many people, like the DM whom I referenced above, see immigration as threatening something essential about Japan's national identity. Second, the title refers to the common slogan on the windows and doors of businesses that are seeking employees. Japan is currently facing a labor shortage, so these signs are all over the country. Finally, the title is an understated reference to the cries of refugees fleeing oppression all over the world. These are people that need help, in a critical and immediate sense. Most advanced industrialized countries could do more to help refugees, but Japan is particularly unlikely to admit these people and grant them asylum.

The thread tying all three of these senses of the phrase "help wanted" together is Japan's extremely restrictive immigration policy and its very small population of foreign residents. Japan's population of foreign residents is among the lowest in the advanced industrialized world, and this is particularly puzzling given its labor shortages, its crisis of *shōshikōreika*, and the ways in which its often takes its responsibilities to the rest of the world very seriously. In this book, I explain why Japan has not yet answered the three different voices asking for help by admitting foreign laborers, particularly foreign nurses, or refugees.

Acknowledgments

Parts of chapter 3 are reproduced with permission from Michael Strausz, "Japanese Conservatism and the Integration of Foreign Residents," *Japanese Journal of Political Science*, 11(2) (2010): 245–64, © Cambridge University Press.

Much of chapter 5 is reproduced with permission from Michael Strausz, "International Pressure and Domestic Precedent: Japan's Resettlement of Indochinese Refugees," *Asian Journal of Political Science*, 20(3) (2012), 244–66, © Taylor and Francis (https://www.tandfonline.com/doi/abs/10.1080/02185377.2012.748966).

Chapters 3 and 5 in this book, which began as dissertation chapters, would not have been possible without my outstanding professors at the University of Washington (UW). My first quarter at UW, I took Elizabeth Kier's International Relations Core Seminar. After the first class, I had pizza with several of my classmates, one of whom said that he could "sense [Kier's] incredible brainwaves vibrating in the room," a sentiment that immediately made sense to many of us. She was a terrific advisor who read everything that I wrote carefully and quickly. This book would not have been possible without her careful and thoughtful feedback.

The same quarter that I took Beth's IR Core, I was a teaching assistant for Steve Hanson's large Introduction to Politics class. Steve believes that, in order to lecture a large group of students, you must make very large hand gestures and speak with great enthusiasm. He coupled these dramatic moves with extremely well-conceived and rich lectures on very difficult topics. Although Steve is a Russia specialist, he gave a terrific lecture on Japanese development in that class. He set a high bar for what undergraduate education can be and what it means to be a comparative politics specialist. I often think of him when I create lesson plans and conduct academic research. His feedback was essential in molding this project.

A few years after I arrived at UW, the university made two simultaneous hires that were the best thing that could have happened to my fledgling career as an academic. UW hired Robert and Saadia Pekkanen, two of the smartest specialists on Japanese politics in the United States. Robert and Saadia also proved to be outstanding mentors who gave very insightful readings on dissertation chapters and terrific career advice.

I wrote much of chapter 4 while on an unofficial "writing retreat" that my spouse, Kate, encouraged me to take, and for which Patricia and Polly Marshall generously offered me the use of their Mammoth Lakes, California, condominium. Thank you to Kate, Patricia, and Polly for that and for just being great.

Chapter 6 was originally a conference paper co-authored with Hannah Goble and later an article manuscript with Adam Schiffer. Although Hannah and Adam are both Americanists, they generously offered to use their statistical skills and knowledge of American politics to give that piece an empirical and comparative flavor. I would like to thank Hannah and Adam for their help.

Much of the research for this book was conducted while I was a visiting scholar at the University of Tsukuba. I am extremely grateful to Yutaka Tsujinaka and Takafumi Ohtomo for being so welcoming and helpful while I was intruding on their university. Jun'ichi Akashi, John Campbell, Ralph Carter, Eric Cox, Erin Chung, Shaney Crawford, Emily Farris, Eric Han, Ben Goldberg, Don Jackson, Yuko Kawato, Gracia Liu-Farrer, Daisuke Matsuno, Kenneth McElwain, Michiya Mori, Megumi Naoi, Greg Noble, Susan Pharr, Glenda Roberts, James Scott, Kay Shimizu, Stephanie Shady, Michael Sharpe, Gill Steel, Kyle Walker, and Toru Yamada all offered useful ideas, thoughts, and/or feedback at various stages of the project. My research assistants Yuka Sasaki, Akina Sumi, Jessika Velazquez, and Shion Yonenuma carefully transcribed many interviews and completed other important tasks, while Katie Nissen did a terrific job creating the maps reproduced in this book. I would like to thank all of my research assistants for their excellent work. Finally, I would like to thank the team at the State University of New York Press—especially Chris Ahn, Chelsea Miller, Eileen Nizer, and Kate Seburyamo—for their help turning this from a "book project" into an actual book.

Research for this book was funded by a Japan Foundation Research Fellowship, a Fulbright Graduate Research Fellowship, and a Northeast Asia Council of the Association for Asian Studies Grant for Short-Term Research Travel. I would like to thank those funding agencies for making this book possible. Although the Maureen and Mike Mansfield Foundation did not directly fund research for this book, the connections that I made as a member of Cohort Three of the Maureen and Mike Mansfield Foundation U.S.–Japan Network for the Future were invaluable to setting up some of the most useful interviews that I conducted for this book, and I am very grateful for that.

It is unlikely that I would have written this book, much less entered graduate school to study Japanese politics, without the warmth and hospitality of my two host families—the Niinumas and the Nejimes. It is hard to express how grateful I am to those families for opening their homes to me, and giving me a taste of Japanese family life. In recent years, two other families—the Matsuno and Fujii families—have also been wonderfully hospitable to me, and I am very grateful to them as well.

My friends and family have been a major source of support throughout my life. My close friends outside of the world of political science—Brian Selfon, Seth Kessler, Danny Zimmerman, Matt Rochkind, David Parzen, Aaron Kobernick, and Abe Cambier—are the best possible friends one could ask for. My parents, Brenda and Richard Strausz, and my sister, Jennifer Strausz, have been unusually supportive of all of my academic (and nonacademic) endeavors. My children, Natalie and Jacob, have changed my life for the better and given me a sense of perspective about the things that are really important. Finally, it is difficult to express the importance of the contribution that Kate has made to this project and to my life inside and outside of academia. Thank you again, Kate.

1

Foreign Laborers, Not Immigrants

We asked for workers, but human beings came.

—Max Frisch, cited in Leitner 1995: 264

Early on during my field research for this book, I sent an email to an interest group representing a sector of Japanese businesses, asking to interview a representative about their stance on immigration. A few days later, a representative from that interest group called me. He said that the group has no stance on immigration, so it might not be a useful interview for me. I replied that I had contacted them on the advice of a well-known economist who told me that the sector that they represent is among those must hurt by Japan's restrictive immigration policy because of the labor shortages that they face. Once I used the word "labor" (the Japanese word *rōdō*), his tone changed. Although they did not have a stance on immigration policy, they had things to say about foreign labor and would be glad to speak with me.

Those conversations were in Japanese, but we also have different words in English for "immigrant" and "foreign laborer," and those words have different connotations. The phrase "foreign laborer" (as well as its Japanese equivalent, *gaikokujin rōdōsha*) focuses on the subject's economic role. However, the word "immigrant" (as well as the Japanese word *imin*, which combines the character for "to move" with the character for "person") stresses the fact that the subject has left some kind of home behind and is thus looking for a new place to live.

This distinction between "immigrants" and "foreign laborers" is a slippery one because these two categories often overlap; many "foreign laborers" become long-term or permanent residents, or even citizens, in their destination countries, while all immigrants with some form of employment are also "foreign laborers." But I begin with this distinction because it highlights the very different reasons that cause people to cross international borders. Broadly speaking, one can speak of those who migrate for primarily economic reasons and those who migrate primarily for other reasons (such as to escape persecution, to accompany family members who have migrated, or because of ties to ethnic or religious groups).

Most advanced industrialized countries have large populations of people residing on their territory who have come for primarily economic and primarily noneconomic reasons. One way that Japan truly stands out when compared with other advanced industrialized economies is that it has very few foreign residents in either category. In 2013, 1.62 percent of people living in Japan were foreign residents. By contrast, 6.96 percent of the residents of the median country in the Organization for Economic Cooperation and Development (OECD 2016b) were foreign residents.[1] In the postwar period, there were important factors pushing foreign residents to immigrate to the advanced industrialized world (such as economic crises and wars) and important factors in the industrialized world pulling foreign residents to immigrate (such as labor shortages and aging populations). These push-and-pull factors operated in Japan, too, and yet Japan has admitted hardly any immigrants. Why not?

In this book, I argue that there are two major factors that have caused the advanced industrialized countries of the world to permit the admission of large numbers of foreign residents (and in some countries, both of these factors operate at the same time). First, many countries have been successfully lobbied by businesses that face labor shortages, generally for low-skilled labor. In these countries, the government has permitted the admission of foreign laborers in large numbers. Perhaps the most famous example of this is the decision by West Germany to admit Turkish guest workers in the 1960s and 1970s. West Germany admitted these individuals as laborers. They were admitted into a country with a blood-based citizenship policy and with the assumption that they would return to Turkey rather than settle in Germany.[2] Second, countries also sometimes admit large numbers of foreign residents when an influential group of elites comes to believe that they have an obligation to admit foreign residents. This obligation may be moral, based on ethnic solidarity, based on a conception of national identity or the national interest, or rooted in an interpretation of international law. Israel's "law-of-return" policy, which gives Jews all over the world a claim to Israeli residency and citizenship, is an example of this, as is America's Cold War refugee policy, when refugee flows from the Soviet Bloc were seen as proof by many American elites of the superiority of American-style capitalism to Soviet-style communism.

Japan has few foreign residents because it lacks either of these factors. Japanese companies have not succeeded in requesting large numbers of foreign laborers from abroad. When Japanese companies have faced labor shortages, the government has responded with "side doors" that permit the admission of relatively small numbers of foreign laborers—including, most famously, the "trainee" program and the favorable treatment given to South Americans of Japanese descent—and, at times, by encouraging companies to move production overseas. But, contrary to what many in the business community wanted, the Japanese state has not granted Japanese business access to foreign labor in numbers that those businesses actually needed to address the labor shortages that they faced.

Moreover, dominant elite conceptions of Japanese national identity suggest that Japan is simply not a country of immigration. Even when Japan permitted the entrance of South Americans of Japanese heritage (so-called *nikkeijin*), they were admitted primarily as laborers, rather than as potential citizens returning to their homeland. In contrast to Israel, for example, where immigrating Jews are almost immediately offered citizenship (Nefesh B'Nefesh 2018), newly entering *nikkeijin* were given "long term residency" visas but there was no influential strain of elite thought which considered *nikkeijin* as "returnees," and they were not given an easy path to citizenship. Moreover, as will be discussed in greater depth below, in the wake of the 2009 financial crisis, *nikkeijin* were paid to leave Japan, provided they promised that they would not return for ten years. This treatment is not consistent with the idea that *nikkeijin* are returnees to their ethnic homeland.

In short, Japan has few foreign residents because the government has rejected requests by Japanese businesses to admit large numbers of foreign laborers and because the dominant elite conception of Japanese national identity suggests that large numbers of immigrants would undermine and fundamentally alter what it means to be Japanese.

This book will proceed as follows. In chapter 2, I outline my theory about the ways in which immigration control policies are made. In chapter 3, I trace the ways in which Japanese governing elites have thought about the appropriate role of foreign residents in Japan by focusing on the moves made by the Japanese government in the 1970s and 1980s to grant some foreign residents in Japan—particularly oldcomer Koreans—access to a variety of new legal rights and protections as well as the failed effort to grant that community of oldcomer Koreans the right to vote in local elections in Japan. Chapter 4 focuses on Japan's decisions to admit (or not to admit) foreign laborers, focusing in particular on the 1989 revision to the Immigration Control and Refugee Recognition Act and subsequent changes. In chapter 5, I discuss Japan's approach to international refugee crises, with particular attention to the Indochinese boat people of the 1970s and 1980s and more recent refugee flows from Myanmar and Syria. In chapter 6, I examine two different proposals from groups of politicians about how to reform Japanese immigration policy: one by politicians from the Liberal Democratic Party (LDP) and the other by politicians from the Democratic Party (DP). In the conclusion, I return to the big question of this book and examine the ways in which the recent emergence of nativist populism in several countries of the West might influence Japan's immigration policy.

2

Help Wanted

Immigration Restriction in a World of Labor Shortages, Aging Populations, and Refugee Crises

I'd be breaking the law to have you work the whole week without a day off, you know. How about getting another job on the side? All the stores are short-handed, so I'm sure they'll be delighted.

—Manager no. 8 in Sayaka Murata's novel
Convenience Store Woman

Shortly after I arrived in Japan to conduct research for this book, I began to notice Help Wanted signs everywhere I looked. There was a large one on the Lawson's convenience store by my apartment in Tsukuba, a small city northeast of Tokyo. At the *koban*, the "police box" just outside of Tsukuba Station, there was a sign hanging in the window that read, Seeking Police Officers for the Ibaraki Prefectural Police Force. The bus that I took from the Tsukuba University campus to the center of town had Seeking Bus Drivers! painted in big letters on its side. I noticed these signs all over Tokyo as well—at restaurants, convenience stores, hair dressers, an "adult goods" shop, and many other places.

Figure 2.1. Percentage of firms having difficulty filling jobs in OECD countries.

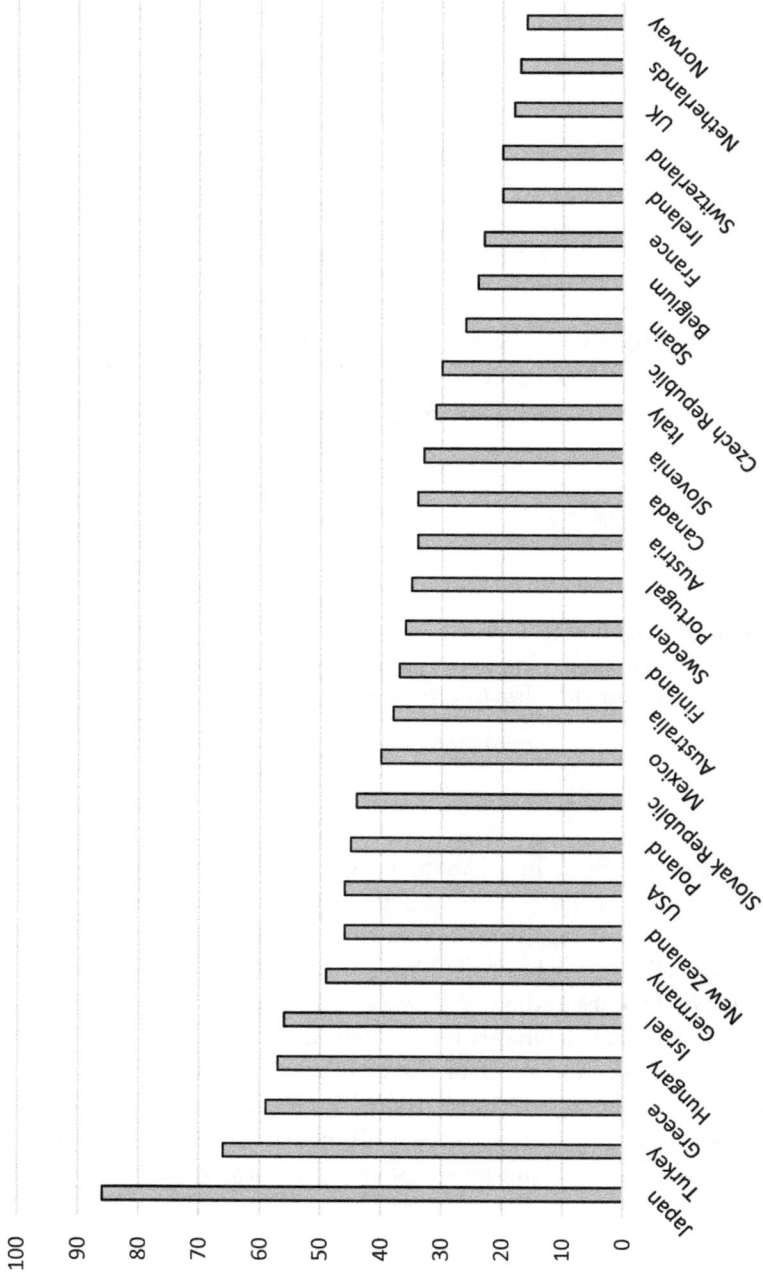

Source: ManpowerGroup 2018. The survey was of over 42,300 employers in forty-three countries and territories in 2016 and 2017. They did not interview hiring managers in seven OECD countries: Chile, Denmark, Estonia, Iceland, Latvia, Luxembourg, and South Korea. However, they did include eight non-OECD countries and regions, and, of their sample Japan had the highest percentage of firms having difficulty filling positions (with 86 percent), followed by Taiwan (73 percent) and Romania (72 percent).

Moreover, these Help Wanted signs reflect a genuine economic trend: Japan is faced with a labor shortage. In 2016, 86 percent of Japanese firms reported having difficulty filling jobs. This number is extremely high, and it is striking in comparison with other countries, as figure 2.1 demonstrates. As figure 2.2 suggests, countries with more foreign residents are less likely to face labor shortages. Japan's problem compounded because of Japan's extremely low birthrate and long life expectancy. In figure 2.3, we can see that an unusually high percentage of Japan's population is over sixty. In 2015, 32.8 percent of Japan's population was over sixty; the next highest numbers were Italy at 28.6 percent and Germany at 27.3 percent.

Figure 2.2. Labor shortages and foreign residents in OECD countries.

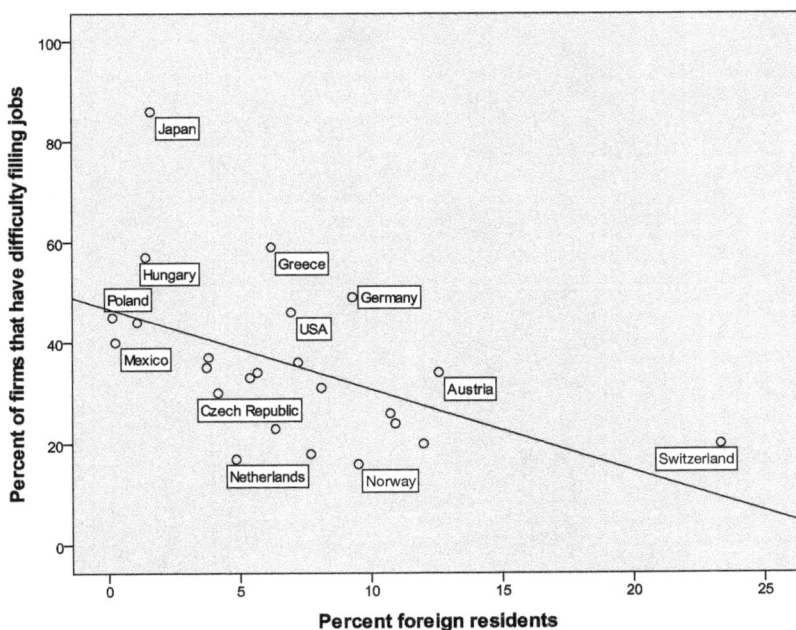

Source: ManpowerGroup 2018 and OECD 2018a. Y-axis data refers to 2016–2017 and X-axis data refers to 2013 (except for France, Ireland, and Mexico, whose data refers to 2012, and Canada and Poland, whose data refers to 2011). Data was not available for Australia, Chile, Denmark, Estonia, Iceland, Israel, Latvia, Luxembourg, New Zealand, South Korea, and Turkey. The correlation represented here is strong (Pearson's r of −.501) and statistically significant (p=.013).

This labor shortage is already having economic consequences for Japan. For example, on March 30, 2016, *Asahi Shimbun* reported that a number of consumer goods, including Tully's Coffee, table salt, tofu, and Suntory Whiskey, would be rising in price, citing rising wages due to labor shortages as one of the causes. In an area where labor shortages are particularly severe—nursing and home care work—the Ministry of Health, Labor, and Welfare announced in early 2017 that it would be advocating a bill at the next Diet session that would increase patients' individual contribution for nursing services from 20 percent to 30 percent of the cost of those services (*Asahi Shimbun* 1/13/2017).

Figure 2.3. Aging populations and foreign residents in OECD countries.

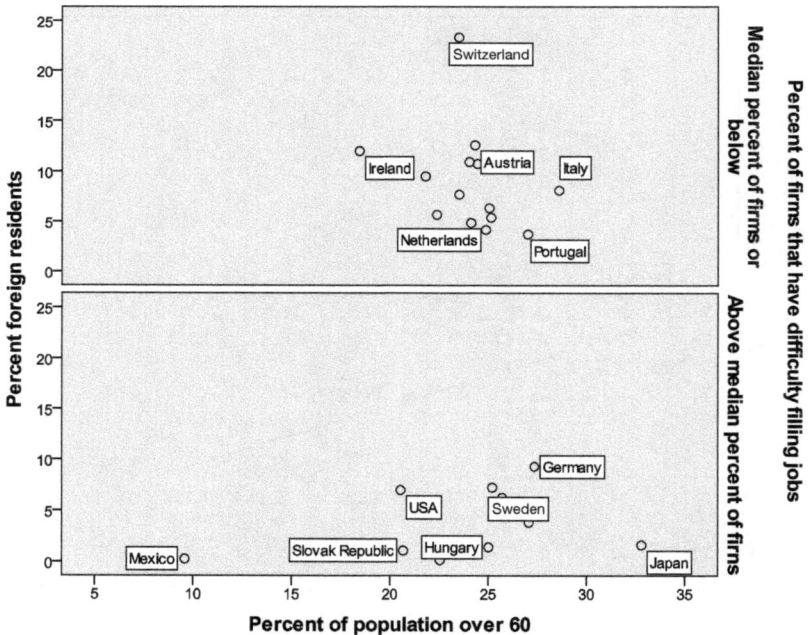

Source: ManpowerGroup 2018, OECD 2018a, and United Nations Population Division 2017. Labor shortage data refers to 2016–2017 and foreign resident data refers to 2013 (except for France, Ireland, and Mexico, whose data refers to 2012, and Canada and Poland, whose data refers to 2011). Population over 60 data refers to 2015. Data was not available for Australia, Chile, Denmark, Estonia, Iceland, Israel, Latvia, Luxembourg, New Zealand, and South Korea.

There is a large pool of laborers that are, in theory, available to address these shortages. Japan is among the wealthiest countries in the world, and there are many people from poorer countries who would gladly work for the wages available for jobs in Japan. Nurses in Japan, for example, make as much as ten times the amount that they would make in the Philippines, Indonesia, and Vietnam (Naiki 2015: 349). In short, there is demand for labor in Japan, and there is a supply of people all over the world who would willingly move there (at least temporarily) to work in jobs that pay much better than what would be available to them in their home countries. And yet, in comparison with other OECD countries, Japan is unwilling to permit labor migration.

Moreover, looking beyond economics, people are fleeing persecution all over the world. In countries such as Syria, Afghanistan, Somalia, Sudan, Guatemala, Honduras, and El Salvador, people with well-founded fears of persecution are fleeing their homes. These people often resettle, temporarily or permanently, in other countries. In response to the civil war in Syria, German chancellor Angela Merkel's government suspended the EU rule whereby Syrian refugees were only permitted to apply for asylum in the first EU country that they reached; this had the effect of making many more Syrians eligible for asylum in Germany (*The Telegraph* 8/24/2015). In contrast, in reply to a reporter's question about whether Japan would join other countries in admitting refugees from Syria and Iraq, Japanese prime minister Shinzo Abe said, "It is an issue of demography. I would say that before accepting immigrants or refugees, we need to have more activities by women, elderly people and we must raise our birth rate. There are many things that we should do before accepting immigrants" (Reuters 5/17/2015).[1]

In short, Japan is unusual as an advanced industrialized country in that it hosts comparatively few labor migrants, virtually no refugees, and relatively small numbers of foreign residents who migrated for other reasons. This is puzzling for three reasons. First, some of the most influential scholarship on immigration control policy suggests that liberal democracies have a tendency toward openness to labor migration. Perhaps the most famous argument in this vein is Gary Freeman's (1995) article "Modes of Immigration Politics in Liberal Democratic States."[2] Freeman suggests that in liberal democracies, immigration policy making tends toward what James Q. Wilson (1980) calls "client politics." That is, the benefits of immigration are concentrated, enjoyed by "employers in labor-intensive industries and those dependent on an unskilled workforce, businesses that profit from population growth (real estate, construction, etc.), and the family and ethnic relations of those making up the immigrant streams." However, "the costs of immigration are diffuse, falling belatedly on the population as a whole" (Freeman 1995: 885). Because the beneficiaries of expanded immigration are well organized, they are able to successfully lobby liberal democratic governments to get what they want, even though their policy agenda is generally opposed by the majority of the public. In Freeman's words, "Client politics is strongly oriented towards expansive immigration policies" (1995: 886).

From the perspective of Freeman's theory, the case of Japan is puzzling. Japan is a liberal democratic state with well-organized groups representing big businesses that have, at various times, requested expanded access to foreign labor. These businesses have faced severe labor shortages at several times (including presently) that make their need for foreign labor more acute. However, for the most part, those requests have not been granted.

Second, Japan is faced with a declining and aging population. This is a problem common to the advanced industrialized world, but it is felt particularly acutely in Japan because Japan has the longest life expectancy in the world and one of the lowest birth rates. It is perhaps because of Japan's rapidly declining and aging population that it appears to have even more severe labor shortages than other countries with a similarly small percentage of foreign residents (see figure 2.3 for a comparative look at Japan). Immigration is often mentioned as a possible solution to labor shortages by a variety of politicians, bureaucrats, and pundits, but little has actually changed in this regard.

Third, Japan generally takes its obligations to the international community seriously.[3] However, it has been much more reluctant than most other advanced industrialized countries to admit refugees.[4] This is more striking when one considers that refugees, in theory, might help Japan address both its labor shortages and its declining and aging population.

Do Potential Immigrants and Refugees Just Avoid Japan?

Previous scholarship gives us several potential tools to explain Japan's comparatively small population of foreign residents. Perhaps this is simply an issue of supply and demand. Many of the legislators and bureaucrats that I spoke with when researching this book suggested that Japan was not admitting Syrian refugees, for example, because Syrian refugees did not want to come to Japan, preferring to move to closer countries with larger Arabic-speaking populations. One Democratic Party (DP) DM argued that Japan has few immigrants because the continued influence of Japan's history of national isolation make it a difficult country to live in for people that are not already accustomed to life there (interview 1156), and a Liberal Democratic Party (LDP) DM pointed to the small foreign communities as a reason that Japan is not an attractive destination for immigrants (interview 1174).

There is some statistical evidence to back up these claims. In an article about the relationship between state treatment of foreign residents and immigrant inflows, Fitzgerald, Leblang, and Teets suggest that even if Japan were to treat foreign residents very well, Japan would remain a relatively unattractive destination for highly skilled migrants because of variables including its lack of land borders, its relatively obscure language, and the relatively small numbers of migrants that live there (2014: 419–23). According to their model,[5] even if Japan permitted dual citizenship, had a relatively short residency requirement for naturalization, permitted children of foreign Japanese residents to become citizens automatically, and did not require Japanese language proficiency for naturalization, it would still be significantly less attractive than any other destination country in their model.

Moreover, Takenaka, Nakamuro, and Ishida (2016) find that immigrants from the West in Japan face what Chiswick and Miller (2011) call "negative assimilation" in terms of wages. For each additional year spent in Japan, immigrants from Western countries make less in terms of wages than immigrants that have been in Japan for less time, holding a variety of other factors constant. This effect does not hold for immigrants from Asian countries, but immigrants from Asian countries also do not make more for each year spent in Japan; years spent in Japan do not appear related to the wages of immigrants to Japan from Asian countries (Takenaka, Nakamuro, and Ishida 2016: 525). Thus, one might argue that immigration to Japan does not appear to pay off over the long term (unlike, perhaps, immigration to other destinations).

However, there are several reasons to think that Japan's small foreign population is not simply a matter of migrants preferring other destinations. In the case of refugees, this is because the primary goal of those fleeing persecution is to escape that persecution. Of course, refugees generally have preferred destinations, but it is difficult to imagine those fleeing ISIS or the Assad regime in Syria, for example, choosing to remain in Syria rather than relocating to Japan.[6] In fact, as figure 5.1 demonstrates, in the last several years, Japan has had a similar number of asylum applicants as the median EU country; in some years, more asylum seekers have applied to Japan than have applied to the median EU country. (This data is discussed in more depth in chapter 5.)

Regarding labor migration, Fitzgerald, Lebang, and Teets partially explain the attractiveness of a given country to migrants with reference to the size of the foreign community that already lives in that country. According to their model, had the Japanese state responded differently to the requests by big businesses in the 1970s and 1980s to admit foreign laborers, contemporary Japan would be a much more attractive destination. In other words, the size of Japan's foreign population is a consequence of previous decisions by the Japanese state, and if we want to explain why Japan is (relatively) unattractive to foreign residents now, we must examine the policy-making process that led to those decisions in the first place.

Moreover, even if Japan is an unattractive destination for labor migration, given its need for laborers, one might think that the Japanese state would respond to the pressures that labor shortages and the declining and aging population have exerted on its economy and society by implementing policies to make it more attractive to foreign laborers. However, while Japan has made some efforts to attract highly skilled laborers such as engineers and business executives, Japan has retained significant barriers to immigration by unskilled workers and workers with skills that do not require graduate degrees, such as nurses and caregivers.

Institutional Explanations for Variation in Immigration Control Policies

Given the dynamic that Freeman (1995) identifies—that public opinion tends to oppose expansion of immigration—it would seem to follow that governments in which the immigration decision-making process is more insulated from public opinion are more likely to support expanded immigration. And, indeed, Breunig and Luedtke (2008) find that ruling political parties in countries with more institutional checks on majoritarianism are more likely to advocate increases in immigration.

Scholars have also noted the importance of institutions in opening some states up to immigration. Some have focused on international institutions such as the EU. In one of the few English-language pieces that specifically addresses the question of Japan's small population of foreign residents, Seol and Skrentny (2009) argue that, unlike Japan and South Korea, European states have permitted families to settle with labor migrants because "supranational institutions at the global and especially European level have created norms or expectations for family reunification for migrants to Europe" (Seol and Skrentny 2009: 594).[7]

Other scholars have focused more on domestic institutions. Joppke (1998, 1999) argues that domestic judicial systems in many advanced industrialized states have been key actors in establishing and protecting a right to family reunification, and Guiraudon and Lahav argue that in addition to international courts and institutions, the "national basic laws and jurisprudence" of European states remain an important factor in shaping immigration control policy (2000: 189). Hollifield suggests that "irrespective of economic cycles, the play of interests and shifts in public opinion, immigrants and foreigners have acquired rights and therefore the capacity of liberal states to control immigration is constrained by laws and institutions" (2000: 150). In short, these scholars argue that judicial systems, constitutions, and other domestic institutions that grant and protect rights in liberal states either force those states to expand immigration in ways that the executive and legislative branches oppose or prohibit those states from deporting unwanted immigrants.

Undoubtedly, both international and domestic institutions shape the way that immigration policies are made. According to the Keefer and Stasavage (2003) data on checks and balances, Japan consistently has the fewest checks and balances in the G7; between 1975 and 2012, Japan averaged 3.6 checks, with a median of 3. Both numbers are the lowest in the G7 for that time period. Thus, one might be tempted to speculate that Japan's small number of checks makes it difficult for interest groups representing labor-intensive businesses to capture the policy-making process and promote immigration.

However, there are three problems with this approach. First, it is notoriously difficult to measure the number of checks in a political system. Knowledgeable Japan specialists have drawn very different conclusions about the number of checks and balances in the Japanese political system, even in regards to the same issue areas. In the case of nuclear energy, Cohen, McCubbins, and Rosenbluth (1995) explain the continued growth of nuclear power in Japan between the 1970s and 1990s with reference to the relatively small number of veto players in the nuclear energy policy-making process. However, Hymans (2015) uses the *large* number of veto players in the nuclear power policy making to explain the persistence of nuclear power gridlock after the Fukushima disaster.[8]

Second, we have reason to be skeptical of the argument that the lack of checks and balances in Japanese democracy means that majoritarianism, rather than elite-led, interest group-driven clientelism tends to win the day. Scheiner's excellent work on opposition party failure in Japan highlights the ways in which the LDP has very effectively used clientelism to stay in power (Scheiner 2006). Had the LDP wanted to please their backers from the business world by admitting foreign laborers, it is relatively easy to imagine them finding a way to do so without paying significant electoral consequences.

Third, states can, in theory, use the lack of formal checks and balances to push through changes with speed and effectiveness. For example, Bedford and Spoonley (2014) argue that the relative lack of checks on executive power in New Zealand—the fact that it is a unitary state and that the executive is permitted to make many changes without legislation—allows New Zealand to quickly follow Canadian and Australian innovations in immigration policy.

Regarding international institutions and domestic counts, one must be careful to avoid granting too much credit to the various courts of the EU or domestic courts for the expanded immigration admission and family reunification policies of European states. There have been important decisions made by European states to expand immigration that cannot be explained by the institutions of the EU or by active courts. Bonjour (2011) notes that in the case of the Netherlands, family reunification policies have often *not* been driven by EU or judicial initiatives, but rather by Catholic political parties as well as shifts in cultural values in the 1960s (that, for example, allowed women to bring their families and laborers to bring gay partners).

Civil Society and Interest Groups

Much recent scholarship on immigration politics in Japan has focused on civil society. Shipper (2008) argues that advocacy groups have in some cases helped immigrants secure access to social services and other benefits. Milly (2014) shows how civil society organizations, working with local governments, have helped to create policies that support foreign residents in new ways at both the local and national levels. Kremers (2014) demonstrates that, while most migrant-related activism takes place at the local level in Japan, an umbrella network of migrant support groups was influential in the 2009 reform to Japan's Trainee and Technical Internship Program.

While Shipper, Milly, and Kremers are right to note the important role that nongovernment organizations (NGOs) have sometimes taken in shaping policy toward foreign residents, the following chapters demonstrate how infrequently civil society groups have been involved in national level immigration control policy making in Japan. Shipper's and Kremers' work shows how rare it is that civil society groups get involved with immigration control policy making. Indeed, Kremers treats the civil society organizations that were involved in the 2009 reform to the Trainee and Technical Internship Program as exceptions to the general pattern of apolitical migrant advocacy civil society organizations, and argues that a number of trends after 2009 appear to have decreased the influence of those somewhat unusual sets of organizations (Kremers 2014: 741). This finding is consistent with my own interviews of civil society actors, which are discussed in chapters 4 and 5.

Other accounts of Japanese politics focus more on interest groups than civil society.[9] An initial glance at these accounts suggests that they are not helpful in explaining Japanese immigration control policy. As noted above, contrary to the predictions of Freeman (1995), the interest groups representing big business have not gotten what they have wanted in terms of immigration policy; Japan has remained quite closed to foreign labor despite severe labor shortages.

One might argue that the case of Japan's immigration policy does not represent a failure of interest group politics, but rather success by those interest groups representing labor in Japan. For example, Vogt

(2018: 49) argues that the lobbying arm of the Japan Nursing Federation (JNF) has been effective in lobbying the Ministry of Health, Labor, and Welfare to limit migration by nurses and caregivers.

However, this example of JNF's success in limiting competition is the exception rather than the rule. In general, there are few examples of labor defeating management in postwar Japanese history. Ikuo Kume's book on Japanese unions focuses on the success of labor in Japan, but he also argues that much of labor's success came through the development of "alliance across business, labor, and the political actors" (1998: 37). When labor and management have completely different views in Japan, management has usually won. As Andrew Gordon argues in the concluding chapter of his book on the postwar history of Japanese labor and management, "corporate hegemony has been stronger and more enduring in Japan since the early 1960s than anywhere in the world" (1998: 196). Thus, even after considering theories of interest group politics, it remains puzzling that Japan has maintained a restrictive immigration policy despite the wishes of the management of major Japanese corporations.

Immigration Restriction as Developmental State Ideology?

A number of scholars explain immigration control policy with reference to the way that policy makers and publics think about and discuss the world and their place in it. For example, Antje Ellermann (2013) argues that the difference between German and Swiss guest worker policies can be explained by different discursive environments in each country. According to Ellermann, important elements of the Swiss polity are animated by a fear of "overforeignization." Although the term "overforeignization" initially was used in Swiss immigration policy making to signal a concern that foreign communities would remain separate from the Swiss polity rather than naturalizing and integrating, this concept became more clearly associated with ethnonationalism by the 1930s (Ellermann 2013: 506–07). Ellermann argues that the meaning and power of the overforeignization discourse in postwar Switzerland (and the relatively weakness of a similar discourse in postwar Germany) explains why Switzerland adopted a rotating system of foreign guest workers while Germany's foreign guest workers were allowed to settle in Germany.

Similarly, Bonjour (2011) argues that Dutch family migration policy was not just about economic needs or about responses to EU directives; values mattered too. Catholic parties supported family reunification (Bonjour 2011: 103), and the cultural revolution of the 1960s led to allowing women to bring their families and people to bring gay partners (98–99). Moreover, the neoliberal norm of "personal responsibility" has justified restrictions in subsequent periods (110). Bonjour concludes by noting that "insight into the dynamics of policy making is only possible if we acknowledge, unlike Freeman and Messina, that policymaking in this field is indeed, to a significant extent, a morality play" (115).

Popular accounts of immigration, along with conventional wisdom, often suggest that Japanese xenophobia has an important role in limiting immigration to Japan. One researcher at an interest group that represents Japan's high-technology sector explained the reluctance of Japan's politicians to even use the word "immigration" as follows: "For a long time an island country mentality has taken root among the Japanese, which suggests that we should not admit foreign residents and that we can only get along with ourselves" (interview 1140). He went on to argue that, although he personally supports immigration, there are some, even in his lobbying group, who prefer not to talk about immigration, although they do still discuss "foreign labor."

The problem with the argument that Japanese xenophobia limits immigration is clear when the argument is considered in comparative perspective. Xenophobia is relatively common throughout the world, and in many countries with large immigrant populations, there is a history of xenophobia. It is not hard to find the influence of xenophobic rhetoric when looking at historical policies and current platforms of major political parties in England, France, the United States, Germany, and elsewhere. If it is relatively common, then why has Japan's xenophobia influenced its immigration policy so much more than other advanced industrialized countries?

Some scholars have looked beyond these claims and linked limited immigration to Japan's developmental state ideology. Seol and Skrentny explain the reluctance of Japan and South Korea to allow migrants to bring their families along with them as follows: "Asian states have an elite political culture that affects migrant settlement outcomes differently from in Europe. Specifically, Asia is still characterized by the repertories and assumptions of a 'developmental state,' which may prioritize economic growth over individual rights, making the region distinct from Europe" (2009, 580). Similarly, Bartram (2000) suggests that Japan did not permit foreign labor in the 1960s and 1970s because of the relative power of the bureaucracy; Bartram quotes Wade's argument that bureaucrats in Japan strive for policies that "can meet a national interest test rather than a clamorous opportunity test" (Robert Wade, cited in Bartram 2000, 25).

Seol and Skrentny and Bartram use the concept of the "developmental state ideology" in different ways. Indeed, Bartram does not even use the phrase "developmental state," although he draws on central claims of Johnson (1982) and Wade (1990)—scholars that have created and refined the notion of the developmental state—to build his argument, and his discussion of bureaucratic dominance is similar to Johnson's and Wade's arguments. Seol and Skrentny suggest that developmentalist ideology causes Japanese bureaucrats to focus entirely on economic growth, while Bartram suggests that developmentalist ideology causes Japanese bureaucrats to advocate policies that harm the economy, focusing on long-term national interest instead. In other words, one can use the notion of the developmental state both to explain focus on growth at the expense of everything else and to explain focus on "national interest" instead of just short-term economic advantage.

Moreover, as Bartram notes, one of the key components of the Japanese developmental state—bureaucratic dominance—had begun to fade as early as 1972 (2000, 26), and yet Japan has remained largely closed off to immigration in subsequent years. To understand the reason for this, we must look beyond the developmental state.

Elite Debates, State/Business Interaction, and a Theory of Immigration Control Policy

I argue that there are two reasons that advanced industrialized states permit the admission of large numbers of foreign residents (see figure 2.4 for a graphic representation of this theory). First, there is employer demand. As Freeman (1995) notes, advanced industrialized economies often face labor shortages, particularly in low-skilled sectors, and businesses in those sectors often lobby their governments for expanded access to foreign labor. Second, countries admit large numbers of foreign resi-

Figure 2.4. Models of immigration control policy among select countries.

		An influential strain of elite thought suggests that significant numbers of foreign nationals have a legitimate claim to residency and membership	
		Yes	No
Labor intensive businesses convince the government to admit foreign laborers	Yes	Countries of immigration (USA, UK, Germany, France, Canada, Australia, New Zealand)	Foreigners as workers, not members (Switzerland, Qatar, United Arab Emirates, Kuwait)
	No	Foreigners as members, not workers (Israel before 1993)	Not countries of immigration (Japan, South Korea, Hungary, Poland, Slovakia, Mexico)

dents when there is an influential group of elites that believe that some foreign nationals have a legitimate claim to residency and/or citizenship. Elites may come to believe that foreigners have a legitimate claim to residency because of their views about *the international role of their state*, because of their beliefs about *importance of a shared ethnic and/or religious heritage*, or because of their beliefs in the *importance of the rule of law*.

Immigration and International Role

Elites in the United States during the Cold War and Germany recently have advocated the admission of refugees, because of their beliefs about the international role of their states. Cold warriors in the United States saw refugee flows out of the Soviet Union and other Communist states as proof of the correctness of the American stance in the Cold War. More recently, Angela Merkel drew on her view of Germany's role in the world when she criticized antirefugee protesters by saying, "I would like to recall that the humane and dignified treatment of every individual who comes to us is part of Germany's national identity" (Eddy 2015). The strain of thought that suggests that Germany has a responsibility to protect refugees was even enshrined in article 16 of Germany's Basic Law, which grants persecuted individuals a right to asylum. Germany is the only country in the world to formally grant this right, and the decision to do so is a direct response to Germany's Nazi past (Joppke 1999, 85–86). The belief of many elites in United Kingdom in the legitimacy of the British Empire was behind the 1948 passage of the British Nationality Act, which gave "the equal right of entry and settlement in Britain" to 800 million people all over the world (Joppke 1999, 101).

Immigration and Shared Ethnic Heritage

A significant portion of elites in Israel and Germany have supported immigration of coethnics and/or coreligionists. Israel's "law of return" grants both entry and citizenship rights to any person that the Israeli state recognizes as Jewish. Similarly, article 116 of Germany's Basic Law granted automatic citizenship to ethnic German refugees fleeing communism (Germany would later use quotas to restrict immigration by ethnic Germans) (Joppke 1999, 63). Although this has not yet been an issue which has led to large-scale immigration because of North Korea's intense restrictions on emigration, in the event of a North Korean regime collapse, South Korea could face a dramatic increase in the numbers of migrants who are legally entitled to citizenship because the South Korean constitution defines anyone from the Korean peninsula as a South Korean citizen (Greenhill 2010, 253).[10]

Immigration and the Rule of Law

Finally, as discussed above, significant numbers of elites across the advanced industrialized world have supported immigration of the family members of labor migrants and/or improved treatment of migrants already living in their countries because of the beliefs of those elites in the legitimacy of international law and/or domestic courts. Even governing elites that believe these policies are misguided generally implement them anyway because of their belief in the rule of law.

In short, states where an influential strain of elite thought suggests that significant numbers of foreign nationals have a legitimate claim to residency and membership include those where an influential strain of elites has (1) a view of their state's role in the world which suggests that some foreigners belong; (2) a belief that at least some co-ethnics belong; and/or (3) a belief that international law compels them to permit immigration. Although these three sets of elite ideas point to a wide variety of different policy outcomes, I combine them for two reasons. First, they are all noneconomic. That is, in countries where an influential strain of elite thought supports at least one of these ideas, there is serious public debate about immigration which presupposes that immigrants are not *simply* foreign laborers. Second, these ideas tend to move together. In countries like France, Germany, and the United Kingdom, there has been an influential strain of elites that has taken up several of these justifications for immigration.

My Explanation for Variation
in Immigration Control Policy

This book argues that these two factors—the nature of domestic political interaction between interest groups representing labor-intensive industries and the state as well as elite ideas about the appropriate role of foreign nationals—are the most important variables in shaping the size and character of a state's population of foreign residents. I point to four ideal typical configurations of immigration control policy in figure 2.4.

I define an "influential strain of elite discourse" as a mode of speaking about foreign residents that is shared by a group of elites that have had the ability to make and/or enforce laws during a nontrivial portion of the postwar years. Thus, for example, the positions of the Japanese Socialist Party (JSP) are not "an influential strain of elite discourse," because the JSP only controlled the office of the prime minister for less than nineteen months between 1994 and 1996, and the JSP never had a majority in either house of the Diet.

I focus on influential strains of elite discourse because I am interested in the ways in which ideas are translated into policy, and ideas that are held by those who never take power are not translated into policy. Of course, noninfluential strains of elite discourse are important to consider as well, because they shape the nature of debate in a given country (and can thus shape influential strains of elite discourse). Moreover, noninfluential strains of elite discourse have the potential to *become* influential in the future if their adherents gain power, and scholars must be attentive to them as well. Subsequent chapters of this book thus address noninfluential strains of elite discourse.

One might raise two objections to this conception of an "influential strain of elite discourse." First, one might object to the suggestion that LDP ideas can be called "influential," because, for example, despite controlling the Diet and the office of the prime minister for the vast majority of the years since its creation, the LDP has not succeeded in amending the constitution, even though there have been many important LDP politicians that have supported constitutional revision, including the current prime minister, Shinzō Abe. However, an idea with the support of some LDP politicians still has to get the support of the bulk of the party (or, in more rare cases, the opposition) in order to be translated into policy. Having the support of an influential strain of elite discourse is a necessary, but not a sufficient, condition for that idea to become a law.

Second, one might object to the exclusion of the rhetoric of the JSP and other minority parties from being considered as an "influential strain of elite discourse" by noting that, when it was the main opposition party, the JSP was often able to use the disjuncture between its radical rhetoric and its relatively moderate politics to get some concessions from the LDP. As Gerald Curtis explains, the LDP "has tried to satisfy some of the JSP's demands as a way to avoid forcing it to act more in accordance with the antisystem stance embedded in its rhetoric" (1988, 123).[11] Of course, I do not deny that minority parties can influence the direction of policy through a variety of channels, including that outlined by Curtis, and subsequent chapters will examine the rhetoric of minority parties as well. However, in order for Japan to decide to admit large numbers of immigrants, I argue that a significant portion of the governing coalition would first have to believe that large numbers of foreigners have a legitimate claim to residency and membership—for reasons that might include Japan's commitment to human rights, Japan's commitment to international law, and/or Japan's responsibility to those with Japanese ethnicity living abroad. As long as significant numbers of bureaucrats and/or members of the governing coalition do not believe that many foreigners have legitimate claim to residency and membership in Japan, we cannot say that there is an influential strand of elite discourse supporting the idea.

In *countries of immigration*, such as the United States, the United Kingdom, Germany, France, Canada, Australia, and New Zealand, an influential strain of elite discourse has accepted the idea that large numbers of foreign citizens have a legitimate claim to residency and membership, and, at various times in the postwar period, labor-intensive businesses have succeeded in convincing the state to admit foreign laborers.[12]

Of course, there is significant variation between these countries, and within each country, there has been significant variation over time. However, because of the totality of their immigration control policies in the postwar period, each of these states has significant portions of foreign residents that immigrated for a wide variety of reasons, including employment, family reunification, fleeing persecution, and educational opportunities.

In countries that treat *foreigners as workers, not members*, there is no powerful strand of elite discourse that argues that foreigners have a legitimate claim to residency and membership. Elites in postwar Switzerland, for example, concluded, based on their own interpretation of pre–World War I Swiss history, that the presence of foreigners must be carefully limited and regulated, and thus there are few foreign residents in Switzerland that are not guest workers on temporary work permits (Ellerman 2013). Even more starkly than the Swiss case, oil-rich countries of the Middle East, including Qatar and the United Arab Emirates (UAE), rely on huge numbers of foreign guest laborers. In each of those countries, foreign laborers make up more than 80 percent of the workforce (Mednicoff 2012, 187). In Qatar and the UAE, foreign laborers are hired based on firm need rather than nationally established quotas, and thus "the presumption from the start is that residence is based on a fixed contract, rather than a more potentially general right" (202).

There are few examples of countries that treat *foreigners as members, not workers*. Perhaps this is because, if there is an influential strand of elite discourse that recognizes that foreigners have a legitimate claim to residency and membership, it is much easier for firms in labor-intensive industries to succeed in convincing the government to admit foreign laborers. Israel before 1993 appears to have been an unusual example of this type. Israel was founded as a Jewish state in 1948, and it retains the "Law of Return" with which it was founded, a law which "permits unlimited immigration of Jews and grants them immediate citizenship on arrival" (Bartram 1998, 310, note 3). Despite this law, there were still labor shortages in many sectors, shortages that were generally filled by Palestinians from the occupied West Bank and Gaza Strip. However, the Palestinian uprising that began in late 1987 reduced the numbers of Palestinians that were able to get across the border into Israel, and thus Israeli companies started to request access to foreign laborers. In 1993, Israel closed the border after a series of murders by Palestinians on Israeli-controlled land. In the aftermath of this, Israel ended up granting permits for foreign construction workers, and this was the beginning of a pattern, whereby "after each bombing or series of individual attacks, the government would close the borders completely to Palestinian workers. Employers would then present demands for more foreign workers and the government would comply, typically granting about 20,000 new permits at a time" (Bartram 1998, 314).

Finally, Japan, South Korea, Hungary, Poland, Slovenia, and Mexico are *not countries of immigration* because there are few foreign laborers and no influential strain of elite thought which suggests that foreign residents have a legitimate claim to residency and membership. That is not to say that no foreign residents live in those countries, of course. The countries that I identify as being nonimmigration countries are those in which less than 2 percent of the population is made up of foreign residents (see table 2.1 for data on these countries in comparative perspective). Here I follow Bartram's (2000) suggestion that it is important to identify negative cases in building and testing theories about migration. When countries have foreign populations that are extremely low relative to their peers, that is an important trend worthy of study by scholars of migration.

Domestic struggles to admit foreign laborers are fought by the state and interest groups in institutional contexts. Thus, to understand those struggles, we must look at both the relative power of various interest groups and the ways in which state decision makers are exposed or insulated from various sources of social pressure. I suggest that Japan has not admitted very many foreign laborers because of the timing of its labor shortages and the ways in which Japanese elites interpreted the foreign work experience of European states.

Japanese industries developed labor shortages that could not be filled by domestic sources later than peer states including France, West Germany, and Sweden. For example, in 1960, when West Germany had

Table 2.1. Percent foreign populations in OECD countries, 2013

Luxembourg	45.81
Switzerland	23.32
Estonia	16.06
Austria	12.59
Ireland	12.00
Belgium	10.92
Spain	10.73
Norway	9.51
Germany	9.30
Italy	8.11
UK	7.71
Sweden	7.24
Denmark	7.08
Iceland	7.03
USA	6.96
France	6.35
Greece	6.21
Canada	5.68
Slovenia	5.39
Netherlands	4.86
Czech Republic	4.18
Finland	3.82
Portugal	3.74
South Korea	1.96
Japan	1.62
Hungary	1.42
Slovak Republic	1.09
Mexico	0.25
Poland	0.14

Source: OECD 2018a. Data refers to 2013 (except for France, Ireland, and Mexico, whose data refers to 2012, and Canada and Poland, whose data refers to 2011). Data was not available for Australia, Chile, Israel, Latvia, Luxembourg, New Zealand, and Turkey.

begun to court foreign laborers, 29.7 percent of Japan's labor force was working in agriculture, compared with only 13.8 percent in West Germany. Japan's percentage of its labor force working in agriculture did not dip below 13 percent until the 1970s (Bartram 2000, 11). This is significant because these Japanese agricultural workers could be hired to address industrial labor shortages in the cities.

In the 1970s, when Japan began to face labor shortages that could not be solved by its indigenous labor force, the pressure on Japanese leaders to admit foreign labor began to intensify. However, the first oil shock of 1973 weakened the global economy and thus suppressed labor shortages in Japan, and therefore there was no significant reform in the 1970s. By the 1980s, when labor shortages began to accelerate, Japanese leaders had observed the experience of European states that had permitted the entrance of foreign workers. Those Japanese leaders concluded, based on the European experience, that foreign labor was a destabilizing force. This idea was related to the commonly held belief—not supported by data—that in Europe immigration has led to an increase in crime.[13] Thus, Japanese elites decided to carve out a different path for Japan, even if it meant undesirable outcomes, including Japanese firms shifting production overseas and, in Bartram's language, "simply to let employers suffer. Suffering, of course, took the form of wage increases, lost opportunities for expansion, and even production cutbacks" (2000, 20).

This piece of the argument has both materialist and ideational components. It is materialist in that, in order for Japanese elites to conclude that foreign labor has unwelcome social costs, it was necessary that they observe such costs elsewhere in the world. If Japan had developed labor shortages that could not be solved with domestic labor reserves at the same time as or before European states developed such shortages, then this theory suggests that Japan would have admitted foreign labor in large numbers.

However, this piece of the argument also has an ideational component, because it focuses on the way that Japanese elites interpret the experience of other states with foreign laborers. As noted above, other states, such as Israel, have admitted temporary foreign labor even after observing the aftermath of such policies in Europe. Indeed, there is not agreement among scholars and politicians about whether European foreign-labor admissions policies were a success or a failure. This book devotes a good deal of attention to the nature of elite debates about foreign labor and foreign residents in Japan in order to explain how Japanese leaders have come to believe that foreign labor leads to social instability (see chapter 4 for further discussion of the evidence in support of this position).

The second reason that Japan is not a country of immigration is that there is not an influential strain of elite thought that suggests that foreign nationals have a legitimate claim to residency and citizenship in Japan. The elites who have controlled Japan since the end of World War II have often spoken of Japan as a one-ethnicity country (*tan'itsuminzoku kokka*). Although this phrase has fallen out of fashion, debates among the conservatives in Japan's governing coalition about the appropriate role for foreign residents in Japan generally take as a given that Japan is primarily a country for ethnic Japanese. The most important national identity debate that I have identified elsewhere has been between "assimilation optimists"—conservatives who believe that relatively small numbers of foreign residents can be successfully incorporated into Japanese society, and "assimilation pessimists"—conservatives who believe that efforts to incorporate foreign residents into the Japanese polity will inevitably fail. Neither assimilation optimists nor assimilation pessimists believe that significant numbers of foreign nationals have a legitimate claim to residency and membership in Japan.[14]

Regarding *the international role of their state*, no influential strain of elite thought in Japan has articulated a vision of Japan's role in the world that requires Japan to admit large numbers of foreign residents for noneconomic reasons. In the case of the *importance of a shared ethnic and/or religious heritage*, although there are significant populations with Japanese heritage in South America to which Japan has given preferential treatment as labor migrants, these individuals have been treated as temporary laborers rather than citizens, and, indeed, those people were given economic incentives to leave during the economic difficulties following the Lehman Shock of 2007 (Kamibayashi 2015, 3). Finally, regarding the *importance of the rule of law*, Japan has a commitment to the rule of law and to complying with international law. However, Japan is not a member of the EU or of a similar international organization that would require it to permit the families of temporary labor migrants to settle in Japan. International refugee law prohibits Japan from sending refugees back to a country where they have a well-founded fear of persecution, so Japan generally avoids doing so. Since international refugee law does not require countries to seek out and grant asylum status to refugees, however, Japan's extremely small refugee population is not a violation of international law (although it can of course be criticized on other grounds).

In sum, Japanese firms have not been able to convince the Japanese state to admit large numbers of foreign laborers (especially low-skilled laborers) because those who control the Japanese state—politicians and bureaucrats—have looked at the rest of the world and concluded that foreign laborers threaten social stability, so they have resolved to limit their entry, even if that meant hurting Japanese industry and the Japanese economy. Moreover, Japan has not admitted large numbers of noneconomic migrants—including refugees and family members of those foreigners who are working in Japan—because such admissions don't appeal to an influential strain of elite thought about the appropriate role of foreign residents in Japan.

Throughout this book, I draw on three major sources of evidence. First, I look at Diet hearings as well as reports by bureaucratic agencies, political parties, interest groups, and activists. These reports are useful for the "raw data" that they provide and give a detailed account of the official positions of various key actors. Second, I refer to interviews that I conducted with a large number of bureaucrats, politicians, interest-group representatives, scholars, and activists. I am grateful to these people for patiently explaining things to me from their very well-informed positions, and I consider their positions in light of one another and in light of other sources of evidence. Third, I examine media accounts of key moments in the making of Japan's current immigration system. I focus primarily on newspaper accounts, and, whenever possible, I examine accounts from multiple newspapers of the same events.

3

Minority Rights and Minority Invisibility

Oldcomer Koreans in Japan

In prewar Japan, everyone said that the Yamato nation was a mongrel (*zasshu*) nation, a mixed nation. People argued in this way even when they were advocating Japanism. However, after the war, something very strange happened. People, including the progressive intelligentsia, began to insist that the Japanese are a homogeneous nation. There is absolutely no foundation for the claim, but this baseless theory is rampant.

—Political Scientist Jirō Kamishima in 1982 (cited in Oguma)

After the international human rights agreements went into effect in the autumn of 1979, the internationalization of our country's legal institutions has steadily proceeded. Although the reform of citizenship law—in which male-female discrimination is deeply rooted—remains an unresolved problem, even in our country, in which a doctrine of an ethnically homogeneous and monocultural purity of blood persists, doors have become open to foreigners in many areas, in a manner suitable to a member of international society. This situation might be called the second opening of Japan, after the Meiji Restoration.

—Yomiuri Shimbun editorial, June 11, 1981

As Japan's posture toward the people of the Korean peninsula changed throughout the twentieth century, elite Japanese thought about the fundamental basis of Japan's national identity also changed. In the years before and during Japan's occupation of Korea (1910–1945), the "mixed-nation theory," which suggested that the Japanese nation was composed of a mixture of migrants from Asia with aboriginal peoples that had lived in Japan before those migrants had arrived, was the dominant elite theory of Japan's national origins. After the war, however, with the end of the occupation of Korea, Japanese elite discourse abruptly shifted away from this mixed-nation theory, which had justified the occupation of Korea, to the theory that Japan was populated by a single ethnic group that had lived in those islands throughout history (Oguma 2002).

Given the sudden prominence of this theory of the centrality of ethnic homogeneity to Japanese national identity in the aftermath of the war, Japanese elites were faced with a challenge—how would they explain the existence of the Korean community that remained in Japan after the occupation of Korea had ended? The way in which Japan's governing, cultural, and business elites have answered this question has shaped Japan's immigration policy more broadly because those elites developed their thinking about the appropriate role of foreign residents in Japanese society largely through their interaction with this community of "oldcomer Koreans" who trace their or their family's time in Japan to before 1945, when Korea was a colony of Japan. In dealing with this community of oldcomer Koreans, the Japanese state has developed ideas and institutions that continued to influence Japan as they decided what do to about future refugee flows and industrial demands for foreign labor.

This chapter examines the evolution of Japanese elites' thought about the appropriate role of foreign residents in Japan—which, for most of the postwar period, was a community largely made up of oldcomer Koreans. In particular, I focus on the period in the 1970s and 1980s when Japan ultimately decided to outlaw a variety of discriminatory practices against oldcomer Koreans. This chapter addresses two related questions. First, given the importance of the idea of Japan as ethnically homogeneous to postwar Japanese elites, why did Japan outlaw discriminatory practices against oldcomer Koreans that by their very existence challenge the idea of Japan's ethnic homogeneity? Second, while extending a variety of rights and protections to oldcomer Koreans and other foreign residents in Japan, why did Japan not grant foreign permanent residents (such as oldcomer Koreans) the right to vote in local elections in Japan? This was a cause that was championed by activists in the old-comer Korean community and supported by the CGP, the party that has been in coalition with the LDP since 1999.

I argue that these two changes—extending a variety of rights and protections to oldcomer Koreans while deciding not to grant that same community the right to vote in local elections—can both be explained with reference to concerns about visibility. Those skeptical that foreign residents had any kind of role in Japanese society were convinced that it was useful to grant rights and protections to oldcomer Koreans because doing so would make that community less likely to protest, and thus decrease its visibility (thereby strengthening Japan's claims to ethnic homogeneity). However, even some of those who believed that foreign residents have some legitimate role in Japanese society saw granting for-eign residents the right to vote in local elections as a bridge too far, as granting foreign residents such a right would increase the visibility of oldcomer Koreans to such an extent that it would be difficult to continue to claim that Japan is ethnically homogeneous (as how can a country with foreigners that do not represent the dominant ethnic group voting be called ethnically homogeneous?).

From the Meiji Restoration to the Separatist Idea

In the years following the Meiji Restoration, Japanese scholars developed two competing visions of the origins of the Japanese people:

> One was the mixed nation theory which argued that the Japanese nation consisted of a mixture between a conquering people and a previous aboriginal people and others, while the second was the homogeneous nation theory, which argued that the Japanese nation had lived in Japan since time imme-morial and that their lineage had been handed down to con-temporary "Japanese." (Oguma 2002: 15)

Both visions continued to have advocates throughout the Meiji period, through the Taisho period, and through Japan's participation in World War II. However, as Japan looked to justify and strengthen its annexation of Korea in 1910, the mixed-nation theory became the most influential explanation of the origins of Japan both among scholars and in the mass media (Oguma 2002: 81–92). As Japan's empire continued to grow, the mixed-nation theory gained more and more influence; even thinkers who had previously been outspoken advocates of the centrality of shared blood to Japan's national identity began to incorporate the central tenants of mixed-nation theory into their writing (110–124).

After the war, the combination of Japan's defeat, the collapse of Japan's empire, and fears shared by Japan's conservative governing elite and the US-led occupation of communism from the Korean peninsula spreading to Japan led to a radical reconsideration of the nature of Japanese identity. In this period, "there were almost no attempts to formulate a vision of Japan as a multi-ethnic state" (Oguma 2002: 298).[1] Instead, elites in Japan began to establish what Keizō Yamawaki calls the "separatist idea"; the idea that foreigners don't belong in Japan, and should be encouraged to leave (2001: 298). The separatist idea makes the following assumptions about Japan's national identity. First, Japanese identity is primarily ethnic, rather than civic. Second, Japanese greatness is intricately linked with ethnic homogeneity. Third, those who are not ethnically Japanese do not belong in Japan for the long term, and an effective way to encourage non-Japanese to leave Japan is to guarantee that they are not extended the same privileges and social protections as Japanese people. Masuyama Noboru, a section chief in the Bureau of Immigration, well summarized the separatist idea's views about foreign residents in 1969: "It is not in the interest of Japan for Koreans to remain here. The line of thinking that suggests that 'if they can, it would be best if they leave' is predominant" (Yamawaki 2001: 295).

Japan's Korean Community

The separatist idea gained power partially because the dominant social organizations that governed the Korean community in postwar Japan agreed with its fundamental assumptions about the ethnic roots of Japanese identity. By 1945, almost 2 million Koreans lived in Japan (Kim 1997: 24; Chapman 2004). The majority of these Koreans came to Japan for employment. Many former Korean peasants migrated to Japan because reforms that ended traditional land-holding patterns (often in ways that benefited Japanese companies) rendered them landless. Japanese companies frequently encouraged migration by Koreans, as Koreans were a source of cheap labor (Kim 1997: 27–34). Moreover, in 1938, Japan began to specifically recruit Korean laborers to alleviate labor shortages in industries such as coal mining. This system of "recruiting" was frequently coercive, and, in 1942, Japan began formally conscripting Koreans to serve as laborers. The statistics regarding this era are difficult to discern; Japanese government statistics suggest that between 1939 and 1945 more than six hundred thousand Koreans were conscripted to Japan, but some scholars put the number at close to 1.5 million (Kim 1997: 118).

From Japan's surrender in 1945 until 1946, around 1.3 million Koreans migrated to Korea, leaving 647,006 in Japan (Kim 1997: 170).[2] The nature of the Korean community in Japan has gradually changed since the end of World War II. The numbers of Koreans who are "old-comers," that is, people that can trace their (or their ancestors') time in Japan to the colonial period, has gradually declined, dipping below 500,000 for the first time in 2000, and standing at 344,744 in 2015 (Data from Zairyū Gaikokujin Tōkei 1964; Ministry of Justice 2016).

These statistics are bit misleading, however, because they ignore the large numbers of oldcomer Koreans who have naturalized and thus taken Japanese citizenship. Although Japanese officials keep annual statistics on naturalizations, they do not ask questions about ethnicity on official government censuses and surveys. The Japanese state thus treats ethnicity and citizenship as two sides of the same coin. This assumption has long been shared by the major organizations that represent Koreans in Japan.

Although most oldcomer Koreans in Japan come from the geographic area that is now South Korea, the formal citizenship status of that group has changed over time.[3] In 1947, while Japan was still under US occupation, the Diet passed a law that required Koreans to carry foreigner registration cards at all times. Those cards identified them as being from Chōsen (Korea) (Chung 2010: 76). This marked a major break with Japan's policy during the colonial period, when Koreans living in Japan were citizens of Japan who could vote and run for office (that policy was consistent with the mixed-nation theory of Japanese national identity, discussed above).

The two dominant social organizations in the Korean community in Japan have been the pro–South Korean Residents Union of Japan (Mindan), and the pro–North Korean General Association for Koreans

Residents in Japan (Chōsen-Sōren).[4] Both groups have historically discouraged their members from applying for Japanese citizenship (Chung 2010: 87). This policy is based on an assumption about citizenship and identity that links national identity with formal national citizenship, an assumption that Mindan and Chōsen-Sōren have shared with the Japanese state. According to this outlook, when Koreans take Japanese citizenship, they renounce their Korean identity. For this reason, the vast majority of Koreans in Japan did not naturalize, but to avoid discrimination they tried to pass as Japanese. This created the strange situation of "over 600,000 highly assimilated Korean permanent residents living within Japan's territorial boundaries without full citizenship rights" (Chung 2003: 35).

After the two regimes were founded on the Korean peninsula, Japan encouraged Koreans in Japan to change their citizenship to Kankoku, which was the Japanese name for South Korea. Those who did not change their citizenship to Kankoku became citizens of North Korea, as the Japanese word for North Korea was Kita Chōsen (recall that "Chōsen" was the citizenship status that Japan gave to all Koreans in 1947).

Many Koreans living in Japan kept Chōsen citizenship either because they supported the North Korean regime or because they did not support either regime on the Korean peninsula, and Chōsen was the default nationality that had been assigned to them (Chung 2010: 78). In 1950, 85.8 percent of the Korean community in Japan were officially citizens of North Korea. That number gradually declined in subsequent years, and, in 1969, more Koreans in Japan were citizens of South Korea than North Korea for the first time (Mindan 1997: 7).

Today, only 31,674 Koreans in Japan are North Korean citizens. 98 percent of those are Special Permanent Residents, which is a status only available to those who can trace their or their family's time in Japan to Japan's occupation of Korea and Taiwan. Figure 3.1 shows where that community lives as of 2017. In terms of oldcomer South Koreans per thousand residents, Osaka has 9.17, Kyoto has 8.1, and Hyōgō has 6.46. Perhaps not surprisingly given the origins of the oldcomer community, the per capita populations of North Korean residents and South Korean oldcomers in a given prefecture are almost perfectly correlated (with a Pearson's r of .914),[5] and there is also a high correlation between prefectures with high per capital populations of South Korean oldcomers and South Koreans who have migrated to Japan since the end of World War II (Pearson's r of .466) (Ministry of Justice 2017).

Figure 3.1. Map of South Korean Special Permanent Residents per thousand people in Japanese prefectures, 2017.

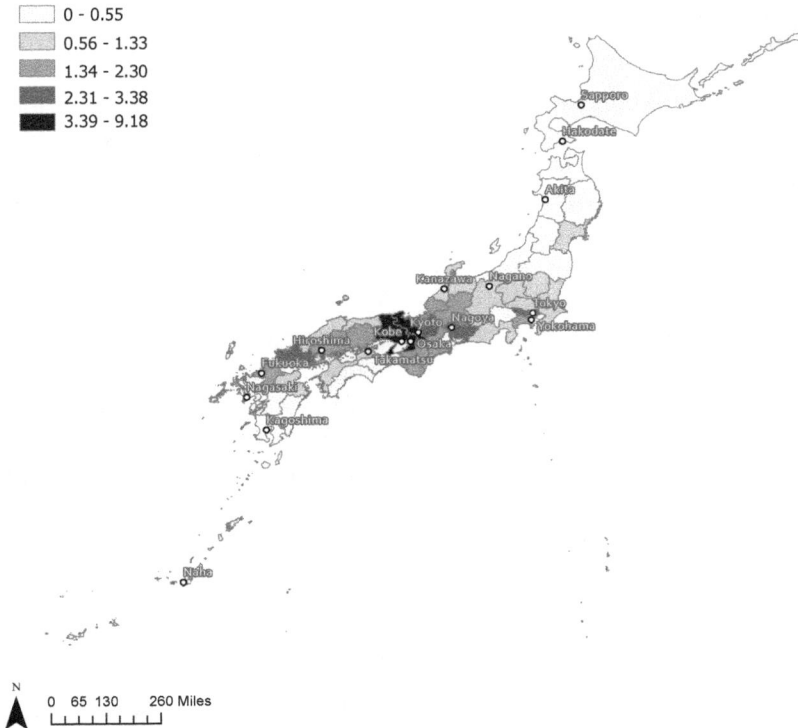

	0 - 0.55
	0.56 - 1.33
	1.34 - 2.30
	2.31 - 3.38
	3.39 - 9.18

Data from Ministry of Justice (Japan) 2017.

The Political Implications of the Separatist Idea

The political impact of the separatist idea was immediately evident in three different policy-making processes: the negotiation of the postwar constitution, the passage of the 1946 Revised Parliamentary Electoral Law, and the formation of citizenship policy in 1952. As the Japanese government and the US occupation authorities (herein called SCAP, for Supreme Command of the Allied Powers) negotiated the contents of the Japanese constitution, the Japanese government succeeded in convincing SCAP to eliminate a proposed article which had stated that "aliens shall be entitled to the equal protection of law" and to change the subject of article 13, which guarantees equal protection under the law and forbids discrimination, from the vague "all natural persons" (*subete no shizenjin*) to "the people" (*kokumin*) (Koseki 1989: 140). The term *kokumin* was later defined in statute to mean "persons with Japanese citizenship" (Hamano 1999: 437).[6]

In 1946 former colonial subjects lost the right to vote and hold office due to the Revised Parliamentary Electoral Law, which was passed with the consent of SCAP (Kim 1997: 143). Also in 1946, the Japanese government instituted a tax that only non-Japanese were required to pay. SCAP allowed this law to pass once it was amended so that citizens of the Allied powers were exempt (Ōnuma 1993 [1978]: 27).

As the occupation drew to a close, Japanese officials realized that, contrary to what they had anticipated, SCAP would not require them to allow former colonial subjects to choose whether or not to keep their Japanese citizenship. Thus, on April 19, 1952, nine days before the peace treaty went into effect, Japan took legal steps to clarify that Koreans and Taiwanese, including those who remained in Japan, were no longer citizens of Japan (Iwasawa 1998: 131, particularly notes 29 and 30). This was consistent with the 1950 revision to the Nationality Law, which confirmed that citizenship in postwar Japan would be conferred through the principle of *jus sanguinis* ("by blood," which means that one's parents—or, in 1950, one's father—must be Japanese in order for a child to be Japanese) (Rao 2017: 71).

The separatist idea continued to influence Japan's approach toward foreign residents after the end of the occupation. In 1966, the year after Japan normalized relations with South Korea, the Immigration Bureau in the Ministry of Justice released a document called *Zainichi Kankokujin no Hōteki Chii Kyōtei to Shutsunyūkoku Kanri Tokubetsu Hō Kaisetsu* (A Commentary on the Agreement on the Legal Status of South Koreans in Japan and the Special Law on Immigration and Emigration), written by Nobuo Tatsumi. This document explained the recently ratified agreement with South Korea and the subsequent law that put that agreement into effect. The document is primarily a standard legal analysis. During the brief discussion of the social problems that faced many South Koreans in Japan, Tatsumi argues,

> According to research from April of 1954, of the Koreans in Japan, the number of people with jobs is 140,714, which

means that 24.3% are employed. Leaving out Koreans and Chinese, 40.4 % of other foreigners in Japan are employed, and therefore the rate [for Koreans] is comparatively low, but Koreans are affixed to our country in a different way than other foreigners, and hence, in addition to wives and children without jobs, as will be explained subsequently, because there is employment instability, it is thought that there is a considerable number of people who are unemployed or close to unemployed. (1966: 17)

Tatsumi then provides a more detailed statistical analysis of the employment situation of Koreans in Japan. However, he does not attempt to analyze the steps that the Japanese government might take to improve this situation. He makes no mention of the possibility that discrimination, the formal denial of social safety-net protections, and the lack of public-sector employment opportunities for foreign residents might be causes of these economic difficulties. The subtext of the report seems to be that, while Japan has faithfully implemented its agreement with South Korea, it is not a very hospitable place for foreign residents, and that won't change anytime soon.

The 1965 agreement between Japan and South Korea recognized those Koreans in Japan who allied themselves with South Korea as permanent residents of Japan. However, those of Taiwanese heritage and those who formally allied themselves with North Korea—two groups totaling 493,099 people in 1969 (*Zairyū Gaikokujin Tōkei* 1970)—still retained an ambiguous legal status. The Immigration Bureau unsuccessfully proposed a law to grant permanent residency status to those two groups four times between 1969 and 1981. The *Asahi Shimbun* suggests that these proposals failed in the Diet because they also contained provisions which would have given the Ministry of Justice increased authority to check the political activities of foreign residents (*Asahi Shimbun* 3/2/1981). In short, the Ministry of Justice acted as if granting permanent residency status for foreign residents must be accompanied by limitations on their political activities; despite the change in residency status, the Ministry of Justice still discouraged foreign residents from considering Japan their long-term home.

These proposed laws were not the only strategies that the Ministry of Justice used to attempt to limit the political activities of foreign residents. In 1969, the Ministry of Justice refused to grant a one-year visa extension to an American citizen for two reasons: a minor visa violation and his participation in a variety of peaceful political demonstrations while in Japan (including anti–Vietnam War protests). The Supreme Court held:

> Even when the conduct of Aliens during their stay is in accord with the Constitution and is lawful, if the Minister of Justice determines that the conduct of the alien is undesirable for Japan from the prospective of propriety, or if it is inferred from the said conduct that there is danger in the future that the said alien will behave in a way that is harmful to Japan's interests, this does not amount to depriving an alien of constitutional protection. (*McLean v. Justice Minister* 1978: 477)

In short, the court gave the Ministry of Justice wide latitude in restricting the rights of foreigners. Even when foreign residents could claim constitutional rights, the ability of the Ministry of Justice to deport aliens for constitutional activities amounts to a *de facto* weakening of those rights.

The Ministry of Justice also aimed to limit the overseas political activities of resident foreigners. In 1977, it denied reentry permits to seven resident Koreans with North Korean citizenship who wanted to travel to North Korea to participate in an "election" of the Supreme People's Assembly, giving the following justification: "Regarding reentry of resident Koreans, because it is limited to humanitarian cases such as visiting graves, there is no precedent for openly political activities such as this case" (*Asahi Shimbun* 11/10/1977). All of these policies are consistent with the separatist idea's assumption that foreigners don't belong in Japan and should be encouraged to leave.

International and Domestic Legal Challenges to the Primacy of the Separatist Idea

Beginning in the 1960s, there were several changes to the international and domestic legal context in Japan that weakened the influence of the separatist idea on Japanese elites. Domestically, local government initiatives and a key court decision were pulling Japan toward a more accepting policy toward foreign residents. Many local governments had been extending benefits to foreign residents since the early 1970s, even in the face of direct requests from the central government to be less generous (Takao 2003: 541–48), and Japanese courts ruled in 1974 that Hitachi was wrong to fail to hire Chǒng-sǒk Pak once they learned of his Korean heritage (Chapman 2008: 33–36); legal scholar Yuji Iwasawa has compared the results of the Pak case on oldcomer Korean mobilization with the impact of *Brown v. Board of Education* on African American mobilization in the United States (Iwasawa 1998: 202, note 331). This trend was particularly troubling to central government bureaucrats because it challenged the conventional dominance of the Japanese bureaucracy over the pace and course of social change. This is something that the Japanese bureaucracy has aimed to protect (Upham 1987).

In one sense, the government's fears proved founded, as in the years after the Pak case, increasing numbers of Koreans in Japan refused to be fingerprinted.[7] This movement culminated in 1985, when around ten thousand Koreans refused to be fingerprinted. In response to both this movement and pressure from the South Korean state, Japan ultimately abolished the fingerprinting requirement in 1991 (Strausz 2006/2007).[8]

On the international stage, Japan ratified the International Covenant for Civil and Political Rights (ICCPR) and the International Covenant on Economic, Social, and Cultural Rights (ICESCR) in 1979. Article 26 of the ICCPR forbids discrimination on the basis of national origin. Some scholars have argued that these ratifications gave human rights groups and Koreans' rights groups in Japan new tools to demand change (Gurowitz 1999). Interestingly, however, even while it was actively working to improve the conditions for oldcomer Koreans in Japan, the Japanese state repeatedly denied that the treaties imposed any new obligations on it regarding its treatment of foreign residents.

Neither of Japan's two reports before the Human Rights Committee from the 1980s acknowledge the existence of any problems with the way in which Japan treats foreign residents. Both reports suggest that equal protection of foreign residents is already guaranteed under Japan's constitution. The 1980 report suggests:

> With regards to the rights of an alien, some provisions of the Constitution refer only to nationals (articles 11, 13, 14, et al.), and others to all persons irrespective of nationality.

However, the Constitution does not purport to exclude an alien from the enjoyment of fundamental human rights, and, therefore, an alien is also guaranteed, by the constitution and other domestic legislation, enjoyment of the rights recognized in the Covenant. (Government of Japan 1980: 2)

The 1987 report makes a similar argument:

The rights of aliens are guaranteed in accordance with the spirit of the Constitution which is based on respect for fundamental rights and international co-operation, with the exception of the rights which are applicable, by definition, only to nationals such as the right to vote. (Government of Japan 1987: 4)

Neither of these statements acknowledges that Japan's ratification of the ICCPR imposed new obligations on the Japanese state.[9] Despite these statements, however, by the time that Japan had ratified these treaties, the elite consensus around the separatist idea had been weakening for some time.

Beginning in the 1960s, governing elites began to express concern that the separatist idea was out of step with the way that the rest of the word treats foreign residents (particularly the advanced industrialized states of the West). The Ministry of Foreign Affairs first formally expressed this idea in a publication in 1965. The publication is a comprehensive study of all laws relating to foreign residents in Japan. It begins with an eleven-page overview and analysis. Early on in the analysis, they discuss the debate about whether the constitution protects the rights of foreign residents. After outlining three different positions on this issue, they argue that, even if the words of the constitution themselves do not protect foreign residents, it is consistent with the spirit of the constitution (*kenpō no shinsei*) to protect the rights of foreigners. In particular, they reference the constitution's emphasis on the theory of natural law, the principle of international cooperation, and the protection of fundamental human rights (Ministry of Foreign Affairs 1965: 2).

Having argued that the constitution protects the rights of foreign residents, they are soon faced with the difficult task of explaining why Japanese law still limits the rights of foreign residents. They argue: "Before the end of the recent war, there were extensive limitations and prohibitions on the possession of rights by foreigners and foreign legal people. These limitations and prohibitions were in large part eliminated after the war, and in contemporary politics only the following items remain" (Ministry of Foreign Affairs 1965: 4). The Ministry of Foreign Affairs thus links restrictions on the rights of foreign residents in Japan with Japan's illiberal prewar system. While the ministry does not explicitly invoke Western models, the implication of the quote seems to be that policies that discriminate against foreign residents are gradually being eliminated from Japanese politics, as Japan's system continues to advance beyond the prewar system.

Throughout the 1970s and into the 1980s, there were increasing calls in popular media for Japan to modify its treatment of foreign residents in accordance with Western practice. In the introduction to a news article on Japan's practice of prohibiting foreigners from becoming professors at Japanese national universities, *Nihon Keizai Shimbun* argued that "with the hosting of the Tokyo Summit and so forth, Japan aims to become opened to international society, but, in terms of becoming a Western-style place where it is easy for foreigners to live, Japan remains at the beginning of such changes" (6/16/1979).[10] This quote is particularly interesting because it assumes that emulating the West is an avenue through which Japan can become open to international society. The article then names countries that have a more effective policy approach than Japan:

> Now, in national universities throughout the country, there are about 290 foreign teachers, but their contracts are almost invariably one-year contracts. If we look at the example of advanced industrialized nations, West Germany, America, and England employ foreign professors the same as citizen professors, and voices saying "let's open up the road of hiring foreigner as regular professors" are increasing from both inside and outside of Japan.

This quote uses a rhetorical device that is extremely common in Japanese newspaper articles and editorials in the 1970s and 1980s: to claim that there is criticism of Japan's existing policy approach, particularly criticism from outside Japan, without providing any specific examples of the sources of that criticism. This is often coupled with favorable reporting on the practice of Western states.

Japanese media also focused on the issue of the citizenship of children born to mixed-nationality couples. Before 1985, Japan had a patrilineal citizenship policy: the children of Japanese women and foreign men were not granted Japanese citizenship. There had been talk about revising this policy as early as 1979, when minister of foreign affairs Sunao Sonoda said during a House of Representatives Foreign Affairs Committee discussion of the ICCPR and the ICESCR that the Ministry of Foreign Affairs would talk with the Ministry of Justice about the possibility of eliminating gender discrimination from Japan's citizenship law. Two families where Japanese women had married foreign men unsuccessfully sued the Japanese government to change this law. On the same day that the Tokyo District Court announced this ruling, the Ministry of Justice announced that it would change Japan's citizenship policy so that either parent could pass on citizenship by 1985, the tenth year of the UN decade of the woman (*Nihon Keizai Shimbun* 3/31/1979: 23).

In an opinion piece critical of Japan's patrilineal citizenship policy, Toshie Kanemori argues that this policy is unconstitutional, and notes the dissatisfaction of the Japanese women's movement with the current policy. He says: "Also, globally, various countries that had previously had a patrilineal citizenship policy, such as West Germany and France, have, with the rise of the women's liberation movement in the 1970s, one by one changed to a policy whereby citizenship could be passed on by either parent." (*Yomiuri Shimbun*, 3/11/1981).

While this purports to explain a global trend, both of Kanemori's examples come from Western Europe, and other critics cite Western examples to criticize Japan as well (*Nihon Keizai Shimbun*, 4/1/1981). Officials at the Ministry of Justice agreed with Kanemori regarding the importance of foreign examples to Japan's citizenship policy. In a move reminiscent of the Iwakura Mission of 1871–1873, when Meiji Era elites went to Western nations to study their governing institutions, in the summer of 1980, the Ministry of Justice sent delegates abroad to examine how other countries have dealt with the problems stemming from the abolition of patrilineal citizenship. They seemed particularly concerned with the problems stemming from dual citizenship (*Nihon Keizai Shimbun* 3/31/1981: 23).

The importance of Western examples was also evident in Diet debates about whether Japan should ratify the Refugee Convention in 1981. The Refugee Convention requires states to extend the same pension benefits to refugees and citizens. Debates about this provision generally accepted the premise that if Japan ratified the treaty and extended pensions to refugees, then it would have to extend pensions to foreign residents, particularly those who had been in Japan since World War II and their descendants. Officials from the Ministry of Health and Welfare, as well as some Diet members, feared that allowing foreign residents to participate in the pension program would be prohibitively expensive, and hence they suggested that Japan should make reservations to articles 23 and 24 of the Refugee Convention, which dealt with pensions (*Nihon Keizai Shimbun* 5/4/1981). At one point the Ministry of Health and Welfare suggested that if Japan ratified the Refugee Convention, then Japan's system of social insurance would collapse (*Nihon Keizai Shimbun* 3/13/1981).

It is interesting to note the Ministry of Foreign Affairs' response to the Ministry of Health and Welfare. Rather than dealing with the economic claims of the Ministry of Health and Welfare, bureaucrats from the Ministry of Foreign Affairs argued, "Of the 80 countries that ratified the treaty, only three developed countries have made reservations, and if we did that, we would be inviting international criticism" (*Nihon Keizai Shimbun* 5/4/1981). In short, it is desirable for Japan to become more like a developed, Western state, and a reservation to the Refugee Convention—which would have allowed Japan to exclude refugees from the national pension plan—is not consistent with that goal.

Hidenori Sakanaka and the Emergence of a Debate about Assimilation

The reforms to Japan's approach to oldcomer Koreans were not simply a response to the disjuncture between policies based on the separatist idea and the policies of other advanced industrialized countries, however. There were changes going on within the oldcomer Korean community that made continued commitment to the separatist idea difficult for elites committed to the idea that Japan's ethnic homogeneity is a crucial component of its identity. Some Korean thinkers in Japan began to talk seriously about "a way to live in Japan as home, without being totally Korean or Japanese but by being '*zainichi*' (resident in Japan)" (Chapman 2004: 34). This new intellectual current developed as the Koreans in Japan attempted to grapple with the changing nature of their community, as the second and third generations of Koreans were born in Japan, attended Japanese schools, and often spoke Japanese but not Korean. By 1974, 76 percent of Koreans in Japan had been born there (*Zairyū Gaikokujin Tōkei* 1975).[11] This demographic trend—Koreans increasingly appearing to be long-term settlers in Japan—was often called *teichakuka* (residentialization).

Teichakuka challenged the expectation of many elites committed to the separatist idea that the most effective way to encourage those without Japanese ethnicity to leave Japan is to make certain that they are not extended the same privileges and social protections as those with Japanese ethnicity. In spite of the fact that Korean residents in Japan were not extended privileges and social protections, the Korean community appeared prepared to remain in Japan. From the standpoint of those elites committed to the idea that Japan's ethnic homogeneity is normatively desirable, this was a worrying trend.

One of the earliest and clearest explanations of why this trend is undesirable can be found in the writing of Bureau of Immigration bureaucrat Hidenori Sakanaka. Sakanaka's essay, "Zainichi Chōsenjin no Taigū [The Treatment of Koreans in Japan]," won a Ministry of Justice Immigration Bureau essay contest in 1975, and its impact on Ministry of Justice rhetoric about foreign residents was almost immediately evident. His essay laid the intellectual foundations for postwar assimilation optimism. He begins by saying that "the reality that, as a heterogeneous group of foreigners, 640,000 Koreans exist in our country's society in an unstable situation, creates all sorts of problems from the standpoints of domestic order and international relations." He goes on to note the issues of most concern to Koreans in Japan: "Koreans in Japan, and Korean groups in Japan, in addition to requesting future legal status, are making increasingly strong requests for lifestyle-based and economic rights including the end of workplace discrimination, financing from public banks, the end of discrimination in public housing, and the granting of child support allowances" (1999 [1975]: 149). Like Tatsumi's 1966 analysis cited above, Sakanaka's essay uses the word "instability" (*fuantei*) to describe the situation of Koreans in Japan. However, unlike Tatsumi's essay, Sakanaka specifically addresses a wide range of factors that create that instability, and he makes specific arguments about solutions that the government should pursue.

Sakanaka notes three ways of thinking about the appropriate treatment of Koreans in Japan: "(1) assimilation (naturalization) policy, (2) a policy of treating them and their descendants as foreigners, and (3) encouraging and forcing them to return to their country of origin" (1999 [1975]: 150). He is critical of each approach; while he dismisses the third approach quickly, arguing that forcibly returning Koreans to Korea or encouraging them to return is contrary to humanitarian ideals and is not likely given the current context, he devotes a bit more attention to the first two ways of thinking about the treatment of Koreans in Japan. Regarding assimilation/naturalization politics, he argues that many Koreans in Japan do not want to take on Japanese nationality for historical reasons. He also claims that, even if they do take such nationality, "the problem remains that, as 'former Koreans,' it is expected that they will still face discrimination" (151).

While this criticism suggests a degree of discomfort with assimilation-driven policies, Sakanaka's criticism of the second way of thinking about Koreans in Japan—the policy of treating them and their descendants as foreigners—suggests that he is also uncomfortable with the idea of Japan continuing to have a large, unassimilated minority population. He argues:

> It is thought that there is a natural momentum pulling second and third generation Koreans in Japan toward "Japanization" in the form of language, customs, and ways of thinking, to the extent that they can carry out a lifestyle in Japan. However, we should indicate that that things that contradict this natural tendency create a situation where ethnic consciousness provides spiritual uplift, and Koreans in Japan can effectively create an ethnic minority consciousness, and there is a strong chance that the root cause—an ethnic minority problem—will remain. (1999 [1975]: 151)

This quote is telling because it reveals that Sakanaka is not actually opposed to assimilation. He is opposed to government policies that promote naturalization as a form of assimilation, because he does not believe that many Koreans want to naturalize, and because he thinks that Koreans will still face discrimination. But in the above quote he suggests that, if the government wants to promote the actual assimilation of Japan's Korean minority (separate from promoting naturalization), it should promote their human rights.

The Sakanaka thesis was not an official statement of policy. However, the fact that it won the Bureau of Immigration's essay contest in 1975 and Sakanaka's subsequent extremely successful career as an Immigration Bureau bureaucrat suggest that it influenced the Immigration Bureau. Moreover, the impact of the Sakanaka thesis on how the Bureau of Immigration discussed foreign residents was immediately evident. The Bureau of Immigration's 1976 periodic report was the first such report in the postwar period to have a section devoted to human rights (see Ministry of Justice 1959, 1964, 1971, 1976). Also, in 1976, the Bureau of Immigration released a white paper that called Koreans "settled" residents for the first time (Chung 2010: 147). Broadly speaking, the Sakanaka thesis marked the beginning of a new emphasis by the Bureau of Immigration in dealing with Japan's Korean minority: focusing on reducing discrimination against Koreans in Japan in order to avoid creating a visible ethnic minority—vocal and unhappy—a minority whose very existence challenged the notion of Japan's ethnic homogeneity.

Changes in the Treatment of Oldcomer Koreans after the Sakanaka Thesis

The Sakanaka thesis and the change in elite thinking that it marked had material consequences for the treatment of oldcomer Koreans and other permanent residents in Japan. In the 1970s and 1980s, Japan made substantial efforts to increase the access of foreign residents to public-sector employment, social safety-net programs, and education, thereby complying with international human rights norms against discrimination against foreign residents. In public-sector employment, the first major change occurred in 1977, when Nippon Telephone and Telegraph (NTT), a public corporation, lifted the requirement that its employees be Japanese nationals and began to employ some Korean residents of Japan. NTT thus joined Japan's other two major public companies, Japan National Railway and the Japan Monopoly Corporation, in hiring foreign residents.[12] Also in 1977, a foreign resident was able to become an attorney for the first time in the postwar period. In Japan, prospective attorneys were required to spend two years at the Supreme Court–led Legal Training and Research Institute, and the Supreme Court did not allow foreign nationals to attend. However, in 1977 a prospective attorney with Korean nationality refused to naturalize, and the Supreme Court changed the rule (Iwasawa 1998: 165–66).

In 1983, the Ministry of Economy, Trade, and Industry revised an order to allow foreign residents to become patent attorneys either under the principle of reciprocity or "when the Minister of International Trade and Industry recognizes it as appropriate." In 1984, the Ministry of Posts and Telegraphs, under pressure from an Osaka citizens' movement, began to allow noncitizens to serve as mail carriers, and in 1986, the Ministry of Home Affairs sent a circular notice to municipal governments encouraging them to treat health nurses, midwives, and nursing positions as technical and thus allow foreign residents to take those positions (Iwasawa 1998: 164–66).

Changes in the social safety net began even earlier. During the 1965 normalization talks between Japan and South Korea, Japan promised to extend national health insurance to South Korean citizens in Japan, which Japan did in 1967. Many municipalities also chose to extend health insurance to other foreign residents, but they were not required to do so. Because the citizenship of Koreans in Japan was fairly fluid—it was not very difficult to move one's citizenship from North Korea to South Korea—this policy had the effect of encouraging Koreans to change their citizenship from North Korea to South Korea, thus weakening the relationship between the Communist North and the Korean community in Japan, which was a desirable Cold War strategy to the Japanese state. In 1982, following the ratification of the Refugee Convention, national health insurance was extended to refugees, and in 1986 national health insurance was extended to all foreign residents who would be in Japan for more than one year (Iwasawa 1998: 169–70).

In 1975, the Ministry of Construction began to allow foreign residents to use public housing, and in 1979 the Ministry of Health and Welfare formally changed its interpretation of the Mother-Child and Widow Welfare laws so that foreign residents were eligible for those programs. In 1982, refugees and foreign residents were allowed to participate in Japan's national pension plan—with the exception of those who were over sixty or over twenty and disabled in 1982. The Refugee Convention did not require Japan to extend pensions to foreign residents, but the idea that if pensions are extended to refugees, they should be extended to foreign residents too was virtually uncontested in Japanese elite public discourse. In 1983, the Tokyo High Court ruled that Japan was required to pay the pension of a Korean man who had been sold a Japanese pension plan before 1982, and, in a move that was rare for Japanese courts, the High Court cited international human rights treaties in its decision (Iwasawa 1998: 171–75).

There were two major changes in education policy as well. In 1975, the public Japan Scholarship Society changed its policy so that some foreign residents could obtain loans for education, and federal policy was changed in 1982 so that foreigners could be hired as full professors at national and municipal universities. Unlike the majority of laws in Japan, DMs, rather than bureaucrats, proposed this law. The version of the law that bureaucrats had proposed was more restrictive of the rights of foreign professors (Iwasawa 1998: 157, 163, note 157).

In sum, Japan prohibited a variety of discriminatory practices against foreign residents in the 1970s and 1980s, and the group that was most impacted by those changes was the oldcomer Koreans who could trace their or their family's time in Japan to the colonial period. These changes were made possible by the weakening elite consensus around the separatist idea, discussed above. Those elites who continued to support the separatist idea began to be challenged by an emerging group of elites who believed that, under some limited circumstances, assimilation of foreign residents was possible and desirable. As a result of these changes, Shipper suggests that oldcomer Koreans are now "at the top of the racialized hierarchy in terms of immigration status and rights" (Shipper 2008: 35). Because these reforms primarily impacted oldcomer Koreans, the reforms were supported by assimilation optimists while being relatively unobjectionable to assimilation pessimists because they were framed as a way to preserve the appearance of ethnic homogeneity.

Indeed, it is possible to extend additional rights to oldcomer Koreans while preserving the appearance of ethnic homogeneity because of the unusual nature of the oldcomer Korean community. As Chung notes, "among advanced industrialized democracies, the foreign population in Japan is one of the only groups for which phenotypical difference is *not* the basis for the formation of new ethnic minorities." Chung goes on to say that in addition to "physical indistinguishability from the dominant Japanese population" (2010: 55), that community also generally speaks Japanese as a first language, and a large percentage of oldcomer Koreans have Japanese names that they use at least part of the time.

The Birth of Assimilation Optimism and Pessimism

In the years after the Sakanaka thesis and the subsequent changes to the legal treatment of foreign residents in Japan, elites in the government, business, and the media began to debate about whether it was possible and/or desirable to assimilate oldcomer Koreans and other foreign residents of Japan in order to preserve the idea of Japan as a homogeneous country. I call those elites on each side of this debate "assimilation optimists" and "assimilation pessimists."[13] Assimilation pessimists are strongly committed to the idea of Japan as ethnically homogeneous and do not believe that it is possible or desirable to assimilate foreign residents. However, assimilation optimists believe that, in some cases, it is possible and desirable to assimilate foreign residents into Japanese society. Assimilation optimists share with the mixed-nation theorists of the prewar period the idea that it is possible for those without Japanese blood to become Japanese, at least in some cases.

Nihon University law professor Akira Momochi clearly articulates assimilation pessimism in an essay in the popular conservative journal *Seiron*. Momochi discusses a 2008 Japanese Supreme Court decision and the subsequent revision of the immigration law to comply with that decision. Before 2008, a child born to an unmarried foreign mother and Japanese father was not granted Japanese citizenship unless the Japanese father acknowledged paternity before the child was born. On June 4, 2008, the Japanese Supreme Court ruled that this was a violation of the constitution's guarantee of equal protection under the law, and on November 18, the ruling coalition agreed to pass a law that granted Japanese citizenship to a baby born to a foreign mother and a Japanese father, even if the Japanese father acknowledges paternity after the baby is born.

Momochi's essay is critical of both the Supreme Court decision and the law. He is particularly concerned with the possibility of babies fraudulently obtaining Japanese citizenship. Toward the conclusion of his discussion of the Supreme Court decision, Momochi argues:

> If citizenship can be conferred with only the "acknowledge-
> ment" (*ninchi*) of a Japanese man, then babies that are born
> and raised in foreign countries, and have never once been
> to Japan . . . can obtain [Japanese] citizenship. This is in
> fundamental contradiction to the principle of a citizenship
> policy that awards citizenship based not only on blood con-
> nections, but also on close relations with our country's society.
> (2009: 123)

In other words, Momochi argues that Japanese blood should be a necessary but not a sufficient condition for the conferring of Japanese citizenship. While states usually confer citizenship by blood (to those born of
citizens) *or* by soil (to those born on the territory), Momochi suggests
that Japan should use *both* principles to restrict access to citizenship even
further. This is consistent with Momochi's conclusion, where he suggests
that naturalization should be made more difficult, noting that, unlike
the United States, applicants for naturalization in Japan are not asked
to pledge permanent allegiance to Japan (127).

Momochi's concern about proposals that he fears make Japanese
citizenship too accessible stem from his views about the stakes in this
kind of argument. He believes that permissive citizenship policies—policies that might obfuscate the meaning of "Japanese citizenship"—might
well destroy Japanese society. This is evident both from the title of his
essay, "Reform of Citizenship Law Will Dissolve Japan," and from the
concluding section, where he argues: "those that do not understand rev-
erence for the nation (*kokka no sonkei*) or the weightiness of citizenship (*kokuseki no omomi*) have combined with those that aim to destroy
the nation like bitter enemies placed in the same boat, and decided to
allow citizenship to be acquired simply with an acknowledgment" (2009:
127).

Momochi clearly believes that changes that make it easier for those
without Japanese ethnicity to access Japanese citizenship pose an existen-
tial threat to something fundamental about Japan. In short, Momochi
believes that it is neither possible nor desirable for foreign residents to
assimilate and become Japanese.

In another *Seiron* article, Nisohachi Hyodo is critical of recent
policies that allow relatively small numbers of nurses into Japan from
Indonesia and the Philippines (these policies are discussed in more depth

in chapter 4). Hyodo argues that instead of admitting foreign workers, Japan should attempt to lure disaffected Japanese, including those not in employment, education, or training (NEETs) and *puutarō* (vagabonds) back into Japanese society, since they are "on the side of Japan" (*nihon no mikata*)(2009: 27). By way of contrast, "the idea that it is ok to shift the responsibility for Japan to cheap foreign labor power is only held by people who have not thought at all about Japanese society or Japanese civilization" (Hyodo 2000: 27). In short, Hyodo believes that it is unthinkable that foreign labor can solve Japanese labor shortages because there is no avenue through which foreigners can become Japanese. It is better to entrust Japan's future to those with Japanese ethnicity who do not want to work than to entrust that future to those without Japanese ethnicity who do.

More recently, novelist Ayako Sano wrote a column that broke with Hyodo's optimism that labor shortages, particularly in the area of elder-care nursing, could be solved with Japanese labor. Sano argues that there are not enough Japanese workers to address these labor shortages. Instead, she argues that these labor shortages can be solved with temporary foreign labor, particularly female laborers from nearby countries. After briefly making the case for this form of temporary foreign labor, Sano makes a rhetorical move that was condemned by many Japanese pundits and even earned condemnation from the South African embassy. She argues that the postapartheid era in South Africa has failed because blacks live in large families which whites cannot adjust to. She concludes her essay by saying that "people work, research, exercise, and do many other things together. However, it is best if people live separately" (*Sankei Shimbun* 5/11/2015). In other words, it is not possible or desirable for the foreign workers about which she writes to assimilate into Japanese society, and they should thus live in separate enclaves, modeled after South African apartheid.

Not all conservative pundits and politicians are as pessimistic about the ability of foreigners to assimilate into Japanese society. A clear articulation of the assimilation optimist's perspective is found in the work of Taikin Tei, a professor at Tokyo Metropolitan University and frequent commentator on issues relating to foreign residents of Japan.[14] In 2008, Tei wrote an article in the popular center-right magazine *Chūō Koron* about proposals to grant foreign residents the right to vote in local elections in Japan. This piece is primarily concerned with Koreans in Japan.

Tei argues that there is a taboo against naturalization within the Korean community in Japan. Tei traces this taboo to the notion that "naturalization is assimilation," and he argues that this notion comes from Chōsen Sōren, the North Korean–affiliated group in Japan. According to Tei, proposals that would grant Korean residents the right to vote, rather than encourage them to naturalize, "makes permanent the discrepancy between the identity and membership of Koreans in Japan" (*zainichi no aidentiti to kizoku no aida no zure wo eizokuka saseru*) (Tei 2008: 130). Moreover, Tei argues that more Koreans want to naturalize than obtain the right to vote. As evidence for this claim, he cites the fact that, while five thousand people showed up to a demonstration in favor of the right to vote for foreign residents in January of 2008, twice that number—ten thousand Koreans—naturalize every year (131).

Instead of granting Korean residents the right to vote in local elections in Japan, Tei suggests making naturalization easier by streamlining the naturalization process for special permanent residents and allowing naturalization applicants to choose from an expanded set of Chinese characters that would include a larger number of characters that are common in Chinese and Korean names.

Tei justifies this proposal by arguing that, in addition to helping Koreans in Japan avoid the identity confusion that comes with holding one nationality while voting in another nation, this proposal would also benefit Japan:

> One thing that is exceptional about Japan compared with other East Asian countries is that, although people have the freedom to leave, there is very little emigration. Japanese people have a feeling of trust toward their own country, and to some degree this is a thing that connects them, about which Japanese people are proud. However, because of this, we should not forget that this has averted Japan from opportunities to build feelings of solidarity with other cultures. (Tei 2008: 132)

In short, making naturalization easier for foreign permanent residents would benefit Japan because it would give Japanese more opportunities to interact with those from other cultures. However, these opportunities would have their limits, as Tei only proposes to streamline naturalization for special permanent residents of Japan. As noted above, this group is almost entirely made up of Koreans who can trace their family's residence in Japan to before 1945. A very large percentage of these people speak Japanese as their first language and are highly assimilated into Japanese society.

Tei rejects a policy that would pose a substantial challenge to the idea that Japan is ethnically homogeneous—granting foreign residents the right to vote in local elections—in favor of a policy that would pose a relatively minor challenge—streamlining the naturalization process for special permanent residents. Tei is an assimilation optimist because he believes that oldcomer Koreans can and should be encouraged to assimilate into Japanese society and that granting foreign residents the right to vote in local elections in Japan without naturalizing would make assimilation less likely.

Voting Rights for Foreign Residents in the Diet

The reforms in the treatment of oldcomer Koreans in the years after the Sakanaka thesis could be justified as making what was then the largest population of foreign residents in Japan less likely to protest, and thus less visible. However, subsequent proposals to grant oldcomer Koreans the right to vote in local elections did not make much progress in the Japanese Diet because of shared concerns by assimilation optimists and pessimists in the LDP that such policies would make it easier for those without Japanese ethnicity to be active members of their community while also being visible as ethnic minorities.

Activists and politicians have made a number of proposals to grant foreign permanent residents the right to vote in local elections. According to Japan's Ministry of Internal Affairs and Communications, as of February 28, 2007, 32 prefectures, 12 ordinance-designated cities, and 1,193 nonordinance-designated municipalities made written requests to grant foreign residents the right to vote in local elections (House of Councilors [HoC], 3/13/2007). The Supreme Court also ruled on this question in 1995, determining that Japan's constitution neither requires the national government to grant foreign residents the right to vote in local elections nor forbids national government from granting such a right.

In the Diet, the CGP—the party that has been the junior partner in a coalition with the LDP since 1998—has unsuccessfully supported proposals that would have granted foreign residents the right to vote in local elections. The CGP was quite persistent about this in the 2000s, raising the issue six separate times between 2000 and 2006 (Chung 2010: 184, note 11). Unlike LDP politicians, CGP politicians cannot always be called assimilation optimists or pessimists; some CGP politicians have explicitly made the case for a multi-ethnic Japan, instead of a Japan where foreign residents either disappear through assimilation or through leaving. CGP DM Tetsuzō Fuyushiba was the most vocal proponent of extending the right to vote to foreign residents when this issue was being regularly debated. In defending a proposed law that would have extended the right to vote to foreign residents in 2004, Fuyushiba makes two kinds of arguments. First, he discusses the desirability of foreign residents voting with reference to what that would mean for Japanese democracy: "[I]t is desirable that people that live in the area can independently and autonomously make decisions regarding regional issues, and as a mature democratic country . . . [T]he cooperative management decisions in regions with exceptionally close relationships [with foreign residents] in daily life should reflect those relationships" (HoR 11/16/2004). Noteworthy here is Fuyushiba's reference to "mature democracy," along with the implication that mature democracies have local decision-making mechanisms with inclusive participation.

After his general statement about the importance of the foreign resident vote to Japanese democracy, Fuyushiba specifically notes the foreign community that would be most impacted by this kind of policy change: Japan's Korean minority. Fuyushiba argues that "for the oldcomer Koreans who have been born, raised, made a living, and will die in this country, regarding that population with their particular historical background, if they would like to, we should treat them the same as Japanese nationals, without limit" (HoR 11/16/2004).

After making this argument with reference to the specific historical and demographic circumstances of the oldcomer Korean population, Fuyushiba also argues that improving the situation of oldcomer Koreans would have a positive impact on Japan's relationship with South Korea. He notes that two different South Korean presidents—Kim Dae-jung and Roh Moo-hyun—both discussed the issue of voting rights for oldcomer Koreans in speeches before the Japanese Diet, and he quotes passages from each speech (HoR 11/16/2004). After South Korea extended the right to vote in local elections to foreign residents (including Japanese citizens) in 2006, Fuyushiba also began to argue that the international relations principle of reciprocity obligated Japan to extend the same right at least to South Koreans (HoC 3/13/2007).

Although Fuyushiba himself generally does not use the phrase "multi-ethnic country," other members of his party have used this phrase to describe a possible and desirable result of granting the right to vote to foreign residents. CGP DM Shigeki Satō argued in a 2004 hearing on constitutional revision that "as we think about what kind of society 21st century Japan is, from now on, I can't help but thinking about the definite possibility that Japan will become a multiethnic country, where people from various ethnicities can coexist, and about how this kind of Japan could do things such as securing our labor force in an era of declining population" (HoR 11/18/2004). Satō notes that granting human rights to foreign residents could make Japan into a multiethnic society, and he expresses concern that the strong opposition to CGP proposals to grant foreign residents the right to vote will make it more difficult for Japan to become multiethnic. In addition to Fuyushiba and Satō, a number of other CGP DMs have spoken in favor of granting the right to vote to foreign permanent residents in local elections, including Taniguchi Takayoshi, the vice minister of public management, home affairs, posts, and telecommunications under Prime Minister Yasuo Fukuda (HoR 1/21/2008), Tetsuo Saitō (HoR 3/6/2006), Yutaka Fukushima (HoR 2/2/2005), and Hidekatsu Yoshii (HoR 11/16/2004).

Aside from the CGP, the other major political party that frequently spoke in favor of granting the right to vote to foreign residents in Japan was the now defunct DPJ. DPJ Upper House DMs including Takashi Yamamoto (HoC 4/6/2005; HoC 12/6/2006), Shinkun Haku (HoC 3/13/2007), and Renhō (HoC 4/23/2008) have all spoken in favor of granting foreign residents the right to vote in local elections. In addition, the former head of the DPJ, Ichirō Ozawa, told South Korean president Lee Myung-bak that he supported extending the right to vote in local elections to foreign residents in Japan in February 2008.

DPJ DMs sometimes attempted to use the issue of extending the right to vote to foreign residents to drive a wedge through the ruling coalition by questioning whether—despite the formal goals of the LDP/ CGP alliance—LDP DMs would ever vote for a law that would grant foreign residents any kind of voting rights. In a 2007 hearing of the

House of Councilors Budget Committee, DPJ DM Shinkun Haku asked CGP DM and the minister of land, infrastructure, transportation, and tourism Tetsuzō Fuyushiba several aggressive questions about the CGP/ LDP alliance including the following: "Because [the right to vote in local elections for foreign residents] is in your ruling coalition agreement, even though you say things like 'the LDP is a different party from mine,' I can't help but thinking that deep down you are embarrassed about [the LDP's behavior]. Can you comment on that?" (HoC 3/13/2007). Haku clearly tried to use the issue to highlight differences between the CGP and the LDP.

However, not all DPJ DMs support extending the right to vote to foreign residents. In particular, both Hitoshi Matsubara (HoR 5/19/2006) and Yukihiko Akutsu (HoR 11/16/2004) have raised concerns that extending the right to vote to foreign residents would benefit North Korea. In a Lower House Foreign Affairs Committee meeting, Matsubara asked Minister of Foreign Affairs Tarō Asō several questions about coop-eration between Mindan, the organization representing South Koreans in Japan, and Chōsen-Sōren, the organization representing North Koreans. When Asō suggests that the two groups differ on whether the right to vote in local elections should be extended to Koreans in Japan—Chōsen Sōren does not support such a policy—Matsubara argues, "I have heard it said Chōsen-Sōren is analyzing whether to support the right to vote for foreign residents in the future" (HoR 5/19/2006). While Matsubara does not specifically speak against granting this right, his skepticism about the motives of the social organizations in the oldcomer Korean community suggests that he would prefer that the community not be granted a larger role in Japanese politics.

LDP leadership has been reluctant to directly criticize proposals to extend the right to vote to foreign residents in local elections—perhaps because of the LDP's coalition agreement with the CGP. The last three LDP prime ministers of Japan—Tarō Asō, Yasuo Fukuda, and Shinzō Abe—all made statements in Diet hearings that suggest that, while they do not support the CGP's policy proposal, they are not willing to issue direct criticism. Abe came the closest to direct criticism when, as chief cabinet secretary, he noted in discussing a meeting with a South Korean official that "regarding the history problem and the issue of the right to vote for foreign permanent residents in local elections, while our opinions and understanding were different, we frankly talked to one another, and

I did not think that [the differences] were important" (HoC 3/13/2007). He does not clarify what specifically these differences were, but the clear implication is that, unlike the South Korean official, Abe does not support granting the right to vote to foreign residents in local elections.

Fukuda and Asō were less direct. Fukuda as prime minister (HoR 1/12/2008) and Asō as foreign minister (HoC 3/13/2007) each argued that the issue needed to be debated more, and Asō specifically mentioned that those who do not support the policy should be included in the debate.

LDP backbenchers have been much more vocal in their opposition to policies that would extend voting rights to foreign residents. In an argument with CGP DM Tetsuzō Fuyushiba, LDP DM Masazumi Gotōda takes the position of an assimilation pessimist, arguing that extending this right does not suit one-ethnicity countries like Japan and other Asian countries:

> You have given America as an example, and one might also say the same thing about Europe. Compared with other countries, Japan is a one-ethnicity country, and America and Europe are multi-ethnic countries. I think that this is a big difference between those countries and our country Japan. Now, while there is a situation of foreign permanent residents obtaining citizenship, there are also many examples of European countries that extend the right to vote in local elections. However, in China, Japan, South Korea, and North Korea, this kind of thing is not allowed. (HoR 11/16/2004)

Unlike the CGP's Shigeki Satō, who sees Japan as moving away from being a one-ethnicity country (and who sees that movement as desirable for economic reasons), Gotōda treats Japan's status as a one-ethnicity country as an unavoidable and unchangeable fact. Moreover, his remarks do not highlight a way in which non-Japanese can become Japanese through assimilation.

Another LDP DM, Tsukashi Akimoto, expresses concern that a foreigner voting has two hearts (*futatsu no kokoro wo motte iru*). He goes on to argue that while a foreigner can definitely be loyal to Japan, those foreigners who are loyal to Japan should give up ties to their previous country by naturalizing: "I don't deny that [a foreigner] could love Japan, but because there is currently a system whereby foreign residents can naturalize, if a foreigner uses that system, he or she receives the right to vote" (HoC 4/6/2005). Unlike Gotōda, Akimoto's statement implies that foreigners can obtain Japanese identity if they love Japan.[15]

It is difficult to imagine the LDP supporting a proposal to grant foreign permanent residents of Japan the right to vote in local elections. While there may be a few LDP DMs who support the CGP's position, those individuals, if they exist, have been silent in Diet debates. That said, the differences between Gotōda and Akimoto's objections to granting foreign residents the right to vote are revealing. While Gotōda and Akimoto's different ideas about the possibility and acceptability of foreigners assimilating lead them to the same conclusion, these two differing perspectives—both still in existence within the contemporary LDP and the Japanese conservative movement more broadly, suggest different possibilities for immigration reform in the future. The possibility of immigration reform in the future in Japan are discussed in more depth in chapter 6.

Japan beyond Assimilation Optimism and Pessimism?

Neither assimilation optimism nor assimilation pessimism—the two major ways of thinking about foreign residents in Japan among the conservatives that dominate the Japanese government—suggests that significant numbers of foreign nationals have a legitimate claim to residency and membership in Japan. Given the dominance of these ways of thinking about foreign residents, we should not be surprised that Japan has admitted so few foreign residents in the postwar period. Assimilation optimists and pessimists share a belief that non-Japanese should not be visible in Japan. This belief can be traced back to the elite movement against the "mixed-nation theory" that coincided with the occupation of Japan and the end of Japanese imperialism. Assimilation pessimists believe that foreign residents should be, for the most part, kept out of Japan, because they are not confident that the idea of Japan's homogeneity could be preserved with any significant, visible foreign presence in Japan. Assimilation optimists believe that foreigners can and should be encouraged to become as "Japanese" as possible so as to reduce, if not eliminate, the visibility of ethnic minorities.

Under what circumstances might we see significant alternatives to assimilation optimism and pessimism emerging as influential strains of elite thought in the coming years? I argue that there are three paths through which alternative ways of thinking about foreign residents might emerge.[16] First, it is possible that the economic and demographic pressures stemming from *shōshikōreika* will become so severe that Japanese elites will have no choice but to find a way to justify the admission of long-term foreign laborers. Chapter 4 will provide a sense of how such a change might happen by examining the way that Japan has admitted foreign laborers (in relatively small numbers) in the past. Second, it is possible that a collapse of the North Korean region or a catastrophe somewhere in Asia will convince Japanese elites to admit large numbers of refugees, and, relatedly, to rethink the appropriate role of foreign residents in Japan. Chapter 5 examines the way that Japan dealt with a major Asian refugee crisis from the 1970s and 1980s—the mass exodus out of Southeast Asia as Communist regimes consolidated power in Vietnam, Laos, and Cambodia—in order to provide a sense of how Japan's response to unexpected refugee flows might look in the future.

Third, it is possible that leaders in Japan will articulate a new way of thinking about Japanese identity that persuades both other elites and the public that challenging the idea of Japan's ethnic homogeneity is possible and desirable. Chapter 6 examines proposals by politicians in Japan's major parties in recent years to shake up Japan's immigration policy and thus, perhaps, Japan's national identity.

4

The Crow Is White

Foreign Labor and the Japanese State

Because we don't have foreign labor in Japan, we have the Trainee
and Technical Internship Program. In Japanese, we have an expres-
sion, "the crow is white," which means that, although we don't
say "labor power," trainees and interns are actually laborers in dis-
guise [just as a "white crow" would actually be a black crow in
disguise]. . . . As a society of elderly people continues on without
young people, those that support society will go away, those that
can activate the economy will go away, and those that care for the
elderly will go away. In short, the country will gradually collapse,
and so to fix this situation, there is no alternative but to gradually
utilize people from foreign countries.

—Interview 1173

In sectors across the Japanese economy, firms are facing severe labor
shortages. These labor shortages have been a topic of serious discussion
by Japanese politicians, bureaucrats, and businesspeople. And yet, until
recently, Japan has been extremely reluctant to turn to foreign labor to
address these shortages. In this chapter, I outline the history of Japan's
responses to labor shortages in order to explain its reluctance to admit
foreign laborers in large numbers. I argue that Japan has been reluctant
to admit foreign laborers for two reasons. First, it developed its domestic

labor shortages late relative to West European states such as France and Germany. Second, Japan's governing elites have come to view Western European labor migration policy as a failure that Japan should take care to avoid emulating.

I begin this chapter with a snapshot of the foreign laborers that are currently in Japan. Second, I outline labor shortages that are currently facing Japan, as well as some of the things that Japan has done to address those shortages. Third, I trace the history of the government's response to requests to use foreign labor to address labor shortages, focusing in particular on the economic and political contexts of cabinet understanding from 1967, 1973, and 1976 and the 1989 revision of the Immigration Control and Refugee Recognition Act. Finally, I trace the (often unintended) consequences of the 1989 revision and subsequent reforms. Throughout this chapter, readers will observe governing elites attempting to balance their desire to address serious labor shortages with their fear of duplicating what they see as the social instability stemming from foreign labor migration in Europe.

Foreign Labor in Contemporary Japan

As of July 2017, there were 2,471,458 foreign residents in Japan (Ministry of Justice 2017), which made up 1.95 percent of Japan's total population (Ministry of Internal Affairs and Communications 2018). Table 4.1 shows the most common countries of origins of foreign residents, and table 4.2 on page 64 shows the six most common visa categories. Three of the visa categories in permit their holders to work in almost any kind of job that a Japanese person could work in (with the exception of government jobs and elected office): permanent resident, special permanent resident, and long-term resident. In most cases, permanent residents are required to have lived in Japan for ten consecutive years and convinced the Ministry of Justice that, among other things, their "permanent residence is regarded to be in accord with the interests of Japan" (Ministry of Justice 2006a).

Special permanent residents are almost all those with Korean heritage whose family moved to Japan between 1910 and 1945, when Japan occupied Korea (some Koreans moved for economic opportunity, and others were brought to Japan and forced to work in Japanese factories).[1]

Table 4.1. Foreign residents of Japan in 2017 by citizenship

China	711,486	28.79%
South Korea	452,953	18.33%
Philippines	251,934	10.19%
Vietnam	232,562	9.41%
Brazil	185,967	7.52%
Nepal	74,300	3.01%
United States	54,918	2.22%
Taiwan	54,358	2.20%
Thailand	48,952	1.98%
Peru	47,861	1.94%
Indonesia	46,350	1.88%
North Korea	31,674	1.28%
India	30,048	1.22%
Other	248,095	10.04%
TOTAL 2,471,458	100.00%	

Data from Ministry of Justice (Japan), 2017.

This community is sometimes called "oldcomer" Koreans to distinguish them from Koreans who have come to Japan since the end of World War II. Long-term residents are those with Japanese ancestry who were permitted to migrate to Japan by the 1989 reform of the Immigration Control and Refugee Recognition Act, which will be discussed in more depth below.

The Engineer/Humanities/International Services Visa (established by law in 2014 and went into effect in April 1, 2015) attempts to combine several different kinds of skilled labor visas under one title. The Immigration Bureau explains on its website: "In order to respond flexibly to the needs of companies, etc. related to the acceptance of foreign nationals in professional and technical fields, the division between 'Engineer' and 'Specialist in Humanities/International Services,' which was based on a division of knowledge (sciences/humanities) necessary for the work, was removed" (Ministry of Justice 2015).

The other largest visa categories among foreign residents in Japan are those of trainees, technical interns, and students. Holders of these two kinds of visas are permitted to work in Japan, but their job opportunities are severely regulated. Foreign students must apply at a regional immigra-

Table 4.2. Foreign residents of Japan in 2017 by visa type

Permanent residents	738,661	33% Chinese, 17.1% Filipino, 15.2% Brazilian, 9.3% South Korean, 4.6% Peru, 20.8% other
Special permanent residents	334,298	89.6% South Korean, 9.3% North Korean, 0.3% Chinese, 0.3% Taiwanese, 0.5% other
Foreign students	291,164	39.5% Chinese, 23.9% Vietnamese, 8.5% Nepali, 5.5% South Korean, 3.3% Taiwanese, 19.3% other
Trainees and Technical Interns	251,721	41.6% Vietnamese, 31.8% Chinese, 10.2% Filipino, 8.1% Indonesian, 3.1% Thai, 2.3% Cambodian, 2.9% other
Engineer/Humanities/ International Services	180,180	41.4% Chinese, 11.7% South Korean, 10.1% Vietnamese, 4.7% American, 4.6% Taiwanese, 3.4% Indian, 24.1% other
Long-term residents	173,317	30.3% Brazilian, 27.9% Filipino, 15.9% Chinese, 6% Peruvian, 4.2% South Korean, 15.7% other
Other visa categories	502,117	33.8% Chinese, 8.7% Filipino, 8% South Korean, 8% Nepali, 5% American, 4.1% Brazilian, 32.4% other

Data from Ministry of Justice (Japan), 2017.

tion control office for permission to work a part-time job (Ministry of Justice (Japan) No Date), and trainees and technical interns are limited to working at the firm that is responsible for their training.[2] After college students graduate, they are permitted to reside in Japan for a fixed period. An administrator involved with international students at a major public university told me that students are usually given ten months to remain in Japan after they graduate but that the Ministry of Justice still expects those students to leave within one to two months after graduating. If they do not leave after one to two months (even if they were given a ten-month visa), the Ministry of Justice begins contacting the university to ask why the recent graduates have not left yet (interview 1145).[3]

Undocumented laborers in Japan have been historically important in driving the government toward reform. Figure 4.1 outlines the ways in which the size of this group of has changed in the last twenty-five years. Given that these are government numbers, they likely understate the numbers of undocumented immigrants. For example, Tessa Morris-Suzuki (2006) demonstrates that tens of thousands of Koreans likely entered Japan illegally between 1946 and the 1970s, but these entrants are not acknowledged in official government statistics.

Even before the government was publishing statistics on undocumented foreign residents for public consumption, the Ministry of Justice's Immigration Bureau was very concerned with this group of people. Until

Figure 4.1. Undocumented foreign residents in Japan.

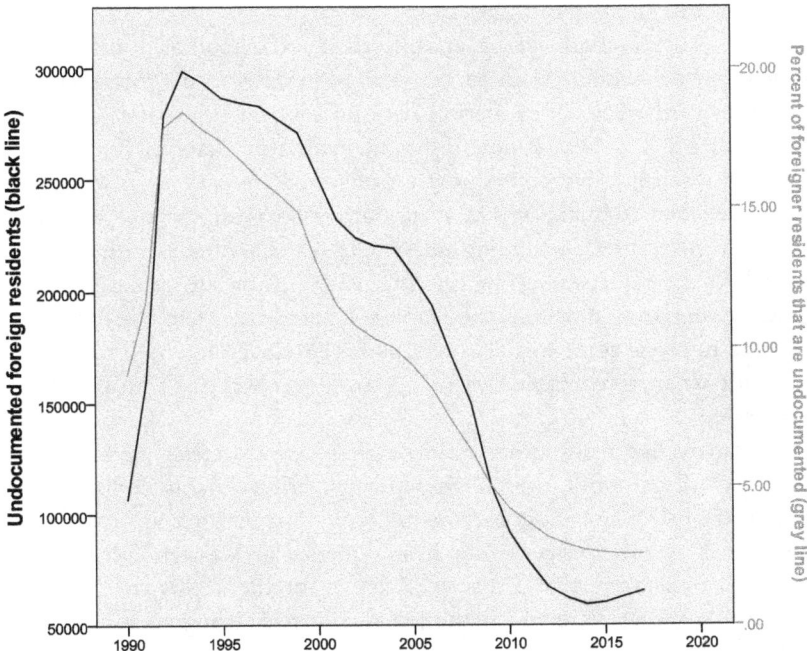

Data from Ministry of Justice (Japan), various years.

1980, the Immigration Bureau's annual reports focused primarily on illegal *entry*. Beginning in 1980s, these reports expanded their focus and began to discuss those illegally *staying* in Japan. It was not until 1985 that the Immigration Bureau used the phrase "illegal work" for the first time (Seigo 1997).

Japan is an island nation, and it is thus very difficult to reach without making the authorities aware of your presence (since airports are carefully monitored and boat journeys are perilous). Given that, most of the undocumented workers in Japan enter the country legally, but either work in jobs that are prohibited by their visa or overstay their visa. Two of my interview subjects had stories about how accidental visa overstays gave them or their employees a scare. A successful American businessman told me about how he realized that his visa was about to expire on a Friday. The following Monday, he went to the immigration office and turned himself in. He was left in a room alone for about two and a half hours (he later learned that this was to reflect on what he had done), and then he was asked to write a letter of apology. After that, his visa was renewed (interview 1129).

A British employee at an international school told me that a teacher at her school confused the expiration date on his foreigner registration card with the expiration date on his visa (these dates used to be different, but there is now only one expiration date for both pieces of identification). He consequently overstayed his visa by a few days, and they had to make several trips into Tokyo (the school was in a different prefecture), including one where the school administrator was asked to act as Japanese-English interpreter, since she spoke Japanese but the employee did not. The employee noted that, had the employee wanted to reveal some mistreatment by his employer, it would have been difficult when a representative of her employer was also the translator (interview 1149).

Japan, like many other countries, takes visa overstaying and other forms of illegal work by foreign residents seriously, and perhaps even more seriously when those overstaying their visas or working in jobs not permitted by their visas are not from America or Western Europe, like the two overstayers that I discussed above. In the 1990s the Ministry of Health and Welfare ended the practice of permitting undocumented foreign residents to buy into the Japanese National Health Insurance program, and many hospitals will not treat undocumented foreign residents (Shipper 2008: 52–53).

Perhaps the most interesting aspect of figure 4.1 is the peak. According to Ministry of Justice estimates, both the number of undocumented foreign residents and the percent of foreign residents that undocumented immigrants compose peaked in 1993, when 298,646, or 18.4 percent of foreign residents were undocumented. This number stayed above 250,000 until the year 2001, when it dipped to 232,121. One NGO representative that I spoke with suggested that the post-2001 dip was related to a government response to the September 11 attack in the United States. He suggested that the national and Tokyo governments specifically aimed to cut visa overstayers in half between 2003 and 2008 (interview 1198).

The pattern in figure 4.1 suggests that despite the 1990 Immigration Control and Refugee Recognition Act, which established the two pillars of low skilled labor migration to contemporary Japan—the Trainee and Technical Internship Program as well as the "long-term resident visa" which was aimed at those with Japanese heritage in South America and elsewhere—there remained significant demand for labor throughout the 1990s. This law and its consequences will be discussed in greater depth below.

Japan's Labor Shortages

As noted in chapter 2, Japan is currently facing severe labor shortages, with 86 percent of Japanese hiring managers reporting difficulties in filling jobs in 2017. Figure 4.2 puts these labor shortages into historical context. While the labor market has generally been good for Japanese job applicants—between 1964 and 2017 there were an average of 1.27 jobs for every new applicant to the job market—there have been three noticeable peaks in that period. In 1972, there were 2.14 jobs for every new applicant, in 1990 there were 2.07 jobs for every new applicant, and in 2017 there were 2.24 jobs for every new applicant. The 1990 and 2017 situations will be discussed later in the chapter. For now, we will dwell on 1971.

In the years leading up to 1971, Japan's economy had been growing extremely rapidly, and the kinds of industries that Japan was specializing

Figure 4.2. Japan's job seeker ratio.

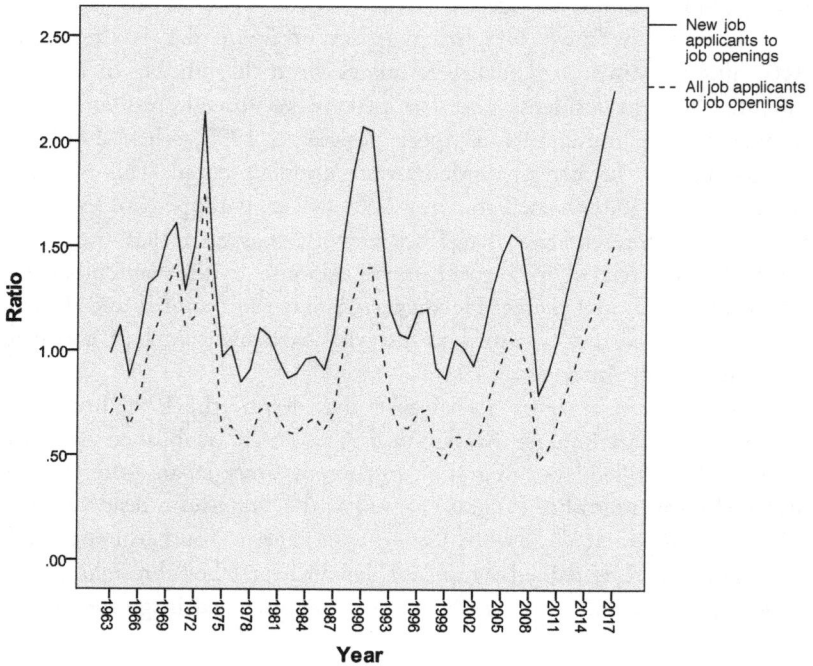

Data from Ministry of Health, Labor, and Welfare (Japan), 2018.

in relied on large numbers of laborers concentrated in urban areas. Before 1971, Japan's growing urban industries drew on workers employed in Japan's agricultural sector, luring them to cities with the promise of better wages. Compared with other countries that were pursing similar kinds of industrialization, such as Germany, France, and the United Kingdom, a large percentage of Japan's workforce remained in agriculture for a relatively long time. This discrepancy is clear when looking at figure 4.3. In 1961, when Germany had already signed guest-worker agreements with Italy, Spain, Greece, and Turkey (Bartram 2000: 11), 28.97 percent of Japan's labor force remained in agriculture. In contrast, only 13.15 percent of Germany's workforce was in agriculture in 1961.[4] Japan's agricultural workforce would not dip below 14 percent until 1973, and the most important interest group representing big business, Keidanren, first asked for Japan to admit foreign labor in 1970 (Yamawaki 2000: 58).

Figure 4.3. Percentage employed in agriculture.

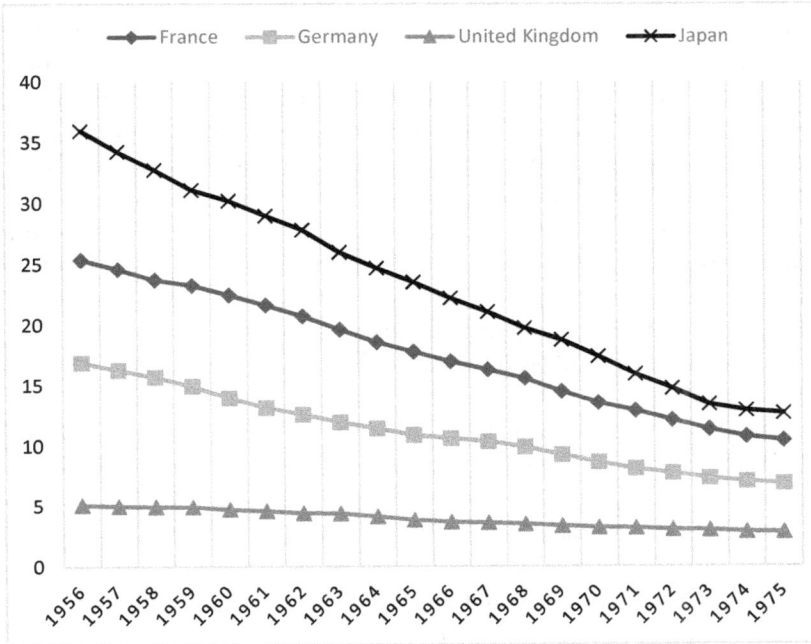

Data from OECD 2016.

Japan's labor shortage did not remain severe for long, however. Just as Japan's job-seeker's ratio reached its 1973 peak, with 2.14 jobs for every new job seeker, the global economy went into a depression, partially related to OPEC's decision to raise oil prices after the Yom Kippur War. By 1975, there were only .97 jobs for every new job seeker in Japan, and only .61 jobs for every job seeker in Japan (see figure 4.2). Thus, there was a relatively short period of time when companies became gravely in need of foreign labor in the late 1960s and early 1970s.

During that short period, Japan announced cabinet understandings dealing with labor strategy on two different occasions—in 1967 and 1973. Both of these cabinet understandings made it clear that Japan would not be admitting unskilled foreign laborers (there was another similar cabinet understanding in 1976, after the severe labor shortages had dissipated). In 1967, Prime Minister Eisaku Sato said on the day that the cabinet understanding was released: "We cannot admit foreign labor power because there is a problem with what kind of legal status those people will have" (*Yomiuri Shimbun* 3/14/1967). In 1973, on the day that the second labor-themed cabinet statement was released, Minister of Labor Tsunetaro Kato said: "In recent years construction businesses and others have asked for Japan to admit foreign labor. However, this cabinet understanding was formulated with an assumption that foreign labor power will not be used" (*Yomiuri Shimbun* 1/30/1973).

Despite these statements, Japan did begin in this period to import foreign labor on a very small scale. Kodama Chemical was permitted to bring in 10 trainees from Taiwan on one-year contracts, and Meiji Seisaku (a hydraulic pump and plastics maker) brought in a handful of trainees and their families on three-year contracts (Clark 1970: 42–43). Between 1965 and 1973, Japan admitted fewer than 331 South Koreans as trainees in the nursing field (Akashi 2010: 75). In October 1970, the Ministry of Labor proposed a plan that would have permitted companies to hire up to 1,000 trainees per year for five years (Clark 1970: 43). Had labor shortages continued for several years, instead of being cut short by the oil shock–related economic collapse of 1973, it seems plausible to suggest that Japanese businesses would have eventually succeeded in convincing the state to expand foreign labor admissions much beyond these small steps.

As noted above, in the 1980s, companies increasingly turned to undocumented migrants to fill their labor shortages. Particularly after the 1985 sharp rise in the yen against the dollar, it became difficult for small- and medium-sized manufacturing and construction companies to reduce costs in order to compete both domestically and abroad (Douglass and Roberts 2000: 6–7). Japanese firms thus turned to foreign labor from two different sources.

First, companies hired foreign students. In 1983, on a visit to Southeast Asia, Prime Minister Yasuhiro Nakasone met with people who had studied abroad in Japan, and he was shocked to hear them say that they did not plan to send their children to study abroad in Japan, and he resolved to fix Japan's exchange student programs. Later that year, Prime Minister Nakasone convened a panel of experts to discuss how Japan might create a Twenty-First Century Foreign Exchange Student Program, and he announced the "Statement About a 21ˢᵗ Century Foreign Exchange Student Policy," which was also known as the "100,000 Exchange Student Plan," because it included that ambitious goal (Tanaka 1995: 182). That goal was particularly ambitious because, in 1984, there were only around 8,000 foreign exchange students in Japan.

Nakasone's plan resulted in a much faster increase in precollege students (who planned to learn Japanese) than in college students, partially because Japanese language schools could act as guarantors, and thus the number of private Japanese language schools increased from 49 in 1984 to 414 in 1990 (Tanaka 1995: 190). As David Chiavacci notes:

> Many operators of these newly funded schools were not interested in offering good language tuition to studious students but were fully willing to act as guarantors for foreign students and to overlook absenteeism from school as long as these "students" paid their school fees. Some imposters even acted as intermediaries for non-existing Japanese language schools and claimed large brokerage fees. In October 1998, Chinese who had been deceived by such imposters demonstrated in front of the Japanese consulate in Shanghai. (2012: 33)

Chiavacci goes on to note that Japan increased its scrutiny on both Japanese language schools and the visa applications of Japanese language students in the late 1980s and thus seem to have alleviated this issue by the early 1990s.

The other large group of undocumented migrants in Japan were Asians who were working while on tourist visas or other kinds of visas that did not permit their holders to work. Japan attempted to combat this path to undocumented work by changing its immigration regulations so that, beginning in 1989 visitors from Pakistan and Bangladesh needed visas to visit Japan, and beginning in 1992, visitors from Iran needed visas (Kashiwazaki 1998: 240). However, as figure 4.1 demonstrates, the numbers of undocumented migrants in Japan continued to grow despite these changes. Akashi suggests that it was a combination of concern about foreign organized crime gangs; human trafficking in the 1990s; and, after September 11, 2001, international terrorism that caused the Japanese state to strengthen its enforcement efforts against undocumented foreign residents (2010: 198–99).

The 1990 System

As the Japanese state moved to push out undocumented migrants and to close loopholes that turned many students into de facto foreign laborers, Japan wrestled with how to create a new program to admit foreign residents that might fill labor shortages. Ultimately, Japan revised the Immigration Control and Refugee Recognition Act in 1989. This revision went into effect in 1990, and thus Jun'ichi Akashi and others call it the bedrock of the "1990 System," for immigration control (in contrast with the 1952 system that went into effect after US occupation) (Akashi 2010: 97).

The 1989 revision to the Immigration Control and Refugee Recognition Act made four major changes to the way that Japan deals with foreign residents; those changes continue to influence Japan today. First, the revision aimed to promote "highly skilled immigration" (Akashi 2010: 97), although there is no official definition of a "highly skilled immigrant," as visas are granted for job types, rather than skill level. There are thirteen visa categories that are generally considered to be "highly skilled" categories, including engineer, professor, and investor/business manager (Oishi 2012: 1082). As a general rule, these categories require at least ten years of education or practical experience after middle school, although in the late 1990s the education requirement for IT professionals was simultaneously standardized at fewer than ten years by Asian counties including Japan, India, Singapore, and Vietnam (Iguchi 2012: 1138–39).

Second, the revision established punishments for firms that hired workers without proper visas and for brokers who brought workers without proper visas. The law also established formal legal definition for "illegal work" activity, as "any activity engaged in by persons outside their residence status, persons who have entered Japan illegally, and for which remuneration or other income is received" (Seigo 1997: 82).

Third, the revision formalized and expanded the process of hiring foreign trainees and technical interns, a process which began before 1990 (Akashi 2010: 106). The Ministry of Justice explained this as an international development program. In the words of Immigration Bureau Chief Kagechika Matano, "The revised law would increase the numbers of trainees that we admit, but this is an important dimension of our international cooperation strategy with developing countries and others" (HoC 11/30/1989b). In short, the formal justification for this law was that it would allow Japan to transfer technical knowhow to the developing world by teaching skills to temporary residents and then sending them back to their countries of origin to put their skills to use. Even at the time, this program was understood by many of its supporters and critics as a de facto low-skilled immigration program, although some supporters followed Matano's lead in discussing it primarily as a development program.

Finally, the 1989 revision established a new visa category called *teijūsha*, or "long-term resident." This category had no work restrictions, and it was open to the relatives and descendants of Japanese citizens. The large numbers of so-called Nikkeijin, or ethnically Japanese people, that took advantage of this new status shocked politicians as well as bureaucrats from the Ministry of Justice and the Ministry of Labor, who had not foreseen this new visa category as a source of low-skilled migration (Milly 2014: 65, Tanaka 1995–20, Akashi 2010: 113–14). In fact, just after the law went into effect, Katsunori Toda, a planning officer from the Ministry of Foreign Affairs, predicted that the *nikkeijin* would be unlikely to settle in Japan:

> The descendants of emigrants to South America cannot be categorized as "foreigners" because of their lineage. The world trend is toward treating those carrying the blood of one's own country the same as nationals of one's own country to the third generation. The descendants of those who have succeeded in the country in which they settled are the ones who come, so there is little likelihood of their settling in Japan—that is the difference between them and other Asians. As far as the Ministry of Foreign Affairs, which allows emigration, is concerned, it would in fact be a problem if they were to return and settle. It would be contrary to emigration policy. In any case, so long as there is a need in Japan and in the country of origin for homecoming work by descendants of South American emigrants, it is the role of bureaucrats to make that as easy as possible. (Cited in Seigo 1997: 11–12)

Toda, as well as many other bureaucrats, was wrong about the attractiveness of the long-term residency visa both to *nikkeijin* and to businesses. The Trainee and Technical Internship Program and the long-term resident visa remain the major sources of low-skilled labor in Japan today.

Noticeably absent from the 1989 revision to the Immigration Control and Refugee Recognition Act is any provision for direct and purposeful admission of low-skilled immigrants. Whenever Immigration Bureau chief Kagechika Matano attended Diet hearings in the months before the revision was passed, he was inevitably asked about this. His answers were remarkably consistent. Here is a typical explanation from an Upper House Budget Committee Meeting, where he is answering a question about what to do about the demand by many businesses for more laborers:

> This problem, other than being an issue of reconciling supply and demand (for labor), will impact the entirety of Japanese business and the Japanese people's life. Because of that, we should carefully analyze the situation from various perspectives, and we should maintain the position of the current revised law that low skilled laborers should not be admitted. (HoC 11/30/1989a)

Later in that same meeting, Kijun Sakurai, a DM from the Socialist Party, asked Matano about how low-skilled immigration had worked out in Europe, and Matano replied:

> We should carefully refer to the countries of Western Europe, especially West Germany and France, when thinking about our own policies. In general, the immigration and residency management of foreign workers in Western Europe has become very restrictive, and countries like France and West Germany are giving foreign laborers subsidies to return to their countries of origin. As a matter of fact, these countries are urging foreign workers to leave. If we think about this, for the countries that have admitted foreign laborers on a large scale, the very existence of those laborers has become a large burden. (HoC 11/30/1989a)

Other DMs discussed the experience of Europe, and especially Germany, with foreign labor several times in Diet hearings in 1989 and 1990, the period spanning the passage of the revised law. The argument that the European experience with low-skilled foreign labor demonstrated the problem of admitting foreign unskilled labor found purchase with DMs from the LDP—Yoshio Nagata (HoC 11/27/1989) and Shun'ichi Suzuki (House of Representatives [HoR] 4/24/1990)—and from the Socialist Party (Mamoru Kobayashi; HoR 4/26/1990).

In short, the opponents of low-skilled foreign labor continued to point to what they saw as the failed experience of Western European states, and in particular, France and Germany. On the other side of the argument were many in labor-intensive businesses that were facing the kinds of labor shortages that you can see in figure 4.2. For example, in the same hearing where Matano made his argument about Germany and France regarding their low-skilled labor immigration policies, Kazuyoshi Shirahama, a Diet member from the CGP, pointed to a Mainichi Shimbun survey of sixty businesses in the greater Osaka region which said that two-thirds of those surveyed wanted Japan to admit low-skilled labor. Between 1986 and 1990, the Ministry of Labor advocated the adoption of a low-skilled immigration system, as did some members of the business community. Ultimately, only the Japan Communist Party voted against the 1989 revision to the Immigration Control and Refugee Recognition Act, because it excluded unskilled workers (Seigo 1997: 94).

Reforms to Foreign Labor Admission After 1990

Following the 1989 revision, Japan has made a number of changes that have impacted what kinds of and how many foreign laborers are admitted to Japan. In this section, I focus on five such changes: the introduction of a "point system"; the increased restrictions on the availability of the "entertainer" visa category; Economic Partnership Agreements (EPAs) with several Asian nations, which permitted the immigration of some nurses and caregivers; the expansion and reform of the Trainee and Technical Internship Program; and the attempt to encourage long-term residents to emigrate.

Point System

A number of countries use some kind of "point system" to give potential labor migrants a score based on their desirability to the domestic economy. Canada was the first country to introduce such a system in the late 1960s, followed by Australia in the 1980s and the United Kingdom in 2002 (Ferrer, Picot, and Riddell 2014: 847). In Japan's case, at the

end of December 2011, the Japanese Ministry of Justice announced that
it would establish a point system in immigration admissions that would
give preferential treatment to highly skilled immigrants; it went into effect
in June 2012. Japan's system grants points to potential foreign workers
based on factors including academic record, employment history, and
salary. The system was weighted to promote immigration by academic
researchers, those with high-level technical skills, and specialists in management and administration (*Yomiuri Shimbun* 12/28/2011).

This system was announced by the Ministry of Justice (i.e., it was
not passed as a piece of legislation), and the Ministry of Justice esti-
mated that it would lead to the admission of 2,000 foreign laborers per
year, which would have been a trivial number in comparison with the
1,170,855 long-term and permanent foreign residents who were already in
Japan with unrestricted work permission, not to mention the 2,033,656
foreign residents in Japan legally in 2012 (*Yomiuri Shimbun* 12/28/2011).

However, the point system actually has resulted in far fewer than
the Ministry of Justice's early estimates. In the first eleven months of the
program's operation, only 17 foreign laborers were admitted on points.
After that, the Ministry of Justice lowered the acceptable point total in
order to promote more immigration (*Yomiuri Shimbun* 4/4/2014). This
reform seems to have worked to some degree; between 2012, when the
system was introduced, and October 2016, 6,298 foreign residents were
admitted through this point system (*Yomiuri Shimbun* 1/18/2017).

When the point system was introduced, highly skilled laborers (i.e.
those with seventy or more points) would be permitted to apply for
permanent residency in Japan after five years of residency (unlike other
foreign residents who would have to wait ten years). In 2017, that period
was shortened; those scoring seventy points or higher would be permitted
to apply for permanent residency after three years, while those scoring
eighty points or higher would be permitted to apply for permanent
residency after one year (*Yomiuri Shimbun* 1/18/2017).

I spoke with two representatives of the reformist business lobbying
group the Japan Association of Corporate Executives (Keizai Dōyūkai)
about the issue of highly skilled foreign labor from the business side.
The Keizai Dōyūkai members that I spoke with both had the impression
that companies that want to hire skilled foreigners do not have trouble
getting the appropriate visas for their employees. One suggested that,
despite this, companies struggle to successfully recruit qualified foreign
workers—not because of government regulations, but because of their

own paucity of international outreach (interview 1128). The other suggested that the legal process of hiring high skilled foreign workers has gotten much simpler in the last few years, and that it is now much easier than it used to be to hire an educated individual with knowledge of Japan but without a specific skill. However, he went on to say that often neither companies nor those individuals with knowledge of Japan are aware of this change (interview 1129).

ENTERTAINERS

In the 1950s, Japan established an "entertainer" visa category at the request of the United States, who wanted English-speaking women (primarily from the Philippines) available to entertain American troops. In 1981, Japan eliminated the requirement that "entertainers" have at least two years' work experience, setting the stage for an expansion of entertainer visas (Shipper 2008: 46). Figure 4.4 shows the increased use of

Figure 4.4. Entertainer visas in postwar Japan.

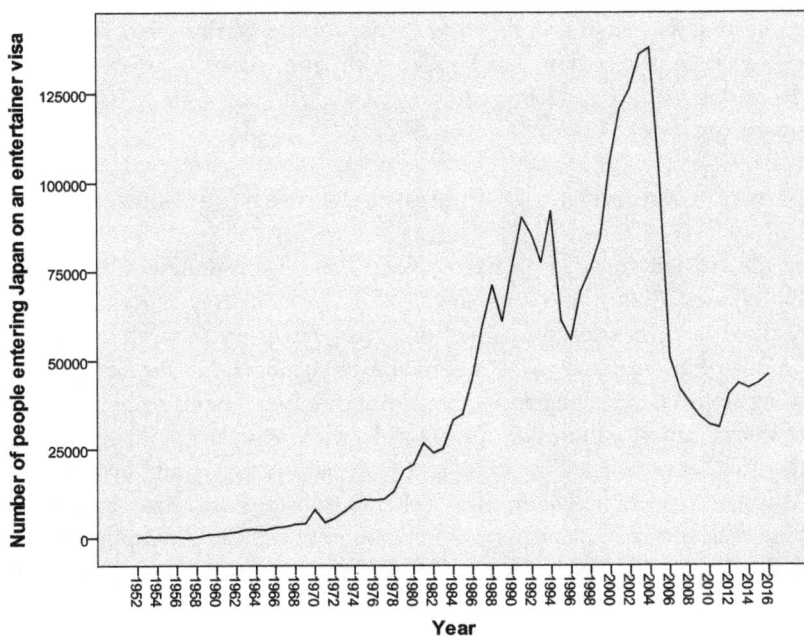

Data from Ministry of Justice (Japan) Various Years.

this visa category beginning in the 1980s. At its peak, in 2004, more than half of the 137,820 people who arrived in Japan on entertainer visas were Filipinas (Shipper 2008: 46).

This visa category had long been criticized for its links to the sex industry and human trafficking. One 1993 study "estimates that over 60 percent of foreign women in this category in Tokyo are forced into prostitution by establishment owners" (Matsuda, cited in Douglass 2000: 94). The Ministry of Justice studied the misuse of the entertainer visa category in 1994, when it issued a report that found that in 92.8 percent of the 444 uses of the entertainer visa that it studied involved violations of immigration law (Akashi 2010: 214). This report confirmed what human rights groups had long been saying, and it led to increased enforcement and a temporary decrease in the numbers of foreign residents who had been entering Japan on entertainer visas. However, this decrease was short-lived, and in 2004, the combination of pressure from domestic human rights groups, the UN Commission on the Rights of Women, and the United States Trafficking in Persons Report caused Japan to make two years of training and/or experience a requirement for the entertainer visa (Shipper 2008: 46; interview 1204).[5] This seems to have addressed the problem with the misuse of that visa, according to a well-known activist that I spoke with, and, relatedly, it significantly decreased foreign residents entering Japan on that visa, as figure 4.4 shows (interview 1204).

NURSES, CAREGIVERS, AND ECONOMIC PARTNERSHIP AGREEMENTS

In the last ten years, Japan has ratified EPAs with Indonesia (2007), the Philippines (2006), and Vietnam (2009). Each of these agreements has resulted in permission for some nurses and caregivers to work in Japan.[6] This is often assumed to be a response to demographic pressures stemming from Japan's aging society, but there are two reasons to be skeptical of this common assumption. First, the Japanese state has explicitly denied the link between labor shortages and nurse and caregiver admissions. The Ministry of Health, Labor, and Welfare's website states that "approving potential nurses and caregivers from Indonesia and the Philippines is not a response to labor shortages in the health service; this training program has been agreed, on the basis of strong requests from the trading partner countries, in order to strengthen economic partnerships" (quoted in Naiki 2015: 344).

Second, the numbers of nurses and caregivers admitted through these programs are far too small to make a meaningful impact on Japan's labor market. Figure 4.5 illustrates the numbers of nurses and caregivers admitted each year. The number has increased each year since 2012, and, in total, 4,695 nurses and caregivers were admitted to Japan between 2008 and 2017. That number is extremely small when compared with the size of Japan's population and its medical sector, and this program has not alleviated nursing shortages. As Ogawa (2012: 571) argues, "the

Figure 4.5. Nurses and caregivers admitted to Japan by Economic Partnership Agreements.

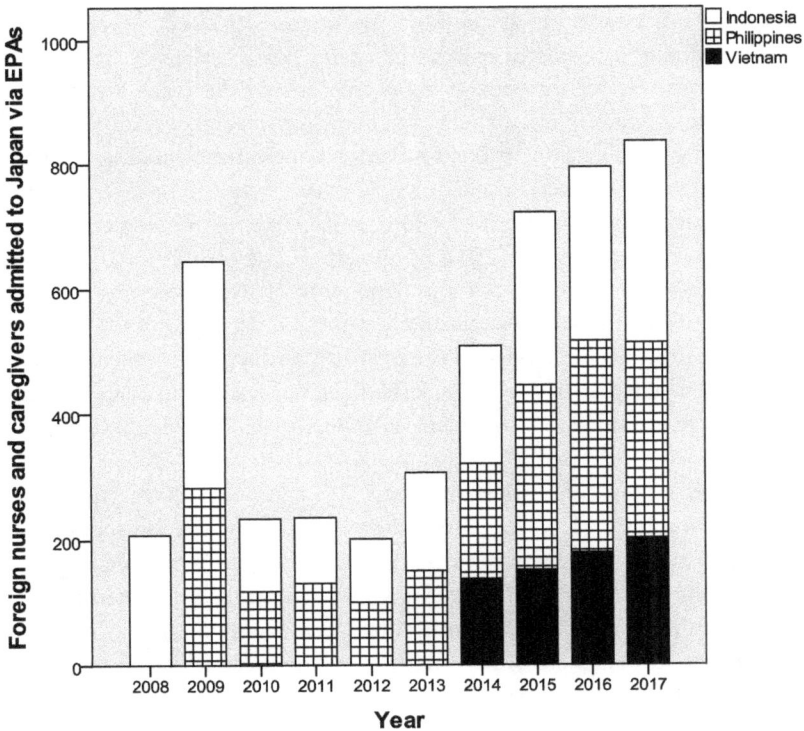

Data from Ministry of Health, Labor, and Welfare (Japan) No Date.

promotion of the migration of care workers to Japan is neither an immigration policy nor a social policy, but a political decision to expand Japan's market to Southeast Asia."

One of the main factors that draws foreign nurses and caregivers to Japan is the wages. The salaries of nurses and caregivers in Japan are as much as ten times the salaries of nurses and caregivers in Indonesia and the Philippines (Naiki 2015: 349). These nurse and caregiver programs begin with six months of Japanese-language training. After that, nurses are permitted to stay in Japan for three years, and caregivers, for four years. During that period, nurses have three chances to take the Japanese nursing exam, and caregivers have one chance (346). If they do not pass the exam, they must leave the country, but if they do pass, they "are given a residence status called 'designated activities' under the Immigration Act, and this status can be renewed without limitation" (343–44). Very few nurses and caregivers pass these exams. In 2012, 11 percent of foreign nursing candidates passed the exam, compared with a 91.8 percent passage rate for the general population taking the exam. In response to these low passages rates, the government has made some adjustments, like writing English translations to disease names and extending the time that foreign candidates had to complete the exam (350–51). Despite these changes, the passage rate for foreign EPA-related nursing candidates remained at 11 percent in 2016 (*Chūnichi Shimbun* 3/26/2016).

One of the most important opponents of expanded admission of foreign nurses and caregivers are interest groups that represent nurses and caregivers in Japan. I interviewed the president and several representatives of a prefectural chapter of the Japanese Nursing Association (Kango Kyōkai), and they expressed several reservations about foreign nurses in Japan:

> Before they come to Japan, they are required to have Japanese ability. However, when they come, they cannot speak Japanese. . . . Moreover, there are cultural differences. We are both from particular cultures and we must come to terms with these differences. Because they have come to Japan, they must do Japanese things. However, there have been those that have not enjoyed doing Japanese things. I want them to understand that, when I come to Japan, I will come into contact with Japanese culture. Moreover, sometimes they send their entire wages back to their home country, and then run

into trouble because they do not have enough money. It would be better if they did not do these things. (Interview 1138)

These concerns, and particularly the concern about the Japanese language ability of foreign nurses, are similar to the reservations that Hōsei University sociologist Chieko Kamibayashi reports about Japanese nurses' opposition to permitting foreign nurses to enter Japan through the Trainee and Technical Internship Program (2015: 6–7).

The representatives of the Japanese Nursing Association that I spoke with were aware of and concerned about nursing shortages in Japan, but they wanted to address these shortages in other ways. They noted that the numbers of people graduating with nursing degrees is increasing but that nurses often give up their careers once they marry and have children and/or once they have to care for their aging parents. Also, it is difficult to maintain jobs when their spouses transfer to different prefectures or even different countries (interview 1138). The representatives were not clear about how they would remedy these problems, but it was clear that they saw finding a solution to these problems, rather than foreign labor, as the key to solving the nursing shortage.

TRAINEES AND TECHNICAL INTERNS

The Trainee and Technical Internship Program was adopted after an intense debate about the topic of whether Japan should permit the admission of unskilled laborers. In the late 1980s the Ministry of Labor was in favor of admitting unskilled labor, while the Ministry of Justice was opposed. The Ministry of Foreign Affairs and the Economic Planning Agency began to advocate programs to provide "technical training" to temporary residents from the developing world. The business community supported some kind of foreign unskilled labor, but they were divided about whether that should be unskilled foreign laborers or trainees. Keizai Dōyūkai's national office, for example, supported a trainee program, while the Kansai branch of Keizai Dōyūkai supported unskilled foreign labor (Milly 2014: 63–64).

Ultimately, as discussed above, the 1989 revision to the Immigration Control and Refugee Recognition Act established a Technical Trainee Program. This program has been gradually expanded. It was initially a one-year training program, but after 1993, trainees could remain for an additional year or two as technical interns. Figure 4.6 outlines the rapid expansion of the Trainee and Technical Internship Programs. In April 2014, the government announced that it would lengthen the Technical Internship Program from three to six years, and it would permit those who had already participated once to apply to participate again (the length was eventually expanded to five years instead of six, however). These changes were linked to the 2020 Tokyo Olympics and to the need for laborers to clean up the nuclear meltdown site at Fukushima (*Yomiuri Shimbun* 4/4/2014; *Yomiuri Shimbun* 2/21/2017).

Trainees and technical interns are concentrated in industries such as construction, food manufacturing, textiles, metals, and agriculture (see

Figure 4.6. Trainees and technical interns in Japan.

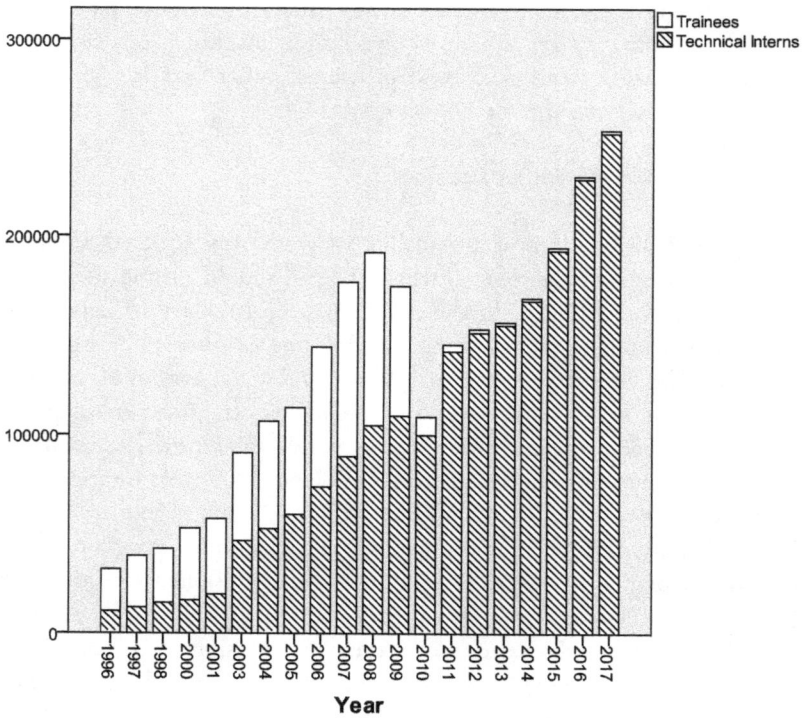

Data from Ministry of Justice (Japan) Various Years.

figure 4.7 for an industry-by-industry breakdown from 2016). These are not among Japan's most internationally competitive industries (automobiles, semiconductors, or other high technology sectors, for example, generally do not make use of trainees and technical interns), but they are industries that are suffering from labor shortages that are related to Japan's declining population.

In the case of agricultural internships, some of Japan's most international competitive farmers are using this program to import laborers from Southeast Asia. When those laborers return after their internships, these Japanese farmers sometimes buy land in Southeast Asia in cooperative ventures with their former interns to establish multinational farming companies (interview 1153). A representative from an agricultural interest group told me that, although labor shortages in agriculture are

Figure 4.7. Trainees and technical interns by industry, 2016.

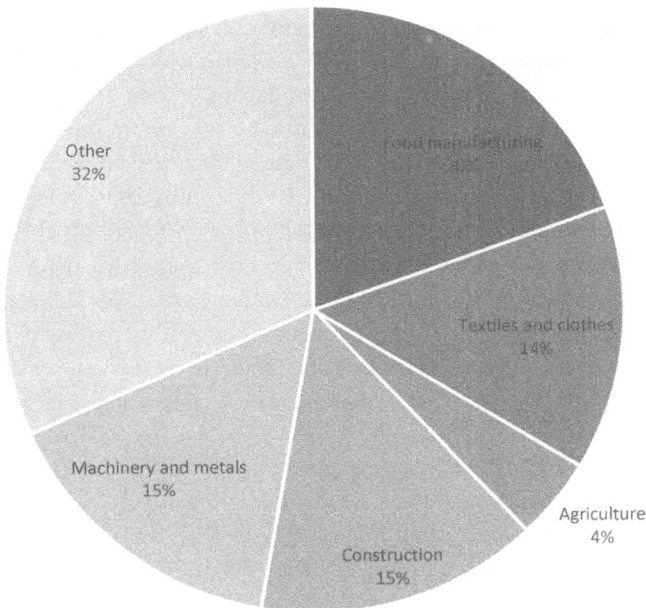

Data from JITCO 2018. Data refers to trainees and those applying to transfer to the technical internship program (which amounted to 98,928 people in 2016). However, JITCO does not publish statistics that break down the technical internship program by industry.

severe overall, the nature of the shortages varies greatly by crop type. He suggested that rice farmers, for example, do not face labor shortages because they have successfully mechanized the rice-farming process (interview 1172).

The Trainee and Technical Internship Program was relatively easy for employers to abuse, and in 2007, they were mentioned in the US State Department's Trafficking in Persons report (Milly 2014: 77). As a result, in 2009, "trainees were formally given the status of workers eligible for the full range of worker protections" (Milly 2014: 69).

Further, the Ministry of Justice convened a panel of outside experts to discuss issues relating to foreign labor in Japan. In 2014, those discussions led to a report about how to repair the foreign trainee program (Kamibayashi 2015: 5). One member of that panel expressed her frustration that, while they were in the process of discussing how to revise and improve the Trainee and Technical Internship Program, Prime Minister Abe went on television and announced that that program would be dramatically expanded (interview 1127).

In November 2016, the Diet amended two laws with a view toward permitting caregivers to be admitted to Japan as trainees while at the same time expanding the protections available to them. These new protections including setting up a new agency to support trainees and fining companies that take the passports of those whom they employee (*Yomiuri Shimbun* 11/19/2016). This marked the first time that trainees would be admitted in service-industry roles (*Yomiuri Shimbun* 11/18/2016).

While media reports did not mention a specific figure goal or quota for caregiver admission, the conservative *Yomiuri Shimbun*, a widely read newspaper that often sympathizes with the LDP, reported that the program was unlikely to put a dent in the nurse and caregiver shortage, which the Ministry of Health, Labor, and Welfare estimates will reach 380,000 by 2025 (11/19/2916).

Shortly after these reforms, in February 2017, the government introduced a variety of additional protections meant to look out for the interests of interns, including a "point system" to rank firms according to how well they treated foreign trainees. Firms would be rewarded if a large percentage passed their National Trade Skills tests and if they paid their interns relatively well. (A firm would earn 5 points for paying its trainees an average of 15 percent above Japan's minimum wage.) Firms would be penalized if they were found to mistreat their trainees or if their trainees went missing (*Yomiuri Shimbun* 2/21/2017).

Despite the fact that the Ministry of Justice still discusses the Trainee and Technical Internship Program in the same section of its reports as it discusses foreign students, the Trainee and Technical Internship Program is now generally recognized to be primarily a foreign-labor program rather than a development program. Only one of my interview subjects, the Diet member that I spoke with who was least supportive of foreign labor in Japan (interview 1123), still discussed the trainee program as primarily an international development program. The idea that the trainee and technical internship is primarily a foreign-labor program is clear when looking at where the trainees go. There is a very strong correlation (.529) between the job-seeker ratio of a prefecture (a measure of labor shortages) and the percentage of that prefecture's population that are trainees and technical interns. That suggests that, as it is currently constituted, the Trainee and Technical Internship Program is attempting (ultimately unsuccessfully) to address Japan's labor shortages. This is also clear when looking at figure 4.8 and the maps in figure 4.9.

Figure 4.8. Trainees and technical interns and labor shortages in Japanese prefectures, 2017.

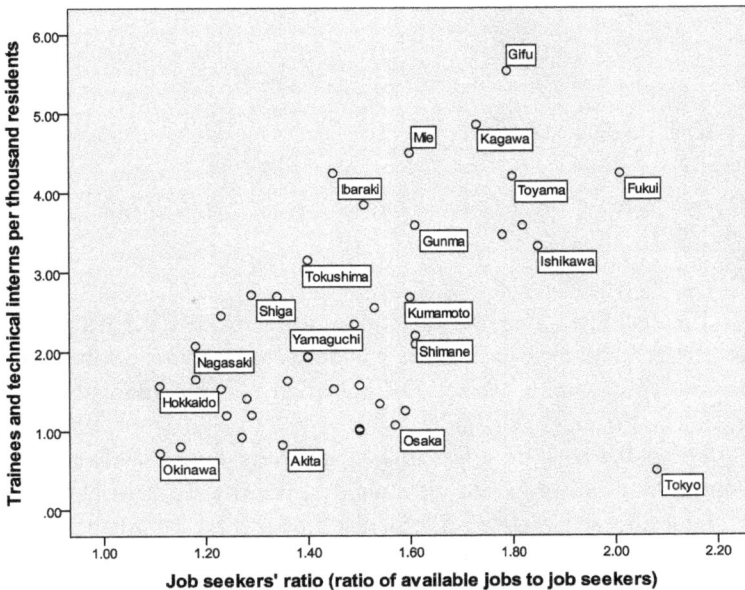

Data from Ministry of Health, Labor and Welfare (Japan), 2018 and Ministry of Justice (Japan) 2018.

Figure 4.9a. Maps of labor shortages and trainees and technical interns in Japan, 2017.

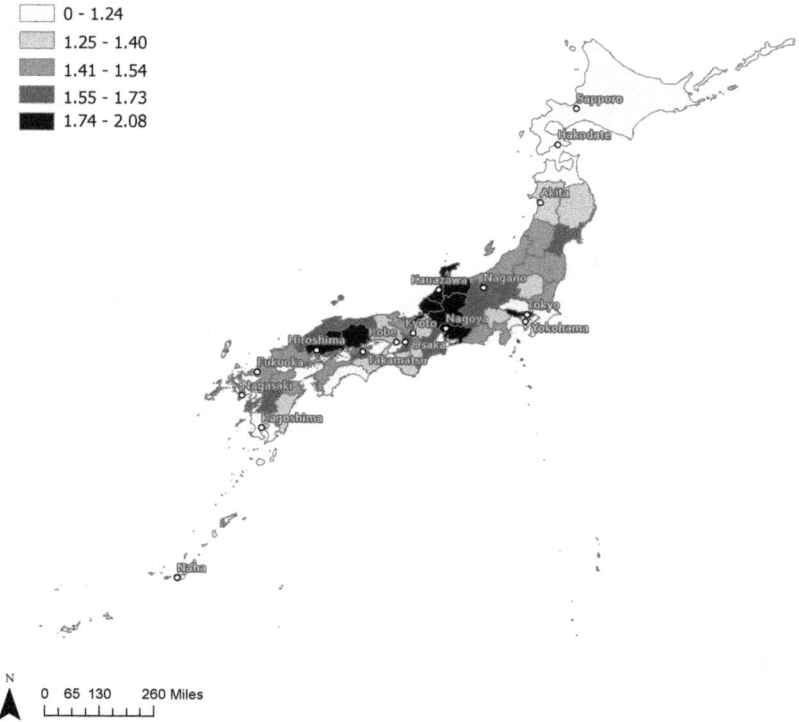

0 - 1.24
1.25 - 1.40
1.41 - 1.54
1.55 - 1.73
1.74 - 2.08

Data from Ministry of Health, Labor and Welfare (Japan), 2018 and Ministry of Justice (Japan) 2018.

The decision to expand the trainee program in a particular sector (caregiving) rather than instituting a wide-ranging immigration policy is consistent with what a senior LDP politician told me about the LDP's foreign labor strategy. He indicated that pro-foreign labor bureaucrats and LDP politicians are advocating a relatively quiet, sector-by-sector foreign labor strategy in order to avoid opposition by far-right groups that might oppose policies that look like broad-based "immigration" policies rather than sector-specific foreign labor policies (interview 1120). A pro-immigration Democratic Party House of Councilors Representative suggested that he supports the LDP's sector-by-sector approach because

Figure 4.9b. Maps of labor shortages and trainees and technical interns in Japan, 2017.

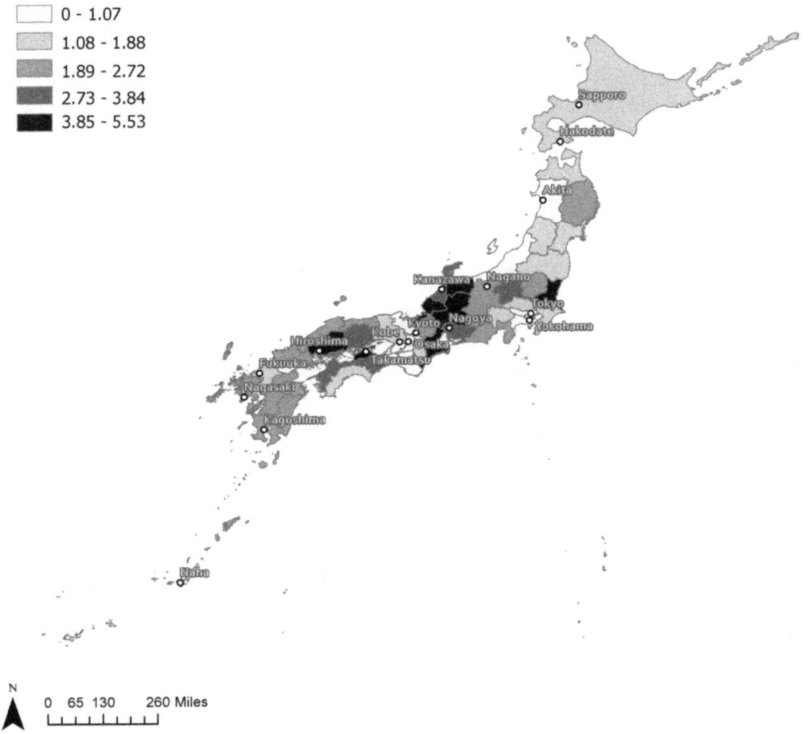

Data from Ministry of Health, Labor and Welfare (Japan), 2018 and Ministry of Justice (Japan) 2018.

he believes that this can lay the groundwork for a broader immigration policy in the future (interview 1156). However, another LDP DM expressed concern particularly with the expansion of the trainee program into nursing and caregiving. He noted that, unlike manufacturing, where trainees and technical interns can take the skills that they learn in Japan back to their countries of origin, nursing and caregiving is different, because the sending countries are not faced with aging countries like Japan. Thus, those "trainees and technical interns" are being trained in tasks that are not in demand in their home countries (interview 1174).

LONG-TERM PERMANENT RESIDENTS

Aside from trainees and technical interns, the other major source of unskilled foreign labor in Japan has been those with Japanese ancestry, who are on "long-term residency" visas. This visa category and status is often associated with those with Japanese ancestry from South America, and as table 4.2 notes, the plurality of those on long-term residency visas in Japan are those with Japanese ancestry who have come from Brazil. Unlike migrants from China and elsewhere in Asia, the vast majority of South Americans in Japan are long-term residents (or permanent residents who initially came to Japan as long-term residents). In 1988, two years before the revision of the Immigration Control and Refugee Recognition Act would go into force, there were only 6,872 people from South America in Japan. By 1991, that number would increase to 153,099. By 2017, that number would increase to 253,633, and almost 96.5 percent of that group had long-term resident, permanent resident, or spousal visas.

Figure 4.10 outlines the changing size of the South American population in Japan. The size of that population has actually decreased every year since 2011. That decrease is linked to the economic downturn of 2008, stemming from the Lehman Shock. Between April 2009 and March 2010, Japan gave fixed payments to long-term residents who would agree to leave Japan and stay away for at least three years (although Japan reserved the right to shorten that period if economic conditions improved) (Milly 2014: 173).

New Visa Categories

As I finish revisions to this book, Japan's labor shortages have continued to get more severe. As noted earlier in this chapter, in 2017 the job seeker's ratio reached its postwar peak, and that ratio has continued to grow. In response to these labor shortages, on December 8, 2018, the Japanese Diet passed a revision to the Immigration Control and Refugee Recognition Act, which, among other things, called for Japan to expand the number of foreign laborers in Japan through a variety of new visa categories in fourteen industries including agriculture, construction, and caregiving (Tokyo Shimbun 12/9/2018; *New York Times* 12/7/2018). Just over two weeks later, the Abe administration announced in a Cabinet

Figure 4.10. South Americans and trainees and technical interns in Japan.

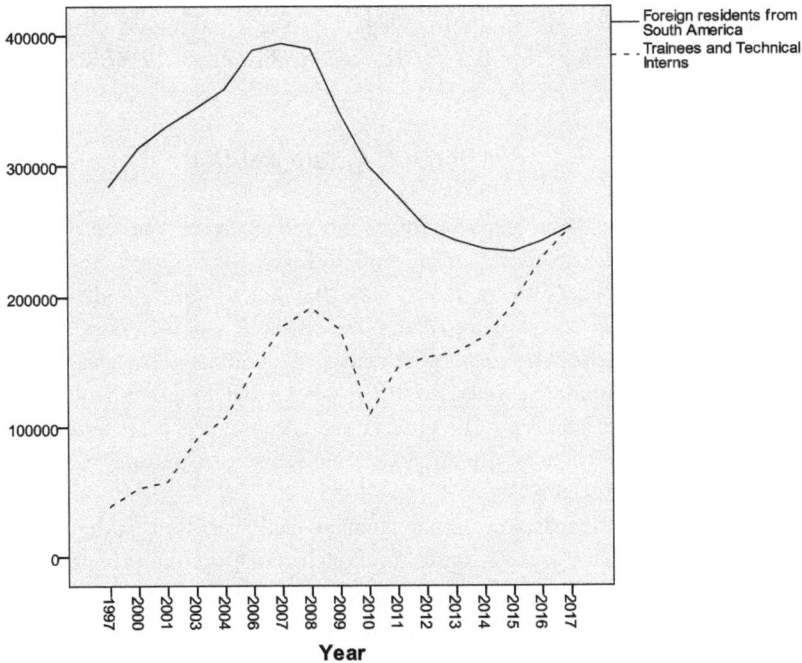

Data from Ministry of Justice (Japan) Various Years.

Understanding that Japan would aim to increase the admission of foreign laborers by 345,150 in the next five years. The Cabinet Understanding also established policies to promote coexistence between Japanese and foreigners, including an office with 100 locations all around Japan that would help foreigners with issues relating to daily life (Yomiuri Shimbun 12/25/2018).

Because these new visa categories will be temporary, Prime Minister Abe and his administration have regularly insisted that this was is immigration policy (see, for example, Mainichi Shimbun 10/29/2018). After a meeting of relevant cabinet meeting in October, Chief Cabinet Secretary Yoshihide Suga said that the policy under consideration was in response to critical labor shortages at small- and medium-sized businesses, and that after the government determined that labor shortages had been solved, the government would cease admissions of foreign laborers (Yomiuri Shimbun 10/11/2018). Many activists and politicians from opposition parties had serious concerns about this law, but the law passed over their objections (Asahi Shimbun 12/7/2018; Tokyo Shimbum 12/9/2019).

A Failure of Interest Group Politics?

Of the six different areas where reforms have been made since the 1989 revision to the Immigration Control and Refugee Recognition Act, only one has actually been reformed in a way that led to substantially more foreign laborers—the expansion of the Trainee and Technical Internship Program. Two of the five areas of reform—the point system and nurse and caregiver admissions linked to EPAs—have led to extremely small increases in foreign laborers. The entertainer visa and the long-term residency visa have both been altered in recent years in a manner that led to far fewer foreign laborers.

Given the labor shortages that Japan is facing, as well as the problems stemming from Japan's aging and declining population, why has Japan remained so reluctant to admit foreign laborers? As many scholars of immigration note (most notably Freeman 1995), large increases in foreign labor, especially unskilled foreign labor, tend to be unpopular with voters. However, those voters tend to be unorganized, unlike the interest groups that represent businesses that might benefit from unskilled foreign labor. And thus, in general, liberal democracies tend to admit large numbers of foreign laborers despite the fact that such a policy tends to be unpopular with voters.

This chapter suggests that Japan has proven to be an exception to this rule partially because Japan came to need foreign labor after similar countries in Europe—particularly Germany—had already admitted large numbers of foreign laborers, and Japanese elites' observation of the European experience strengthened the anti-immigration resolve of Japanese politicians and bureaucrats. In the late 1960s, when Japanese industry first began to develop severe labor shortages that could not be addressed by hiring Japanese agricultural workers away from their farms, Japan rejected calls from industry for foreign laborers, and these calls did not persist beyond 1973 because of the global recession stemming from the oil shock. By the late 1980s, the next time that Japan developed severe labor shortages, Japanese elites were able to observe almost thirty years of European experiences with foreign labor, and, in general, those elites concluded that the European experience with foreign labor was a failure.

Many elites continue to believe that about the European experience. I interviewed one politician in 2009 who was making the case that Japan should double the size of its foreign labor force, but he wanted to be clear that the numbers that he was speaking with were still less than European countries (interview 1099). An anti-immigration member of the CGP expressed concern that a Japan that admitted low skilled immigrants would "face the same issues that Europe faces" (interview 1123). A very senior LDP politician suggested that the very limited temporary guest-worker programs of Dubai are a better model for Japan than European countries because "these people will not stay in the countries where they work" (interview 1141). Another LDP politician argued that Singapore, Hong Kong, South Korea, and Taiwan are the best models for the future of Japan's foreign labor policy "because they accept laborers but not families" (interview 1115).

However, unlike the immigration debate from the 1980s, there now seem to be some politicians from conservative parties that are willing to point to the German experience with foreign labor as a positive one. At a 2016 Diet committee meeting, LDP politician Kōnosuke Kokuba said, "In Germany, foreign laborers have made great effort to advance the latent growth of the economy. However, on the other hand, Japan does not have an immigration policy. If we had one, then I think we would be completing the important task of bearing the burden of Japan's future like a treasure for each one of our children" (HoR 2/26/2016). Similarly, in 2014, Yuzuru Nishida of the conservative Party for Future Generations said in a Diet hearing: "If, despite the example of West Germany, we had temporarily admitted foreign laborers, our economic situation would be better, and we might have avoided labor shortages" (HoR 4/8/2014).

In short, it is possible that the Japanese elites—even those affiliated with conservative parties and ideologies that have traditionally opposed immigration—are beginning to change the way that they think about the costs and benefits of Europe's experiences with immigration and thus the future of foreign labor immigration to Japan. In the language of chapter 3, there are at least some politicians that are moving beyond the schism between assimilation optimism and pessimism—two approaches to immigration which suggest that foreign residents in Japan should be indivisible and the foreign population should be small. There is a more specific discussion of who the immigration reformers are and what they want in chapter 6.

5

Asylum as Exception

While it has gradually improved the way that it treats its oldcomer Korean community and opened some doors to unskilled foreign labor—most notably through its trainee program and the preferences that it grants to foreigners with Japanese ancestry—Japan has remained extremely reluctant to admit refugees. In 2017, for example, it granted asylum to 20 people (while 19,629 applied that year), and in 2016, when 10,901 applied, only 28 were granted asylum (Ministry of Justice 2018a, 2018b).

Japan's refugee policy makes it an outlier among industrial democracies, as table 5.1 suggests. In 2016, Japan had a refugee population of 2,512, substantially below the OECD median of 18,302. Its refugee population is even more striking when compared with its overall population and the size of its economy. In 2016 there were only 0.02 refugees living

Table 5.1. Refugee populations in OECD countries, 2016

	Refugees	Refugees per thousand residents	Refugees per million dollars of GDP
Mean OECD country	151,981	4.48	0.11
Median OECD country	18,302	1.79	0.04
Japan	2,512	0.02	0.0005
OECD countries with values smaller than Japan's	10	0	0

Data from OECD (2018b and 2018c), and UNHCR (2018). Population data was from 2013 and 2014, and GDP data was from 2016. Data was not available for Greece or Latvia.

93

in Japan for every thousand residents, and 0.0005 refugees for every million dollars of GDP. These numbers are both the lowest in the OECD. Figure 5.1 compares asylum requests and successful asylum cases in Japan and the EU. Between 2008 and 2017, the numbers of those *requesting* asylum in Japan and the median EU country were relatively similar, with Japan sometimes surpassing the median EU country (the mean EU country's asylum requests are much higher than the median, driven by a relatively small number of countries including Sweden, Germany, France, Belgium, and the United Kingdom). Figure 5.1 also shows the stark and consistent difference between annual asylum approvals in Japan and in typical EU countries. Between 2008 and 2017, those receiving asylum in a given year in Japan only made up 1.19 percent of those applying for asylum in that year. Conversely, in the median EU country during the same years, successful asylum requests made up 8.99 percent of those applying for asylum in those years. The difference between Japan and the EU has expanded in recent years. As noted above, in 2017, 19,329 people applied for asylum in Japan, and only 20 were granted asylum (an additional 45 were permitted to stay in Japan for humanitarian reasons). In the median EU country in 2017, by contrast, 4,148 people applied for asylum, and 720 people were granted asylum.

In this chapter, I suggest that the primary concern of Japanese officials who have been faced with refugee flows has been that the expectations that present refugee admissions might set a precedent for future behavior. Thus, Japanese leaders decided to admit refugees only after they became convinced that such admissions would not make it more difficult to deny other refugee populations admission in the future. This is clear when looking at the overall orientation of the bureaucrats who currently determine refugee admissions as well as Japan's decisions to admit groups of refugees. This concern with limiting the precedent through which Japan might be compelled to admit large populations of refugees in the future is consistent with both dominant schools of thought among Japan's governing conservatives about the appropriate role for foreign residents in Japan—assimilation optimism and assimilation pessimism

Asylum in Contemporary Japan

Japan has consistently created its refugee policy in a manner that avoids setting a precedent that suggests that it is a major refugee-admitting

Figure 5.1. Annual asylum applications in Japan and the European Union.

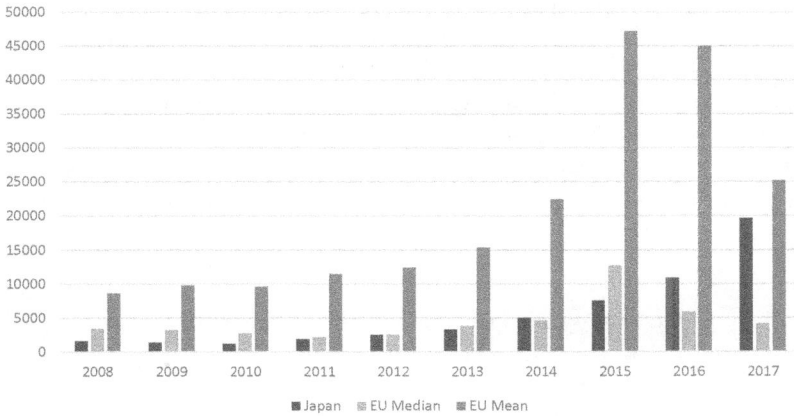

Successful asylum claims as a percent of annual applications.

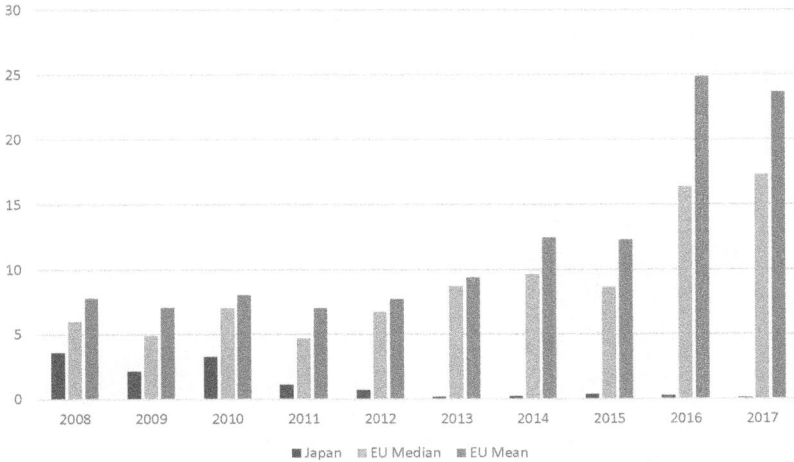

Data from Ministry of Justice (Japan) 2018a and 2018b and Eurostat 2018a. For the purposes of this graph, "successful claims" include only those who were granted formal asylum on their first application (the EU refers to this as being granted "Geneva Convention Status"). Those who win appeals and those who are permitted to stay on humanitarian grounds are not counted as "successful."

country. As one activist that I spoke with explained, "Japan's government does not want to show signs that Japan will start admitting more refugees" (interview 1170).

Figure 5.2 demonstrates both the relatively small number of individuals who apply for asylum in Japan and the even smaller number of those whose applications are approved. I spoke with an individual who is involved with the asylum approval process at the Ministry of Justice about why Japan's asylum approval rate is so low, and he pointed at a map that included data on which regions of the world produce refugees

Figure 5.2. Asylum applicants and asylum approvals in Japan.

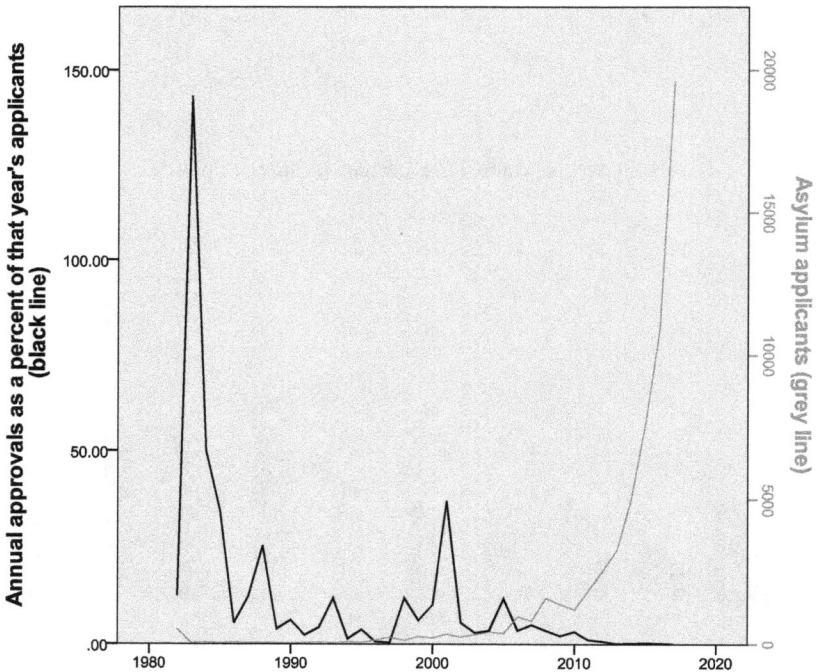

Data from Ministry of Justice (Japan) 2018a and Ministry of Justice (Japan) 2018b. The reason 1983's value is over 100 percent is that, while 530 people applied for asylum in 1982, Japan was only able to reach a decision in 166 of the cases. Many of the remaining cases were decided in 1983, but only 44 new people applied for asylum in 1983.

and internally displaced people. He argued that these days European states tend to get asylum seekers from Syria and other countries with civil wars, where many of them likely have legitimate claims to asylum, but asylum seekers in Japan tend to come from countries that are not involved in wars, which suggests that they are less likely to have legitimate claims to asylum (interview 1205).[1] This concern was echoed by an LDP DM who explained Japan's small refugee population by saying that "those applying for asylum in Japan are economic refugees [which is not a category of refugee recognized in international law]" (interview 1174).[2]

The Ministry of Justice official that I spoke with argued that "it is not the case that Japan's asylum standards are strict, but rather that the people coming to Japan are not fleeing wars or similar situations. There are just not many people near Japan that can be called refugees" (interview 1205). It is difficult to measure the relative strictness of a country's asylum policy, and Japan is sometimes willing to permit failed refugee applicants to temporarily stay in Japan on humanitarian grounds. Between 2005 and 2017, it granted asylum to an average of 22.58 people per year but permitted 127.47 people per year to remain in Japan (at least temporarily) for humanitarian reasons (Ministry of Justice 2018b).[3]

In other words, Japan seems reluctant to grant asylum, but it is also somewhat reluctant to send asylum applicants back to an area where they are likely to face persecution. An activist for refugee rights told me an anecdote that illustrates both of these tendencies of Japan's refugee policy (which he referred to as a "maniac" policy in our English-language interview). He told me about a leader from an anti-Assad group from Syria. The individual's asylum claim to Japan was denied because, although he could prove that he was a member of an anti-Assad group, he could not prove that he was a leader with a third-party source such as a newspaper article that mentioned his name. Because he could not prove that he was a leader, the Japanese government was not convinced that he would be targeted by the Syrian government. However, he was granted humanitarian status and permitted to remain in Japan on a temporary basis, without access to language classes or job-market training. The activist went on to say, regarding the outcome of this case and similar cases, "They have no way to survive. We are creating criminals;

Japan is not affordable. Particularly, their children could contribute to our country, in an era of labor shortages" (interview 1170). In short, reliance on humanitarian status is clearly bad for the refugees, but it also seems to be bad for Japan, as those with humanitarian status remain in Japan without a way to take care of themselves and are not permitted to alleviate labor shortages. Despite these drawbacks, it seems plausible that the Ministry of Justice has a strong preference for humanitarian status over asylum because it retains control over the ultimate outcome of asylum cases, instead of creating legal precedents in asylum hearings that they may not be able to reign in during future asylum cases.

In addition to accepting refugees passively, by waiting for individuals to arrive and then request asylum, countries can also actively seek out particular kinds of refugee admissions. For example, counties may adopt policies stating how many refugees they will adopt in a specific situation. Japan has adopted this kind of policy three times in the postwar period. It adopted its first targeted refugee admissions program to admit those fleeing Southeast Asia after the Vietnam War. More recently, it has adopted much smaller programs to deal with refugee flows out of Myanmar and Syria.

Indochinese Boat People and Japan

Between 1975 and 2005, Japan allowed 11,319 refugees from Vietnam, Laos, and Cambodia to resettle in Japan (Akashi 2010: 94, note 55). As figure 5.3 demonstrates, Japan gradually increased the number of Indochinese refugees that it admitted, and in 1985, it instituted a quota of ten thousand Indochinese refugees, a number it eventually surpassed. Why did Japan decide to break with its past and admit Indochinese refugees for permanent resettlement in substantial numbers?

Japanese leaders have wanted to limit refugee flows into Japan because postwar elites have not seen refugee flows into Japan as demonstrating something important regarding Japanese identity. Had ethnic Japanese been oppressed in large numbers outside of Japan, or had Japanese elites come to believe that refugee flows into Japan demonstrate the superiority of Japan to its adversaries, then elites may have come to welcome refugee flows. However, in the absence of these two conditions, elites saw refugees as a troubling challenge to their ideas about the importance of ethnic homogeneity.

Figure 5.3. Japan's annual admissions of and quota for Indochinese refugees.

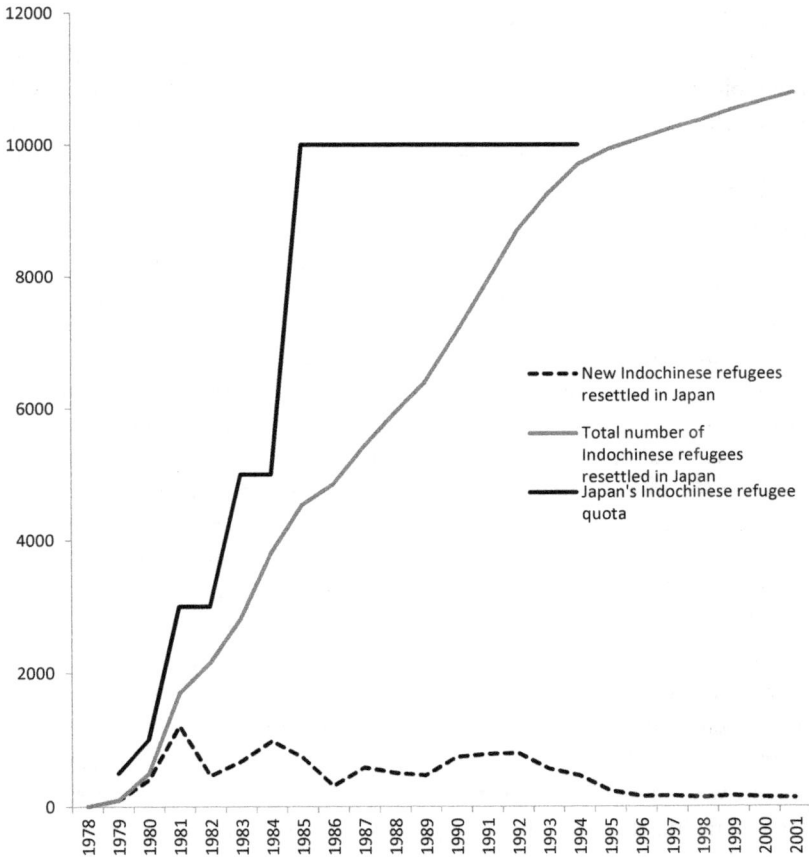

Data from Takahashi (2002: 52) and Akashi (2010: 78). Japan ended its quota for Indochinese refugees with a Cabinet Understanding in December 1994, and Japan stopped resettling Indochinese refugees in 2005. Between 2001 and 2005, Japan resettled 522 Indochinese refugees, but I was not able to find an annual breakdown, and thus this number is not reflected here (Akashi 2010: 94, n.55).

FOREIGN PRESSURE AND JAPAN'S ADMISSION OF INDOCHINESE REFUGEES

There is substantial debate among scholars about the role of foreign pressure in Japanese policy making. On one side is Calder's famous formulation that Japan is a "reactive state" that makes its foreign policy in response to pressure from Western countries (1988: 519–20).[4] On the other side are those who argue that during the Cold War, Japan was able to use its strategic importance to take a less active role in international society than the West would have preferred. Hellman argues that during the Cold War, Japan existed in "a U.S.-made 'international greenhouse,' in which Japan has flourished free from the costs and uncertainties of full participation in international political and security affairs" (1990: 225). Similarly, Pyle argues that foreign policy in Cold War Japan was governed by the "Yoshida Doctrine," whereby Japan took a less active role in international society and "concentrate(d) on the rapid economic growth that would restore Japan's standing in great-power competition" (2007: 32).

Much of the scholarship on Japan's refugee policy suggests that Japan's response to the Indochinese refugee crisis provides evidence in favor of Calder's perspective because Japan only allowed refugee resettlement after international criticism. In her book about Japan's response to a variety of international norms, Flowers argues that Japan ratified the UN Convention Relating to the Status of Refugees (herein the 'Refugee Convention') in 1982 but failed to subsequently comply with the norms underlying the treaty because of tension between Japan's "identity as a member of international society" and its domestic norms (particularly the influential idea that Japan is ethnically homogeneous) (2009: 66). However, in her discussion of Japan's decision to begin allowing resettlement of Indochinese refugees, she argues that beginning in 1978, "European countries and the United States began to heavily criticize Japan, the second-wealthiest country in the world and the wealthiest in the region, for not taking its share of the responsibility" (42). While she goes on to argue that this pressure was not motivated by material concerns, because Japan was already making large fiscal contributions to relief efforts, she does not point to any causes of Japan's decision to admit Indochinese refugees as residents other than this international pressure.

Flowers's argument here is not anomalous. Honma argues that "more than anything else, the thing that caused the Japanese government to change its policy [towards Indochinese refugees] was strong appeals from the US government" (1990: 31). Other scholarly accounts make similar arguments about the key role of foreign pressure in convincing Japan to admit Indochinese refugees (Morris-Suzuki, 2010: 237; Akashi, 2010: 77).[5]

These scholars are correct that foreign pressure played a role in convincing Japan to resettle Indochinese refugees in numbers with no precedent in Japanese history. However, this account is unsatisfying for three reasons. First, unlike foreign pressure regarding whaling and trade issues in the 1970s and 1980s, foreign pressure regarding Indochinese refugees was not accompanied by material threats. Second, official statements of foreign pressure on Indochinese refugees were often stated in the mildest possible terms (again, unlike official statements on issues such as whaling and trade). Third, a substantial number of Japanese elites believe that Japan's "ethnic homogeneity" is a key element of Japan's national identity and an important source of Japan's prosperity (Strausz 2010). For politicians and bureaucrats who believe this, resettlement of Indochinese refugees—people without Japanese ethnicity—would pose a grave threat to Japan, and it is thus difficult to imagine them giving in to international pressure that was stated in weak terms and not accompanied by material threats. However, as I will discuss below, even Yasuhirō Nakasone, the LDP politician who famously declared as prime minister that "things are easier in Japan [than in the United States] because we are a homogeneous society" (*New York Times*, 11/15/1984), supported Japan's resettlement of Indochinese refugees.

This chapter suggests that *neither* Calder's image of Japan as a reactive state nor Hellman's description of Cold War Japan as prospering in an American-made greenhouse is helpful in explaining the puzzle of Japan's Indochinese refugee policy. Calder is right to note that the fragmented nature of authority in Japanese politics, combined with the decentralized nature of political parties under the single nontransferable-vote multimember-district electoral system that Japan had until 1994, made it difficult for Japanese leaders to articulate an independent vision in foreign policy and thus led to a Japan that often "responds to outside pressures for change, albeit erratically, unsystematically, and often incompletely" (1988: 528–31). However, Hellman and Pyle are also right to note that during the Cold War, the importance of Japan to American strategy made it costly for the United States to carry out threats against Japan, and thus gave Japan some flexibility in resisting foreign pressure. In short, Cold War Japan was caught between a domestic political structure that discouraged an independent foreign policy and an international system that limited the consequences when it made decisions that were unpopular with its allies.

In this kind of international and domestic environment, Schoppa's (1997) decision to explain the effectiveness of foreign pressure on Japan with reference to the way that this pressure interacts with domestic politics and elite debates is particularly useful. The next section of this chapter will demonstrate that we cannot understand Japan's Cold War refugee policy without reference to the belief—commonly held in policy-making circles—that opening its doors to Indochinese refugees would not set a precedent that would make it into a major refugee-receiving state.

INDOCHINESE REFUGEES BEGIN TO ARRIVE IN JAPAN

On April 30, 1975, just as the last American helicopter evacuated Saigon, around one hundred Vietnamese living in Guam approached the Japanese consulate and requested asylum (*Asahi Shimbun* 5/1/1975). On May 6, the Ministry of Education sent a communication to heads of private and public universities clarifying the position of the Ministry of Justice regarding the more than one thousand students from Cambodia and Vietnam currently at Japanese universities. According to the communication, old passports would be accepted as identification until Japan formally established relations with the new regimes. Students who wanted to stay in Japan after graduation would be treated on a case-by-case basis (*Yomiuri Shimbun*, 5/7/1975).

On May 11, 1975, nine refugees who had fled Vietnam in makeshift boats reached Chiba on an American container ship that had rescued them at sea. Before arriving in Japan, the American ship had called at Indonesian, Singaporean, and Malaysian ports, but all three of those countries had refused to allow the refugees to disembark. One day after their arrival in Japan, the refugees were flown to Guam, where they would submit applications for asylum to the United States (*Yomiuri Shimbun* 5/13/1975).[6] Between May 1975 and June 1979, 2,250 Indochinese refugees arrived in Japan or were born in Japan (Cabinet Secretariat 1980: 8–18). The vast majority of those refugees were given temporary residency status while Japan searched for countries where they might settle. Of the 2,250 refugees, only 10 were given long-term residency status (*Asahi Shimbun*, 6/28/1979).

Japan began to change its approach to Indochinese refugees in 1978. Most significantly, on April 28, 1978, Prime Minister Takeo Fukuda announced that Japan would begin to accept refugees as settlers, rather than just temporary residents (Mukae 2001: 105–7). The screening criteria for aspiring settlers were strict; among other requirements, settlers needed a Japanese guarantor or adoptive parent, and they also needed to prove that they would "carry out a virtuous life as a member of society" (Cabinet Secretariat 1980: 52). The Japanese media suggested that the timing of this announcement was related to Fukuda's scheduled visit to the United States five days after the announcement was made (*Nihon Keizai Shimbun*, 4/28/1979). Around one year later, on April 3, 1979, Japan instituted its first refugee quota in a Cabinet Understanding and relaxed the requirements for resettlement; potential refugees were no longer required to secure a guarantor as a prerequisite for attaining residency status (*Nihon Keizai Shimbun* [Evening Edition] 4/3/1979). This quota was set to five hundred; it was smaller by many orders of magnitude than the quotas of other advanced industrialized states. This number was gradually raised throughout the 1980s, reaching ten thousand in 1985 (See figure 5.3 for a graphical representation of the changing quota over time, and see table 5.2 for a comparison of Japan's Indochinese refugee admissions with other G7 countries).

In early September 1977, the United Nations High Commissioner for Refugees asked the Japanese Embassy in Geneva if Japan would start accepting Vietnamese refugees as permanent residents (*Nihon Keizai Shimbun* 9/16/1977). Later that same month, Foreign Minister Iichirō Hatoyama had a brief meeting with UN secretary general Kurt Waldheim, and Waldheim asked Japan to respond more generously to the

Table 5.2. Japan's resettlement of Indochinese refugees compared with G7 countries, 1975–1994

	1975–81	1982–1994	Total
USA	421,351	390,234	811,585
Canada	77,588	57,960	135,548
France	72,626	22,976	95,602
England	15,441	4,266	19,707
Germany	19,371	47	19,418
Japan	1,209	7,226	8,435
Italy	2,856	216	3,072

Data from Cabinet Secretariat (1987 & 1994: 11).

Vietnamese refugee issue. Hatoyama replied that he and Prime Minister Fukuda agreed that Japan should improve its refugee policy (*Yomiuri Shimbun* [Evening Edition], 9/27/1977).

Several months later, in May of 1978, Prime Minister Fukuda met with Secretary General Waldheim. Fukuda told Waldheim that Japan was changing its refugee acceptance policies, but it could not change them too much, because "our country is an island nation without room for Vietnamese refugees to settle, but if fixed conditions are provided, we would like to admit refugees" (*Nihon Keizai Shimbun* 5/5/1978). On December 14, 1978, the Ministry of Foreign Affairs announced that Japan would increase its admissions of refugees as residents.[7] This announcement was made on the same day that Japan's ambassador to the United States told Japanese prime minister Ohira that the United States would like Japan to increase its admissions of Indochinese refugees as residents (*Yomiuri Shimbun* 12/15/1978).

American criticism of Japan's refugee policy was most concentrated and intense in the months before Japan was to host its first G7 summit, scheduled for June 28–29, 1979. In May, an anonymous Japanese government source told a *Yomiuri Shimbun* reporter that President Carter voiced criticisms of Japan's refugee policy in a meeting with the Japanese prime minister (*Asahi Shimbun* 6/19/1979). On June 7, Richard Holbrooke, assistant secretary of state for East Asian and Pacific affairs, made a statement at a U.S. House of Representatives hearing to the effect that the administration hoped that Japan would improve its refugee policy, although he criticized other countries' admissions of Indochinese refugee policy as well (Mukae 2001: 113). On June 16, Japanese government reports indicated that the United States had asked Japan to expand its annual Indochinese refugee quota from five hundred to 10,000 (*Yomiuri Shimbun* 6/17/1979).

During his visit to Japan for the G7 meeting, President Carter criticized Japan's refugee admissions on several occasions, although his public criticisms were extremely mild, and certainly more muted than Japanese press reports of his private criticisms. On June 20, Carter told the Japanese press that "the United States is accepting a very large number of refugees. Japan has accepted very few. I think that when Prime Minister Ohira was over here, the total number of refugees accepted in Japan was only three." Carter went on to note Japan's financial support of refugee protection efforts. He also suggested that Japan might have a more difficult time than the United States admitting refugees because Japan is ethnically homogeneous, while the United States is "a nation that is comprised of refugees or immigrants" (USGPO 1980: 1150–51). In a town meeting in Shimoda, Japan, Carter echoed similar themes, saying that "Japan has been very generous in its financial contributions, but because of the homogeneous nature of your own society, Japan has not yet decided to receive very many of the Vietnam refugees" (USGPO 1980: 1173).

JAPAN'S INDOCHINESE REFUGEE POLICY BEGINS TO CHANGE

In the midst of this criticism, Japan made some changes to its refugee policy. On May 9, 1979, it granted residency status to a Vietnamese woman and her two children—the Iguchi family. (Iguchi is actually a Japanese name; Ms. Iguchi was the widow of a Japanese man; *Asahi Shimbun* [Evening Edition] 5/9/1979.) On June 18, Prime Minister Ohira announced that Japan must "seriously consider" expanding its annual quota beyond five hundred (*Asahi Shimbun* 6/18/1979), and immediately following the G7 meeting, he publicly pledged to expand Japan's admissions of Indochinese refugees (Dobson 2004: 37). In the years following the G7 Summit in Tokyo, Japan gradually expanded its quota for Indochinese refugees, but the quota did not reach ten thousand—the size that the United States had requested—until 1985. Prime Minister Masayoshi Ohira announced one of those quota increases—the 1980 increase in the annual quota from five hundred to one thousand—on a trip to the United States, and an unnamed source close to the Prime Minister indicated that President Carter had asked Japan to help out more with Cambodian refugees on that visit (*Nihon Keizai Shimbun* [Evening Edition] 5/10/1980).

International pressure on Japan to increase its support of Indochinese refugee efforts was not always effective, however. At the June 20–21, 1979, International Conference on Indochinese Refugees in Geneva, Switzerland, the Malaysian representative proposed to establish a refugee processing center in Okinawa (*Nihon Keizai Shimbun* 7/4/1979). The governor of Okinawa, Junji Nishime, had earlier indicated his support for allowing Indochinese refugees to settle there as agricultural laborers. Nishime argued that this would deal with both Okinawa's underpopulation problem and Japan's international image: "Japan has been criticized internationally for its refugee admissions, so I thought we could admit some refugees" (*Nihon Keizai Shimbun* 6/23/1979). However, Japan's representative at the UN meeting, Foreign Minister Sunao Sonoda, did not support the establishment of a refugee-processing facility on Okinawa (*Nihon Keizai Shimbun* 7/21/1979), and on the second day of the UN meeting, Asao Mihara, the director general of the Okinawa Development Agency, made it clear that the central government did not support Governor Nishime's attempt to settle Indochinese refugees there (*Nihon Keizai Shimbun* 7/22/1979).

In sum, particularly in the late 1970s, Japan faced international criticism, especially from US and UN representatives. Moreover, Japan's efforts to permit resettlement of increasing numbers of Indochinese refugees often coincided closely in time with that criticism. However, it is important to note three things about that criticism. First, unlike other issues regarding which Japan faced international criticism in the 1970s and 1980s—including trade and whaling—the criticisms discussed above were not linked with threats of sanctions or other material threats. Second, the criticisms were often expressed privately, and when expressed publicly, they were put in the mildest possible terms. In his rebuke of Japan during his stay in the country for the 1979 G7 conference, American president Jimmy Carter made a point that sounded like it could have come from the mouth of a Japanese conservative opponent of refugee admissions; Carter argued that Japan's reluctance to allow refugee resettlement was understandable because of Japan's ethnic homogeneity. Third, international pressure on Japan was most intense in the late 1970s, and yet, as figure 5.3 demonstrates, Japan continued to admit Indochinese refugees through the 1980s and into the 1990s in the absence of continued international pressure.

THE INDOCHINESE REFUGEE IN JAPANESE PUBLIC DISCOURSE

In 1980 and 1982, Japan's Cabinet Office took polls regarding public opinion on Indochinese refugees. In the 1980 poll, respondents were asked: "[T]he government has set a residency quota indicating that we will try to allow 500 Indochinese refugees to resettle in Japan. What do you think about this quota of 500 people?" In response, 22.8 percent of those polled thought the quota should be expanded, 38.2 percent thought the existing quota was appropriate, 11.4 percent were against all refugee resettlement, and 27.1 percent were undecided (Cabinet Office 1980). In other words, 49.6 percent of respondents either wanted to keep the quota at five hundred or did not support any resettlement of refugees, and only 22.8 percent wanted additional resettlement. Despite this unfavorable political climate, the Japanese government raised the quota first to one thousand in 1980, then to three thousand in 1981.

By the 1982 poll, public opinion had moved in the direction of greater support for government policy. Respondents were asked about their opinion of the current quota of three thousand. Of those asked, 7.4 percent thought that this number should be substantially increased, 42.5 percent thought that thus number should be increased somewhat (*aru teido fuyasu beki*), 29.1 percent thought it should not be increased, 0.4 percent had a different answer, and 20.5 percent were undecided (Cabinet Office 1982). While it is thus possible to argue that post-1982 increases in the quota were consistent with public opinion, this data from the Cabinet Office indicates that the quota increases in 1980 and 1981 were not popular.

Moreover, those most concerned with Japan's treatment of refugees—NGOs—were also not particularly focused on convincing Japan to increase the numbers of Indochinese refugees that it admitted. NGOs were much more concerned with the treatment of refugees once they reach Japan than with promoting policies which would encourage Japan to admit more refugees (Flowers 2009: 55–56).

Japan's judiciary has also not been active in encouraging Japan to admit refugees. Courts have been extremely unlikely to rule against the government, particularly in human rights cases (Hamano 1999; Iwasawa 1998). One case where Japanese courts declined to invoke international refugee law occurred in 1976, when the Japanese Supreme Court ruled that Japan could deport a South Korean, Su-gil Yoon, despite the very real possibility that he would be arrested as a political prisoner in South Korea. The Supreme Court's decision overruled a lower court decision from 1969 that had suggested that the principle of nonrefoulement of refugees was a part of customary international law and that deporting Mr. Yoon was therefore a violation of international law (Mukae 2001: 100). In other words, the Japanese Supreme Court was reluctant to use international refugee law to compel Japan to be more generous in its refugee policy.

Without pressure from the judiciary or the public, why did Japan decide to admit Indochinese refugees as residents? In the 1980 public opinion poll, those that supported some refugee resettlement (either at current levels or at an expanded level) were asked for the reason for their stance, and the two most common answers were that it was necessary for humanitarian reasons (46.4 percent) and that it was Japan's duty as a member of international society (41.2 percent) (Cabinet Office 1980). These two reasons—humanitarian concerns and concern with Japan's international image—are the two arguments most commonly advanced by supporters of Indochinese refugee resettlement in the Japanese government and the Japanese media as well.

In a 1978 Diet hearing, Tadamasa Kuroki, councilor to the Cabinet Secretariat, was asked about Japan's reason for deciding to allow long-term settlement by Vietnamese refugees. After explaining the policy change, Kuroki suggested that to decide to allow refugee resettlement "was an entirely humanitarian conclusion" (HoR 5/10/1978). In a 1979 Diet hearing, Democratic Socialist Party DM Renzō Yanagisawa was critical of Japan's failure to admit more Indochinese refugees. Among other things, he asked, "when Prime Minister Fukuda said that 'a human life is weightier than the earth' [during the 1977 Japan Airlines hijacking], did he mean to refer to only Japanese people" (HoC 3/26/1979)? Yanagisawa thus suggested that Japan had a responsibility to all people, not just the Japanese, and therefore, Japan should offer more assistance to Indochinese refugees.

While advocates of resettlement of Indochinese refugees did sometimes cite humanitarian concerns, arguments that focused on Japan's international image were much more common. During a 1978 hearing of the House of Representatives Foreign Affairs Committee, CGP DM Yoshimi Nakagawa asked Minister of Foreign Affairs Sunao Sonoda about how Japan can allow refugee settlement, given that Japan is a one-ethnicity county. In his reply, Sonoda agreed that this was a problem but noted that "at international meetings, there is strong opposition to the idea of Japan opening its door but not allowing residents, and even allowing residency in small numbers. We have no choice but to think about . . . allowing residency in Japan" (HoR 12/20/1978). The following year, in his opening address to a plenary session of the House of Representatives, New Liberal Club DM Yōhei Kōno said that "Regarding Vietnamese refugees, the government initially paid no attention, and we admitted fewer refugees than Papua New Guinea, which has brought international criticism" (HoR 9/6/1979). Soon after assuming office as prime minister, Yasuhiro Nakasone argued in a speech that Japan needs to build more refugee centers for Indochinese refugees and then argued that "the fundamentals of our diplomacy should be based on a thorough recognition of the importance of an expanded international responsibility and role" (HoC 12/10/1982).

In addition to Diet members, representatives of the Japanese bureaucracy were concerned with the impact of Japan's refugee admission policy on Japan's international image. In 1979, the Japanese representative to the UNHCR, Hitoshi Mise, criticized Japan's refugee policy with reference to the policies of other countries: "Japan's system of refugee admissions until now has been inadequate when compared with foreign countries" (*Nihon Keizai Shimbun* [Evening Edition] 4/20/1979). A Ministry of Foreign Affairs representative was clearly referring to Japan's international image when he or she complimented Japan's 1981 expansion of its Indochinese refugee quota to three thousand with the argument that "in sum, by means of this, we have entered the same level as a small or mid-sized European state" (*Asahi Shimbun*, 4/28/1981). The same year, a Ministry of Foreign Affairs publication specifically cites a statement from Prime Minister Masayoshi Ohira that "as we get through the refugee crisis, the real door for our country's internationalization has been opened" (Ministry of Foreign Affairs 1981: 8).

This focus on Japan's international image was common in the major Japanese newspapers as well.[8] An editorial in *Nihon Keizai Shimbun* (6/23/1979) argued that Japan's quota of five hundred Indochinese refugees was far too small and should be raised to ten thousand in order to be comparable with other countries. Similarly, a 1977 opinion piece by Yasunari Magami was critical of the paucity of Japan's admissions of Indochinese refugees when compared with Western states (*Asahi Shimbun* 9/15/1977), and a news analysis piece in *Nihon Keizai Shimbun* (9/22/1977) compared Japanese refugee admissions unfavorably with the admissions of Western states as well as Israel, Hong Kong, and Taiwan.

After the 1979 International Conference on Indochinese Refugees, *Yomiuri Shimbun*'s editorial page advocated increased refugee admissions, arguing that "even if we lay out the particular nature of Japan which has not allowed us to admit refugees, the experience of Minister of Foreign Affairs Sonoda [at the conference] clearly indicates that these will not have persuasive power internationally" (*Yomiuri Shimbun* 7/23/1979). This perspective was not limited to opinion pieces and editorials. A news article in the evening edition of *Nihon Keizai Shimbun* (4/20/1979) called countries like the United States, Canada, and England "Advanced Countries for [Refugee] Settlement," attaching the word "settlement" (*teijū*) to the word for "advanced industrialized countries" (*senshinkoku*).

In short, the argument that Japan should allow the resettlement of Indochinese refugees (and later, that Japan should allow the resettlement of *more* Indochinese refugees) in order to improve its international image was a common one in late 1970s and 1980s Japan. It was an argument supported by a substantial proportion of the Japanese public (although, as of 1980, not the majority), and it was also an argument voiced by LDP leadership, opposition party DMs, Japanese bureaucrats, and opinion pieces or editorials in at least three of Japan's major daily newspapers: *Asahi Shimbun*, *Yomiuri Shimbun*, and *Nihon Keizai Shimbun*. However, this argument did not have universal acceptance; there were powerful opponents of resettlement of Indochinese refugees. Opponents of Indochinese resettlement generally made one or more of the following arguments: (1) Japan is a small, resource-poor, and overpopulated country; (2) if Japan begins to admit Indochinese refugees, it will one day be faced with massive numbers of refugees from other trouble spots; and (3) refugee admissions undermine Japanese society because Japan is ethnically homogeneous.

The first argument, that Japan is small, resource poor, and overpopulated, was most often attributed to Michio Setoyama, minister of justice between 1977 and 1978. In a 1977 House of Councilors Budget Committee meeting, Setoyama argued that, while it would be nice if Japan could allow for the resettlement of Vietnamese refugees, "our territory is extremely small, and our population is large, and in this kind of situation, it is not clear whether refugees could be nicely integrated into Japanese people's lifestyles" (HoC 12/191977). He made similar arguments in several other Diet hearings (HoR 2/14/1977; HoR 4/25/1978).

Bureaucrats also made the argument that Japan was too small, resource poor, and populous to allow refugee resettlement. The argument was articulated in reports from the Liaison and Coordination Council for Indochinese and Displaced Persons (herein the "Liaison Council;" an interministry working group that was established in 1977 to deal with the Vietnamese refugee crisis and later given jurisdiction over crises in Laos and Cambodia) (Cabinet Secretariat, 1980, 1987–1994). This argument also came up in discussions between mid-level bureaucrats in

June 1977. On the same day that the chief cabinet secretary, the minister of justice, the minister of foreign affairs, and the director general of the prime minister's office met to discuss the possibility of allowing the settlement of refugees who lacked another place to go, midlevel bureaucrats in a related meeting indicated that they believed that Japan was too overpopulated to admit refugees for settlement and that it should instead make financial contributions to UN efforts to help refugees and improve the situation of refugees temporarily in Japan (*Asahi Shimbun* [Evening Edition] 9/12/1977).

The second argument—that if Japan admits Indochinese refugees it might one day be overrun by other populations of refugees—was made by bureaucrats on a number of occasions. On September 20, 1977, the day that the Liaison Council was created, *Yomiuri Shimbun* cited an anonymous government source who was concerned with the possibility of Japan's admitting refugees as residents. In addition to noting concerns about overpopulation and population density, *Yomiuri*'s government source argued that resettlement of Indochinese refugees might lead to an explosion of interest from other Asian refugees: "If we allow refugees to settle in Japan, then there is a fear that there will be continuous flows of refugees from other Asian countries as well, and for the present all we can do is improve our refugee policy that had been insufficient until now" (*Yomiuri Shimbun* 9/18/1977). A Ministry of Justice bureaucrat made a similar argument: "Regarding the admission of Vietnamese refugees, there is a fear that this admission would spur a flood of refugees from other countries" (Yomiuri Shimbun 9/28/1977).

The third argument, that Japan cannot allow large-scale refugee resettlement because it is ethnically homogeneous, was also voiced a number of times throughout the refugee crisis. In June 1975, less than two months after the first Vietnamese refugees arrived in Japan, Umao Kagei, the director of the Immigration Bureau (in the Ministry of Justice) argued that Japan should not allow Vietnamese refugees to resettle in Japan. In addition to citing Japan's size, overpopulation, and the difficulties refugees might have in finding jobs, Kagei argued that "we Japanese people, for historical and geographical reasons, have been an ethnic group that has always been homogeneous" (HoR 6/25/1975).

The Liaison Council did not explicitly voice this third concern, that refugee admissions pose a challenge to Japan's homogeneity, in its annual publications. However, the 1987 publication contains the following argument about why some countries have admitted large numbers of refugees:

> Countries that have admitted large numbers of refugees, such as America, Canada, Australia, France, either originated with a tradition as immigration countries or had a background of involvement with the Indochinese countries; also, countries such as Switzerland and Sweden, had a tradition of caring for disabled people based in Western European humanism. (Cabinet Secretariat 1987: 19–20)

Earlier in the same document, the Liaison Council argued that while Japan cannot accept a large number of refugees like the United States, it has helped out in other ways, including monetary support (Cabinet Secretariat 1987: 2). In short, the Liaison Council argued that because Japan is not an immigration country—a concept that is closely related to ethnic diversity—it cannot accept refugees.

An anonymous member of Japan's delegation to the 1979 International Conference on Refugees and Displaced Persons in Southeast Asia made a similar point to a Japanese reporter. The delegation member argued that "on top of the fact that we have little land and high population density, other cultures cannot get used to living in our monoethnic society" (*Nihon Keizai Shimbun* July 7/23/1979). In other words, the speaker is suggesting that Japan's tradition of monoethnicity is fundamentally incompatible with large-scale refugee admissions.

Interestingly, even proponents of resettlement of Indochinese refugees often assumed that this resettlement would undermine Japan's ethnic homogeneity. Even when Minister of Foreign Affairs Sunao Sonoda said "we have no choice but to think about . . . allowing residency in Japan" (HoR 12/20/1978), he was responding to a statement by a DM that such admissions will be difficult because Japan is homogenous, and he indicated at the beginning of his reply that he agreed with the questioner's concern. This assumption is also clear in an editorial in the conservative *Yomiuri Shimbun* that was written in the wake of the 1979 conference. The *Yomiuri* editorial (7/23/1979) argued in favor of resettlement of larger numbers of Indochinese refugees, and it concluded with the argument that "we are requesting changes in the social and spiritual climate in our country, in which other ethnicities are firmly rejected." In short,

Yomiuri argued that in order to admit large numbers of Indochinese refugees, Japan would have to change its ethnic homogeneity.

Given these widespread concerns about the difficulties of refugee resettlement—that resettlement would be difficult because of Japan's population density and resource scarcity; that resettlement of Indochinese refugees may make Japan into a destination for large numbers of refugee populations in the future; and that refugee resettlement would undermine Japan's core identity as a one-ethnicity country—why did Japan eventually agree to allow the resettlement of Indochinese refugees? In addition to pressure from America, the UN, and other international sources, DMs and bureaucrats that were reluctant to allow refugee admissions agreed to allow the resettlement of Indochinese refugees because they came to believe that such a policy would not set a precedent that would cause Japan to become a destination for large-scale refugee resettlement. Thus, they came to believe that the challenges to Japanese society—including Japan's population density, resource scarcity, and ethnic homogeneity—would be relatively minimal.

There were two claims regularly made in official discussions of the Indochinese refugee situation that suggested that Japan would not become a major refugee destination even if it allowed Indochinese refugee resettlement—most Indochinese refugees did not *want* to resettle in Japan, and the Indochinese refugees are a "special case" and not refugees under the Refugee Convention. When asked about the relatively small numbers of Indochinese refugees resetting in Japan, bureaucrats and members of the cabinet often cited polls taken among the refugees themselves indicating where refugees wanted to settle. In a 1977 Diet hearing Yamano Katsuyoshi, the head of immigration inspection at the Bureau of Immigration, argued that "when refugees arrive, we ask them where they want to go, and they all have a particular country in mind . . . The United States is overwhelmingly the first choice, followed by France and Canada" (HoR 10/261977). Democratic Socialist Party DM Rō Watanabe asked whether some refugees might want to stay in Japan but do not understand that as a possibility, and Yamano answered that UNHCR officials have also conducted their own independent inquiries, and they have also found that few refugees want to remain in Japan.

Moreover, as the refugee crisis continued, increasing populations of Indochinese refugees in other countries made Japan a relatively less attractive resettlement destination. By 1985, when Japan established its quota of ten thousand Indochinese refugees, the existence of substantial populations of Indochinese refugees in other G7 countries ensured that those other countries were more desirable destinations than Japan. See table 5.2 for data on both Japan's slow start in Indochinese refugee resettlement and its relatively small total admissions of Indochinese refugees. This argument was made explicitly in a 1980 Diet hearing. When asked about why so few Indochinese refugees wanted to stay in Japan, Hiro Murazumi, chair of the Liaison Council, said:

> [W]hen I have asked refugees why they want to go to other countries, they mention that they have relatives in America. After the fall of Saigon 130,000 Vietnamese went to America, and after that America has continued to admit large numbers. Because of that, many people think that, if I have to leave my country, I want to go to a place with people I can rely on. (HoR 3/5/1980)

Murazumi's answer suggests that even those who opposed resettlement immediately after the Vietnam War may have come to support resettlement later because they came to think that even a Japan that was welcoming to Indochinese refugees would be a less desirable destination than countries with large numbers of Indochinese already living there. The record also suggests that this argument was effective; the only examples I could find of DMs or bureaucrats expressing concern that admitting Indochinese refugees might set a precedent that would make Japan into a major refugee destination came from 1977. While reports from the Liaison Council continued to express concern about both Japan's size and ethnic homogeneity, these arguments are not inconsistent with the idea of making a one-time exception to Japan's antirefugee admission policy. In short, the Liaison Council's reports serve more as a warning that Japan cannot become a major refugee destination than an argument against the admission of Indochinese refugees.

Japanese government officials also took pains to argue that those fleeing Indochina were not refugees according to the Refugee Convention. The Refugee Convention includes a very specific and relatively narrow definition of who is legally considered a refugee. According to the 1967 Protocol Relating to the Status of Refugees, a refugee is someone who is "outside the country of his origin . . . owing to a well-founded fear of

being persecuted for reasons of race, religion, nationality, political opinion, or membership in a particular social group" (cited in Barnett and
Finnemore 2004: 85). Because of the tremendous numbers of those fleeing
Vietnam, Laos, and Cambodia—as many as 3 million people would flee
from these countries in what was "the largest mass departure of asylum
seekers by sea in modern history" (Kneebone and Rawlings-Sanaei 2007:
12)—it was often difficult to establish whether each individual met this
definition, and thus "although the Convention definition itself was not
changed to accommodate new refugee flows, in actual practice UNHCR
applied an expanded definition to deal with the larger refugee movements
of the 1970s in Cambodia, Laos, and Vietnam" (Barnett, 2002: 248).

Japanese bureaucrats and politicians noted this de facto expansion
of the definition of refugee and used it to suggest that Japan's resettlement
of the Indochinese does not have any implications for how Japan might
deal with people who are refugees under a strict interpretation of the
Refugee Convention. During a 1981 hearing on the Refugee Convention
(which Japan ratified on October 3, 1981), Hirome Ōtaka, director of
the Immigration Bureau, made it clear that the Japanese government did
not consider Indochinese exiles to be refugees as defined by the Refugee Convention: "the Vietnamese 'refugees' can apply for refugee status.
However, it is difficult to make a general statement here about whether
they are actually refugees according to the treaty. Without examining the
situations of each individual, it is difficult to confirm that they are refugees" (HoR 5/27/1981). Shortly after ratifying the Refugee Convention,
Yasuhiro Nakasone, director of the Administrative Management Agency
and future prime minister, was asked about the future of Japan's refugee
policy. His reply began:

> There are two kinds of refugees. One kind are people exiled
> for political reasons (*seijiteki bōmeisha*), who are refugees
> according to the Refugee Convention. There were 316 of
> these people in Japan last year. They came from Poland,
> Afghanistan, Czechoslovakia, and other countries, and they
> all wanted to settle in other countries. The other are Viet-
> namese refugees, sometimes called "boat people" for short.

Nakasone goes on to argue that unlike political exiles, Japan has had to
allow the resettlement of some Indochinese refugees because of pressure

from countries that have already settled large numbers of Indochinese refugees, such as the United States (HoC 5/24/1982).

This perspective is also evident in government publications and statements from Japanese bureaucrats. In 1987, two years after Japan established its 10,000 quota, the Liaison Council published a report which argued that Indochinese refugees are not refugees according to the Refugee Convention and that Japan was granting those people refugee status because that is what the UNHCR and UN General Assembly had requested (Cabinet Secretariat 1987: 11). This interpretation of the Refugee Convention has not been limited to the Liaison Council; a Ministry of Foreign Affairs bureaucrat has criticized the annual refugee quotas of other countries because he suggested that, in order to fill those quotas, countries frequently admit people that are not refugees as defined in the Refugee Convention (interview 1098).

The Japanese government's interpretation of the Refugee Convention suggested that Japan did not consider itself legally obligated to treat those fleeing Indochina as refugees, and thus this interpretation gave Japan a great deal of leeway in dealing with other crises. Even after the Tiananmen Square massacre in 1989, the Liaison Council's annual reports did not mention political refugees from China in their discussion of "refugee flow conditions," although the introductory sections of each report after Tiananmen Square did discuss the problem of Chinese posing as Indochinese refugees (Cabinet Secretariat 1990–1994). In the years following the Tiananmen Square massacre, Japan did not grant refugee status to Chinese students residing in Japan who were involved with democracy activism (Mukae 2001: 190–97).

In short, Japanese politicians and bureaucrats came to believe that Japan's decision to admit 10,000 Indochinese refugees would not set a precedent that would make it more difficult for Japan to prevent future refugee flows into Japan for two reasons. First, from the earliest discussions about Indochinese refugees, Japanese politicians and bureaucrats emphasized that the vast majority of them did not want to resettle in Japan. Thus, even if Japan allowed resettlement of the Indochinese, it did not run the risk of resettling hundreds of thousands of refugees. This risk only decreased as the crisis persisted and the size of Indochinese refugee populations in countries such as America, Canada, and France grew.

Second, Japanese politicians and bureaucrats frequently argued that the people fleeing Indochina were not refugees as defined in the Refugee Convention. Thus, those leaders could treat the lenient screening procedures that Japan eventually developed for Indochinese refugees as exceptional, and they could suggest that Japan's quota for their resettlement was a response to a particular international crisis rather than a new policy direction.

Refugees in Twenty-First-Century Japan

Since Japan has ended its Indochinese refugee admissions program in 2005, it has continued to make refugee policy in a manner that avoids setting a precedent that suggests that it is a major refugee-admitting country. This is clear when looking at Japan's approach to asylum applicants, its approach to refugees from Myanmar, and its approach to Syrian refugees. In December 2008, Japan announced that, between 2010 and 2012, it would admit thirty refugees per year from camps on the Thai-Myanmar border (*Yomiuri Shimbun* 12/28/2008). This program was extended through 2014, although only eighty-six refugees were admitted in the end, fewer than the thirty per year that the program would have permitted (*Japan Times* 9/26/2014). After 2014, it announced that it would begin to admit Burmese refugees from camps in Malaysia. Japan had trouble filling its small quotas because the selection criteria that it established was "based the assumption that there would be many applicants for resettlement in Japan" (Takizawa 2015: 226). Thus, Japan established restrictive criteria to screen refugees from Southeast Asian refugee camps. It would only admit those the UNHCR deemed as in need of protection and that would easily integrate into Japanese society. It also chose to admit nuclear families rather than single individuals. However, because of these restrictive criteria, residents of refugee camps often chose to apply for asylum in other countries with less restrictive policies instead (Takizawa 2015: 227).

The Democratic Party of Japan (DPJ) controlled the government as this policy was implemented (The DPJ controlled the government between 2009 and 2012). One DPJ House of Councilors representative said that there were those in the DPJ that wanted to create refugee admissions programs aimed at countries other than Myanmar too, but these DPJ efforts were stifled by resistance from the Ministry of Justice and the Ministry of Foreign Affairs (interview 1152).

In May 2016, a few weeks before it was to host a G7 summit, Japan announced that it would permit 150 Syrian refugees to attend college there beginning in 2017 (*Asahi Shimbun* 5/19/2016). These refugees will actually be on student visas (interview 1205), meaning, as one CGP DM who opposed of expanded immigration in the Japanese Diet told me, "the beauty of this program is that they go back after 4 years" (interview 1123). It turned out that this anti-immigration DM's optimism was misplaced, however. In February of 2017, the Japanese government announced that 300, rather than 150, Syrian refugees and their spouses and children would be able to come to Japan as students and would not be required to leave after their studies were complete (*Asahi Shimbun* 2/3/2017).

Although some supporters of expanded refugee admissions have criticized the small status of this program, a Democratic Party representative from the House of Councilor with a history of supporting refugees was skeptical that Japan could admit many more Syrian refugees; he noted legal, social, and financial barriers that would have to be removed before such admission would be possible (interview 1156).

In sum, Japan's overall orientation toward asylum seekers, as well as the policies that it has designed to admit refugees from global crisis points including the aftermath of the Vietnam war, the repressive regime in Myanmar, and the Syrian civil war, have been designed in a way that permits the Japanese state to retain maximum discretion as to who gets in and for how long. Even when it established a goal of admitting 10,000 Indochinese refugees (a goal that Japan ultimately exceeded), Japan minimized the precedent that such activity would set for its dealings with other refugee populations in the future.

This is largely because, although some elites have criticized aspects of Japan's refugee admission and asylum policies, there has not been an influential strain of elite thought that has articulated a vision of Japan's identity and role in the world in which refugee admission plays a crucial role. The contrasts with countries like Germany, the United States, and Israel are very telling here. Each of those countries has admitted refugees or others without an immediately obvious economic role to fill because an influential group of elites viewed such admission as part of what it means to be American/German/Jewish. Of course, refugee admissions are controversial in those countries as well, with many powerful opponents (indeed, Donald Trump was extremely critical of refugee admissions as he campaigned for president, and since being elected, his administration has taken dramatic steps to decrease the numbers of people that qualify for asylum in the United States). However, in many other countries in the world, there has been an influential strain of elite thought that has articulated a vision of that country's national identity and/or its role in the world that includes admitting refugees. There has not yet been an influential group of Japanese elites that has articulated such a vision for Japan.

6

Is Another Japan Possible?

Public Opinion and Immigration Reformists

The title of this chapter is a reference to the book *Another Japan Is Possible*, edited by Jennifer Chan (2008). While Chan's book asserts that "another Japan is possible" by referring to a variety of new social movements in Japan, in this chapter I will focus on those in the Japanese government attempting to create a "new Japan" through immigration. Are there powerful elites aiming to push Japan to admit foreign residents beyond the relatively modest levels acceptable to immigration optimists? And if so, where did they come from, and what do they want?

In order to answer these questions, this chapter begins with a careful look at the two most prominent immigration reform proposals that came out of Japan's major political parties: the 2003 article in the magazine *Voice* by six DPJ Diet members and the 2008 white paper by a group of 80 LDP Diet members. Although they had their differences, each of these proposals called for Japan to admit 10 million immigrants.

After examining these proposals in detail, this chapter looks at the subsequent fate of immigration reformers in Japan. I assess these proposals and their aftermath with a view toward answering two questions. First, are these relatively recent developments evidence that the Japanese state is close to deciding to admit foreign labor on a large scale? Second, do these recent developments demonstrate that there is an influential strain of elite thought developing that suggests that foreign residents have a legitimate claim to residency and/or citizenship? In short, this chapter will show that Japan does not appear to be on the cusp of a radical shift in its immigration policy. In the years since the major immigration reform proposals of 2003 and 2009, most of the Japanese elites that advocated major reforms that went beyond what would have been acceptable to assimilation optimists either lost power or became less supportive of the idea of transforming Japan.

Making Japan a "Country to Long For?"

In 1999, Taichi Sakaiya, the director general of the Japanese government's Economic Planning Agency, suggested that Japan should consider admitting substantial numbers of highly skilled immigrants to help mitigate its declining population. Sakaiya's idea formed the basis for a July 1999 Cabinet Understanding (Komai 2007: 22). These kinds of ideas have also gained support in the business community. A few years after this Cabinet Understanding, the two largest interest groups representing big business in Japan—the Japan Federation of Employer's Associations (Nikkeiren) and the Japan Business Federation (Keidanren)—each argued that Japan should actively promote immigration to help address population decline.[1]

As far as I can tell, the first time that a group of politicians offered a proposal for large-scale immigration into Japan was in 2003, when DPJ House of Councilors DM Kei'ichiro Asao and five of his colleagues from both houses of the Diet published an article in the magazine *Voice* called "A Plan to Admit Ten Million Immigrants: Let's Make Japan 'A Country to Long For'" (Asao et al. 2003). The proposal justifies its call for large-scale immigration with reference to Japan's declining and aging population. Asao and his colleagues begin by painting a bleak picture of the consequences of Japan's population problem. They note the oft-discussed questions about who will pay for the care of the elderly as the country continues to age and Japanese firms moving their operations overseas to find more laborers. They also note more general problems not necessarily directly associated with *shōshikōreika*, including "an education system in shambles, destruction of the environment, extreme centralization of civic authority and bureaucratic bloat, party politics that seem exhausted and low voter turnout that reflects mistrust of politics" (142–143).

They suggest that they will sketch a broad outline of some proposals that will reinvigorate Japan, and the first proposal that they mention is the proposal from the title of the article: Japan should admit 10 million immigrants. They suggest that these immigrants should not be thought of as a solution to labor shortages or as a means of doing jobs that Japanese young people don't want to do, but rather as "human resources to become a driving force of the Japanese economy" (Asao et al. 2003: 145). Asao and his colleagues advocate admitting people with specific skills that the Japanese economy needs, such as those knowledgeable about technologies used in car manufacturing and programmers of video game software, and they suggest that it would be particularly useful to have immigrant entrepreneurs, since they argue that entrepreneurship is an area in which the Japanese are not very strong (146).

They argue that the reason for the main criticism of Japan by foreigners is that "in Japan there are not equal opportunities" for Japanese and foreign residents. To help create an economy and society that better guarantee equal opportunities and rewards success in economic competition, they use the rest of the article to advocate a variety of political reforms, including direct election of the prime minister, reducing the numbers of Diet members, radically changing the missions of the two houses of the Diet, and promoting the idea of regions of Japan developing their own local identities by, among other things, cutting subsidies by the national government to regional governments (Asao et al. 2003: 146–48).

Asao and his colleagues' *Voice* article did not seem to make a big splash in the Japanese media. It was not reported on at all in the *Yomiuri Shimbun* or the *Tokyo Shimbun*. *Sankei Shimbun* published an opinion piece by Kei'ichi Iwasaki that was critical of the *Voice* article (*Sankei Shimbun*, 8/24/2003). Iwasaki suggests that the *Voice* article is likely to influence the DPJ's manifesto, and indeed, the month after the *Voice* article was released, the DPJ announced five changes to its manifesto. Two of these changes—the proposals to "abolish all national government expenditure-specific subsidies for local governments within four years" and "cut the number of Diet seats and personnel costs of public servants by 10 percent within four years" (*Japan Times* 10/6/2003) are suggested by the *Voice* article. However, the immigration-related proposals are not mentioned in that or other future manifestos of the DPJ.

In other words, this article by Asao and colleagues does not represent the majority position of DPJ DMs. The DPJ (which changed its English name to the "Democratic Party" [DP] in 2016 after merging with another party) has long been divided on questions relating to immigration. Although senior party leadership has, at times, supported proposals to grant foreign residents the right to vote in local elections in Japan, those proposals have not been included in the party's "manifesto" because of a lack of consensus among party members. One DP candidate for the House of Representatives told me that, although he personally supports expanding foreign labor in Japan, he feels that he cannot express that opinion in public because he fears "strong opposition from the right wing" (interview 1122). When the DPJ was in power (between 2009 and 2012), Masaharu Nakagawa, a high ranking DPJ politician, suggested at a news conference that Japan should promote immigration, and he reported that "my office was met with a deluge of angry calls and a pile of faxes protesting the move, with my ministry similarly swamped with calls to such an extent that our job was temporarily paralyzed" (*Japan Times*, 3/3/2017).

Another DP Diet member who supported immigration suggested that, before the DP would be able to become a party of immigration it would have to convince Japanese labor unions that immigration is in their economic interest (interview 1190). This Diet member went on to cite South Korea as an example for Japan to emulate; he argued that South Korea ended the "trainee" program that they had modeled on Japan and introduced an unskilled labor visa category partially because South Korean labor unions were concerned with how the "trainee" category allowed employers to take advantage of workers.[2]

"National Opening to Human Resources!"

On June 12, 2008, a group of 80 LDP DMs released an unusual document. Titled "National Opening to Human Resources! An Opinion on a Japanese-Style Immigration Policy" (complete with the exclamation point), it proposed that Japan should change its immigration and citizenship policies in a number of substantial ways. Perhaps most controversially, the report suggested that Japan should change its immigration admission policies so that 10 percent of its population would be comprised of immigrants; this would involve admitting roughly 10 million foreign residents to Japan (interesting, this is the same figure that DPJ members Asao and colleagues proposed six year before).

This proposal was surprising because of both its magnitude and its source. At the time when the proposal was released, there were

127,692,000 people living in Japan, of whom 2,217,426, or 1.74 percent, were foreign residents (Ministry of Internal Affairs and Communications 2016). This group of DMs was thus proposing to increase the population of foreign residents in Japan more than five times over.

Regarding the source, it was particularly interesting that DMs from the LDP wrote this proposal. The LDP is a center-right political party that had governed Japan either alone or in coalition between 1955 and 2009 (with a ten-month break from 1993 through 1994). During that lengthy period of LDP rule, Japan did very little to encourage immigration, and LDP politicians have regularly noted that, unlike countries such as Canada and the United States, Japan is not a country of immigration. As discussed in chapter 4, when the LDP-led government did revise the Immigration Control and Refugee Recognition Act in 1990, this revision was done in a way that discouraged permanent residency in Japan and encouraged immigration by those with Japanese ethnicity (Chung 2010: 151–53). In contrast, the 2008 proposal makes explicit efforts to encourage immigrants to stay in Japan for a long time, and does not advocate preferential treatment for those with Japanese ethnicity.

This 2008 proposal of the LDP Diet Members Caucus for the Promotion of Foreign Human Resources (herein "the Caucus") marked the first time that a group of LDP DMs advocated large-scale admission of immigrants. The Caucus was formed in December of 2005. It was inactive until 2008, when Hidenao Nakagawa, an LDP Lower House DM who had previously served in major cabinet and party positions, including secretary-general and chief cabinet secretary, assumed the chairmanship (Akashi 2010: 268; Akashi and Ogawa 2008: 69). As one Japanese political reporter explains, "there were other party study groups that discussed issues relating to foreign residents, but someone with the political importance of Nakagawa becoming the head of the Caucus had a significant influence on that group" (cited in Akashi and Ogawa 2008: 69). Nakagawa said that he advocated expanding immigration to Japan because of "concern over the plummeting economic growth rates and concern for the shortage of workers in caregiving" (Roberts 2012: 59).

Although he was not formally a member because he was not a Diet member, retired Ministry of Justice bureaucrat Hidenori Sakanaka (the same bureaucrat discussed in chapter 3) is also widely associated with the Caucus and its proposal. The *Japan Times* called Sakanaka the "plan's mastermind" (6/19/2008), and Sakanaka subsequently released a plan of his own through his Immigration Policy Institute (2009) that also called on Japan to admit 10 million immigrants.[3] Sakanaka has long sought to shape public debate about immigration in Japan (see Sakanaka 1999 and Sakanaka 2005 for other examples). After his retirement from the Ministry of Justice, Sakanaka has focused much of his energy into promoting the idea that Japan should become a country that supports immigration.

In addition to the initiative of key figures such as Nakagawa and Sakanaka, there were two other major factors that influenced the timing of the Caucus's proposal. First, there is the desire by many Japanese firms (and their representative interest groups) for more labor power. This desire led to the 1990 immigration reform, but as figure 4.2 demonstrates, by the mid-2000s, firms began to face labor shortages that they had not faced since the years surrounding the 1990 immigration reform. In 2006, 2007, and 2008, the ratio of jobs available to first-time job seekers was 1.56, 1.52, and 1.25. In short, firms were struggling to fill jobs.

Second, by the time the Caucus formed and made its proposal, there was the widespread perception that Japan's dual problem of a population that is both declining and aging—*shōshikōreika*—is not going away anytime soon. As Schoppa (2006: 151) notes, it was not until the late 1990s that the Japanese government's official estimates stopped predicting that birth rates would eventually rebound, and therefore that the problem of *shōshikōreika* would not just solve itself. All of the Caucus's members with whom I spoke cited *shōshikōreika* as the main problem that they saw the Caucus attempting to address.

The Caucus's proposal is labeled as a draft and is specific about establishing goals; there are twenty-one goals established in the proposal that are attached to "deadlines" of between one and five years. This proposal was much more specific and clearer in its targets than the *Voice* article by DPJ DMs from 2003. These goals range from having the Japanese government make a public declaration to the world that Japan is now an immigration country within one year (LDP 2008: 4) to establishing educational programs that will help Japanese people to think more favorably about other cultures within three years (LDP 2008: 8). The LDP lost control of the Lower House of the Diet and, hence, the prime ministership, in a landslide election on August 30, 2009, a little over one year after this draft document was released, and thus, even if the LDP was entirely committed to this document, it would not have been possible for the party to implement many of the goals outlined.

However, as discussed below, some of the goals have been implemented by either the bureaucracy or by the Abe administration that won back power for the LDP after 2012.

The proposal is clear about its rationale for advocating large-scale immigration into Japan. The first sentence in the document is "Japan is faced with an aging society such that no country in the world has ever experienced." When I interviewed members of the Caucus, it was clear that they also thought about immigration policy as primarily a solution to the problem of *shōshikōreika*. As one House of Representatives Diet member explained:

> It is important to start debate on immigration. There are some people who are opposed to even debate about immigration. For some, I don't know, some psychological barrier or whatever. But we are losing population. The labor market is shrinking fast. A lot of people . . . argue that if we are successful in bringing the women and senior citizens back to the labor market, we don't need to talk about immigration. Now, that is not true. The speed of population shrinking is so fast that if we are successful in bringing women and senior citizens back in the labor market, we still have 1 million people short by 2040–2050, that time frame. So it is important to start debate on starting work visas. (Interview 1099)

Aside from *shōshikōreika*, the proposal is also justified on humanitarian grounds (because it includes refugee admissions) and as a development program (because it includes calls for overseas Japanese language education, and because foreign trainees who decide to return to their countries of origin will bring new skills with them).

All four Caucus members that I interviewed mentioned disagreement within the LDP about the wisdom of admitting large numbers of immigrants. One House of Representatives DM suggested that the eighty-member Caucus did not represent the majority position within the party (interview 1097). Another House of Representatives DM indicated that "within the LDP, there are some right-wing elements who oppose any foreigners" (interview 1099). He concluded the interview with this statement: "I think [immigration] is a very important issue, not many politicians would do it because they don't want to be shot from behind."

This suggests that he thinks that opponents of the proposal, while not particularly vocal, have both strong preferences and a good deal of power within the party. The degree of support for immigration among LDP Diet members is assessed quantitatively below.

In addition to arguing that Japan should aim to be an immigration country, the proposal also specifically sets a goal of admitting 10 million immigrants in fifty years. It is this specific goal that drew the majority of media attention (*Sankei Shimbun* 6/13/2008; *Tokyo Shimbun* 6/13/2008; *Yomiuri Shimbun* 6/9/2008). This was not a popular goal with the members of the Caucus that I interviewed. This is most clearly illustrated in an excerpt from a conversation with the most outspoken Diet member whom I interviewed:

> INTERVIEWER: I am researching the LDP Diet Member Caucus for the Promotion of Foreign Human Resources' proposal from last year.
>
> DM: Ten million whatever?
>
> INTERVIEWER: Yeah, that proposal.
>
> DM: Yeah, no one really cares.
>
> INTERVIEWER: Okay, what do you mean no one really cares?
>
> DM: I mean, come on. We have 120 million [people in Japan] and you want 10 million [immigrants]? Snore. (Interview 1099)

The other House of Representatives Caucus member whom I interviewed was similarly dismissive about the 10 million target: "The idea of suddenly admitting 10 million is, from my perspective, nonsense" (interview 1097). This DM also suggested that the figure of 10 million was actually a compromise, as some estimate that Japan would need as many as 30 million immigrants before 2050 to solve its population problems. Although they saw the goal of 10 million immigrants as exaggerated and designed to catch attention rather than to immediately become government policy, members of the Caucus were more committed to the idea of using foreign labor to address *shōshikōreika*. This point will be further discussed below.

The proposal suggests that immigrants should be encouraged in six categories: high skilled laborers, people wanting to come to Japan for job training, exchange students, the families of immigrants, immigrants with humanitarian concerns including refugees and Japanese wanting to leave North Korea, and the very wealthy (the proposal calls this last group 'investment immigrants' or *tōshi imin*). The proposal advocates establishing a point system for admitting immigrants, where applicants are awarded points based on the extent to which they qualify in one or more of these groups. As noted in chapter 4, the Ministry of Justice did establish a small-scale version of this point system in 2011.

The proposal acknowledges the existence of criticism of Japan's Trainee and Technical Internship Program. The Caucus begins the final section of the proposal by noting that "the Trainee and Technical Internship Program, about which concerns about human trafficking and other similar problems have often been expressed, should be abolished as our foreigners' job training program is established." One significant difference between the existing Foreigner Skills Training Program and the program that the Caucus proposed is the time frame. While at the time the Caucus wrote its proposal, foreign trainees could not stay in Japan for longer than three years (Komai 2001:38), the Caucus proposes that trainees should be able to stay in Japan for as long as four years, and then, "for those who have finished the program and wish to work in Japan, if they can establish that they have a job as a regular worker in a firm from an industry related to the one where they did their training, they will be allowed to stay in Japan with the legal status of either 'skilled worker' or 'resident.'" As noted in chapter 4, the Trainee and Technical Internship Program has indeed been expanded in a manner similar to this; technical interns can now stay for six years and reapply to the technical internship.

The Caucus also proposes radically expanding nurse and caregiver admissions policies. The proposal would establish a goal of admitting three hundred thousand nurses and caregivers to Japan by 2025 (as noted in chapter 4, Japan permitted caregivers to be admitted as trainees in 2016; this proposal was on a much smaller scale than the Caucus's proposal). Interestingly, while the Caucus recommends that Japan adopt almost all of its policy positions unilaterally, the two exceptions to this are the expanded nurse and caregiver admissions policy and the foreign trainees' program. Both of these policies, according to the Caucus, should be implemented through EPAs. However, subsequent reforms in both of these areas have been implemented unilaterally, rather than through EPAs.

The proposal also specifies a number of ways that Japan should make itself friendlier to foreign residents once they have arrived in Japan. The proposal suggests that "there is a need to build a social and economic system that is capable of serving the needs of immigrants." This concern was echoed in several of my interviews. The House of Councilors DM who had a leadership role in the Caucus argued that "the minds of typical Japanese are still resistant to the idea of foreigners" (interview 1096) while another DM argued that the chief obstacle to the Caucus's proposal becoming law was "general [xeno]phobia of Japanese people" (interview 1099).

Perhaps most radically, the proposal suggests that Japan should change from a blood-based to a (limited) soil-based citizenship policy: "Regarding the children of people that are permanent residents of Japan, after they are born they should have Japanese citizenship (and retain dual citizenship until the age of 22)." Moreover, the proposal also recommends that Japan should ease the requirements for granting permanent residence status. If implemented in a serious way, these two proposals would encourage increasing numbers of people without Japanese ethnicity to become Japanese citizens, and this would be a serious challenge to those who believe that Japanese ethnicity is a key component of Japanese identity.

The proposal is also noteworthy for its choice of frames. The proposal notes in more than one place that expanding the use of humanitarian justifications for immigration would allow for the admission of those Japanese who live in North Korea and wish to return to Japan. This seems like an attempt to capitalize on the Japanese media attention that the issue of the Japanese abducted by North Korea had received in recent years. Moreover, the proposal argues that immigration would actually "revive the latent power of Japanese civilization" in four ways.

First, immigration would give Japanese industry the opportunity to compete with foreign companies that are currently overtaking Japan. Second, Japan's history of mutual coexistence between Buddhists, Christians, and practitioners of Shintoism suggests that it should be able to incorporate immigrants from different ethnic backgrounds: "the Japanese, who have inherited 'tolerant' genes from continuously living with people with diverse values, have the potential to successfully build a 'society of multi-ethnic coexistence' with any of the world's ethnic groups."[4] Third, Japan has a beautiful natural environment and a rich cultural heritage which more than eight million foreign tourists come to see every year. Fourth, there are already "people with an immigrant background" living in Japan. In short, this section of the proposal seems designed to answer potential critics who might argue that immigration will undermine Japanese culture. This section suggests that immigration will preserve the Japanese economy and hence Japanese culture, that toleration of difference is actually a part of Japanese culture, that immigrants will be drawn to Japan because of its natural beauty and culture and will hence appreciate that (and perhaps help to keep Japan's ancient culture alive), and that there are already immigrations in Japan who have not undermined Japanese culture.

One of the DMs I interviewed went even further than the proposal in this regard, arguing that the Japanese have lost some kind of cultural essence that immigrants from Asian countries might help to restore:

> The character of Japanese young people is declining rapidly. They are not patient anymore. Traditionally, Japanese people are very patient, and they are very serious, but now, the young people are changing so rapidly, very different from so-called Japanese people. Thus, it is very challenging to find people to work at nursing homes. Therefore, I strongly suggest that Japan should admit laborers from serious Asia (*majime na ajia*) to work in nursing homes. (Interview 1097)

In this quote, the DM suggests that the key element of Japanese national identity is civic rather than ethnic. That is, one can be "Japanese" if one has virtues like patience, while another who lacks those values is not truly Japanese, even if this latter person has Japanese ethnicity. Although he did not go quite as far as his peer, the other House of Representatives DM with whom I spoke suggested that a high degree of Japanese language ability is a much better criterion for immigration admission than Japanese ethnicity (interview 1099). In short, this second DM also suggests that inherited traits are a less essential component of Japanese identity than learned traits such as the ability to speak Japanese.

Did the Foreign Human Resources Caucus Matter?

The text of the proposal suggests that another Japan is indeed possible, specifically regarding immigration. The text suggests the introduction and expansion of many different visa categories, some of which would include unskilled laborers. This suggests that the Caucus members had reconciled themselves with the demands of labor-intensive industries to admit foreign labor. Second, in its discussion of Japan as an "immigration country," as well as its proposals to admit the families of laborers and increasing numbers of refugees, the proposal suggests that its authors believe that foreign residents have a legitimate claim to residency and/ or citizenship. In short, if this proposal's vision had become law in its entirety in 2008, we might now be discussing Japan as a "country of immigration," in the language of chapter 2.

However, there are two reasons to be skeptical that Japan is moving in this direction. First, the only of the Caucus's proposals that have been enacted since 2008 involve foreign labor, mostly temporary foreign labor. This includes the point system, the expansion of the trainee system, and the expansion of caregiver admissions. However, none of these changes has been made in a way that will lead to anything like the 10 million immigrants that the Caucus aimed for. Relatedly, despite the Caucus's plea that Japan should begin to refer to itself as an "immigration nation," the word "immigration" remains controversial among many elites in Japan, including those within the LDP, even those who, like Prime Minister Abe, support expansion of foreign labor. Also, the Caucus's calls for Japan to implement policies that make Japan a friendlier place for immigrants, including the call to establish educational programs that help Japanese people think more favorably about other cultures and to "build a social and economic system that is capable of serving the needs of immigrants" have not yet been heeded.

The second reason that we should be skeptical about the extent to which the Caucus's proposal is changing Japan involves the ultimate fate of Caucus members, particular those that were serious about immigration reform. 2009 was a bad year for the LDP, as they lost control of the

House of Representatives in a landslide. Even given this overall context, it was somewhat worse for candidates who were members of the Foreign Human Resource Caucus. Only 19.6 percent of LDP candidates won their SMDs in 2009. Nonmembers of the Caucus did slightly better than that, with 20.4 percent winning their SMDs, while Caucus members did slightly worse, with only 15.4 percent winning their SMDs.

Perhaps not surprisingly, Caucus members were much more likely to agree with the statement on Masaki Taniguchi 2009 survey of candidates for the House of Representatives that "Japan should promote the admission of foreign laborers" than were non-members (See table 6.1 for a summary of the positions of Caucus members on this question).[5] 45.8 percent of Caucus members agreed with that statement, while only 10.4 percent disagreed (a difference of 35.4 percent). In contrast, 30 percent of LDP House of Representatives DMs who were in the Caucus agreed with the idea that "Japan should promote the admission of foreign laborers," while 25.8 percent disagreed (a difference of only 4.5 percent).

Only 9.1 percent of Caucus members who agreed that Japan should expand foreign labor won SMDs, while 19 percent of Caucus member who neither agreed nor disagreed won their seats (all five Caucus members who disagreed with that statement ended up winning proportional representation seats). In short, it was a bad electoral environ-

Table 6.1. Reaction to the statement "Japan should promote the admission of foreign labor" by LDP house of representatives candidates who were members of the Caucus for the Promotion of Foreign Human Resources

	Percent that agree	Percent neutral	Percent that disagree	Agree minus disagree	Agree minus disagree among all LDP House of Representatives DMs
2009	45.9%	40.4%	10.4%	35.5%	6.3%
2012	22.9%	51.4%	25.9%	−3%	−10.1%
2014	21.9%	62.5%	15.6%	6.3%	−17.6%

Data from Masaki Taniguchi, 2009, 2012, 2014. "Agree" includes those who "somewhat agree," and "disagree" includes those who "somewhat disagree." In this table I focus on those that were members of the Caucus in 2008, when they released their controversial policy proposal. I thus exclude those who joined after 2008 and include those who resigned after 2008.

ment for all LDP candidates, but it was particularly bad for those who both joined the Caucus and expressed clear support for foreign labor. The electorate appeared to punish representatives who were too strongly proimmigration.[6]

Caucus members themselves seem to have internalized this message. In the years after the election, Caucus members and former Caucus members who remained in politics seem to have grown somewhat cold on the prospect of importing foreign labor into Japan (although, as table 6.1 demonstrates, less cold than DMs from the LDP as a whole). In 2012, only 22.9 percent of Caucus members and former Caucus members running for a House of Representatives seat agreed that Japan should promote the admission of foreign labor, and in 2014, only 21.9 percent of those candidates agreed.

Diet Members, Public Opinion, and Immigration in a Postcaucus Japan

What lesson have Japanese elites taken from the fate of the Caucus's proposal and Caucus politicians? How has public opinion on immigration shifted in the years since the 2009? Figure 6.1 demonstrates overall Diet-member thinking on the utility of foreign labor to Japan, as well as DM thinking by party at every election since 2009. Two things are noteworthy in figure 6.1. First, recent Diets have tended to have more pro-foreign labor members than anti-foreign labor members. Despite the punishment that proimmigration Caucus members took in the 2009 House of Representatives election, and the movement of those Caucus members away from pro-immigration stances, Diet members who won seats in the 2010 were even more pro-foreign labor than in 2009. And, after all elections since 2009 (with the exception of 2014), there were more pro-foreign labor than anti-foreign labor members.

Second, despite the incredible demographic and economic pressures on Japan in recent years, there has not been a Diet in the years after the Caucus made its proposal in which the majority of DMs support foreign labor. Indeed, the 2010 House of Councilors was the only election in which more than 40 percent of the winners support increasing foreign labor admissions. Thus, any Diet proposal to convince Japan to admit foreign labor is likely going to have to convince a significant number of those without a position on foreign labor to sign on.

Figure 6.1. Diet members' views on whether Japan should promote the admission of foreign labor.

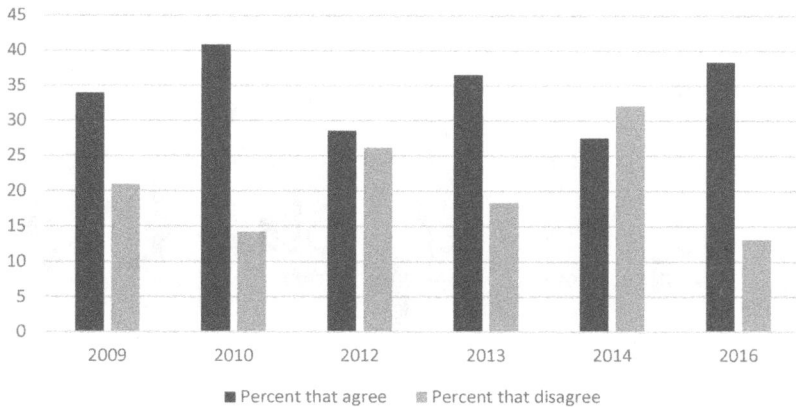

Data from Masaki Taniguchi, 2009, 2010, 2012, 2013, 2014, 2016. Agree includes those who "somewhat agree," and disagree includes those who "somewhat disagree." The House of Representatives surveys (2009, 2012, and 2014) had an average response rate of 94.5 percent, and the House of Councilors surveys (2010, 2013, and 2016) had an average response rate of 53.9 percent.

The obstacles to reform proposals in the short term become starker when looking at figure 6.2. While many more CGP and DPJ politicians have supported than opposed increasing admission of foreign labor, DMs from LDP and communist parties have been much more volatile in their assessment of the utility of expanded foreign labor for Japan. This is particularly noteworthy with regards to the LDP, as it has been the senior partner in the governing coalition since 2012. After two of the six elections since 2009 (the 2012 and 2014 House of Representatives elections), more LDP DMs opposed than supported expanding foreign labor, and after the 2013 House of Councilors election, the percentage of LDP Diet members that supported expanding foreign labor was equal to the percentage that opposed expanding it (both groups made up 26.2 percent of LDP DMs).

Contrary to the suggestions of Caucus members who saw the xenophobia of the Japanese people as an obstacle to large-scale immigration reforms, the Japanese public has not been consistently more against foreign labor than the Japanese Diet. Figure 6.3 suggests that, while the Diet

Figure 6.2. Diet members' views on whether Japan should promote the admission of foreign laborers, by party (percent that agree minus percent that disagree).

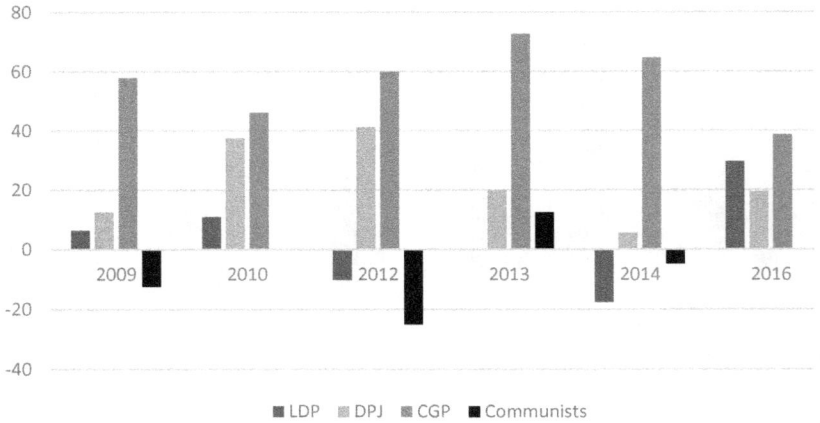

Data from Masaki Taniguchi, 2009, 2010, 2012, 2013, 2014, 2016. Agree includes those who "somewhat agree," and disagree includes those who "somewhat disagree."

Figure 6.3. House of Representatives DMs' views and the public's views on whether Japan should promote the admission of foreign labor, by party (percent that agree minus percent that disagree).

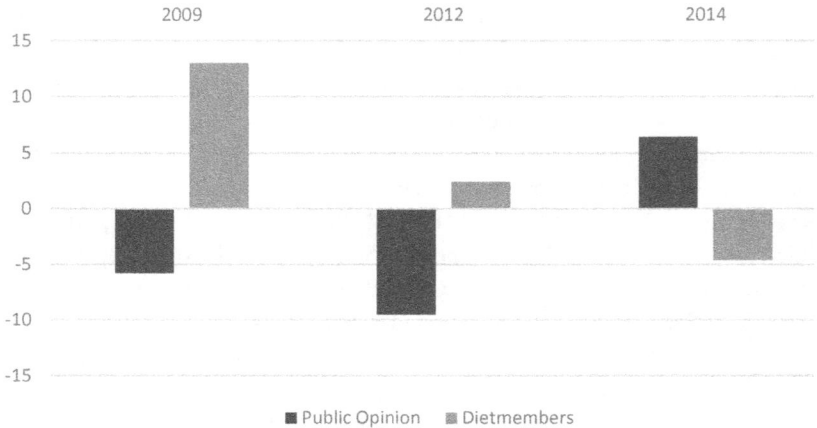

Data from Masaki Taniguchi, 2009, 2012, 2014.

was more supportive of foreign labor than the public in 2009 and 2012, in 2014, the public was substantially more supportive of foreign labor than the Diet; 32.1 percent of the Japanese public agreed with expanding foreign labor, while only 27.5 percent of the House of Representatives agreed (25.7 percent of the public disagreed, while 32.1 percent of the House of Representatives disagreed).[7]

Interestingly, of the three elections for which data are available (Taniguchi does not include a foreign-labor question on his public opinion survey before House of Councilors elections), the correlation between prefectural public opinion and Diet-member opinion on immigration has seemed to be strongest when the public is more opposed to foreign labor than the Diet. See figures 6.4, 6.5, and 6.6 for visual illustrations

Figure 6.4. Public opinion and House of Representatives DMs' views on whether Japan should promote the admission of foreign labor, by prefecture, 2009 (1 means strongly agree with admitting foreign laborers; 5 means strongly disagree).

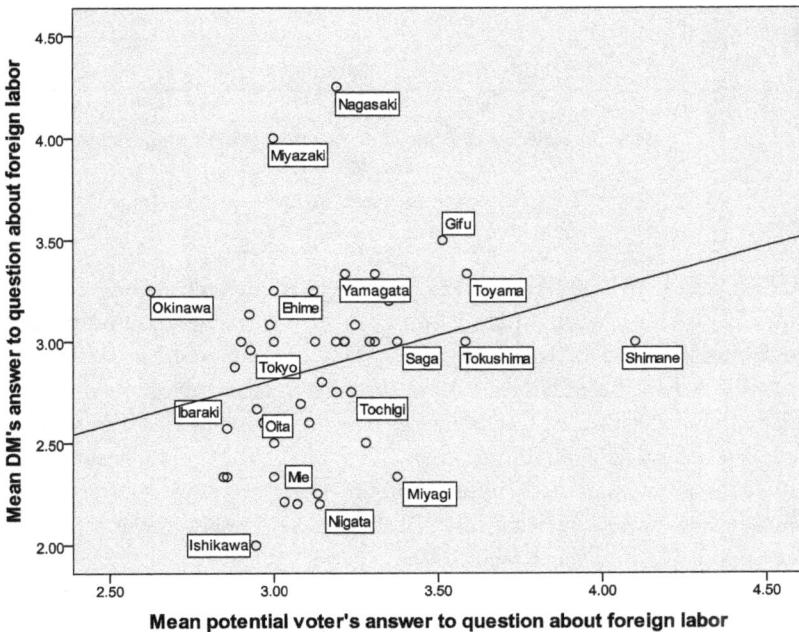

Data from Taniguchi, 2009.

Figure 6.5. Public opinion and House of Representatives DMs' views on whether Japan should promote the admission of foreign labor, by prefecture, 2012 (1 means strongly agree with admitting foreign laborers; 5 means strongly disagree).

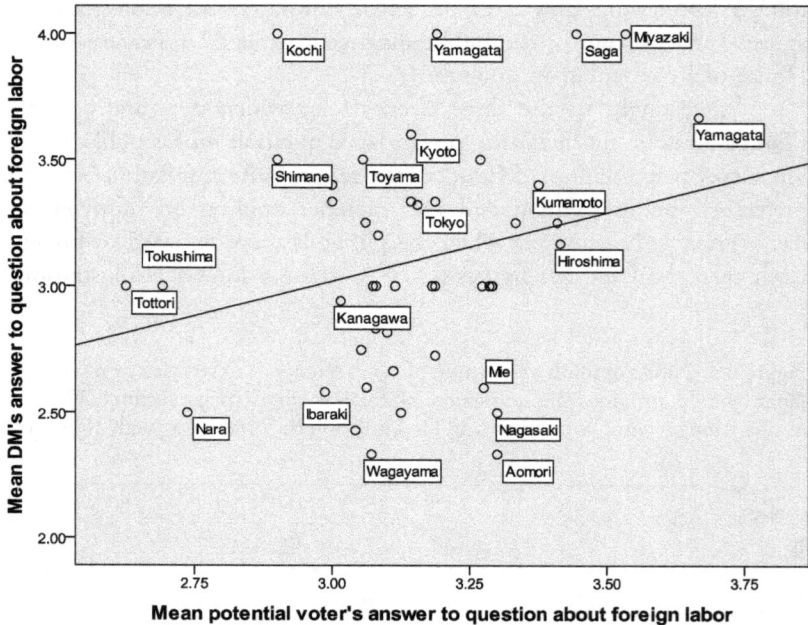

Data from Taniguchi 2012.

of this trend. In 2009 and 2012, there were moderately strong correlations between prefectural public opinion and the average opinion of that prefecture's House of Representatives DMs on foreign labor. However, in 2014, when the public was more supportive of immigration than the Diet, the correlation was actually negative (although it was also weaker and less statistically significant than 2009 and 2012).[8] This means that in 2014, prefectures with public opinion that was more supportive of foreign labor were somewhat more likely to elect representatives that were *less* supportive of foreign labor.

The relatively weak negative tendency from 2014 is likely a reflection of the fact that in 2014 voters made their decisions on who to vote for on issues other than candidates' stances on immigration. But it

Figure 6.6. Public opinion and House of Representatives DMs' views on whether Japan should promote the admission of foreign labor, by prefecture, 2014 (1 means strongly agree with admitting foreign laborers; 5 means strongly disagree).

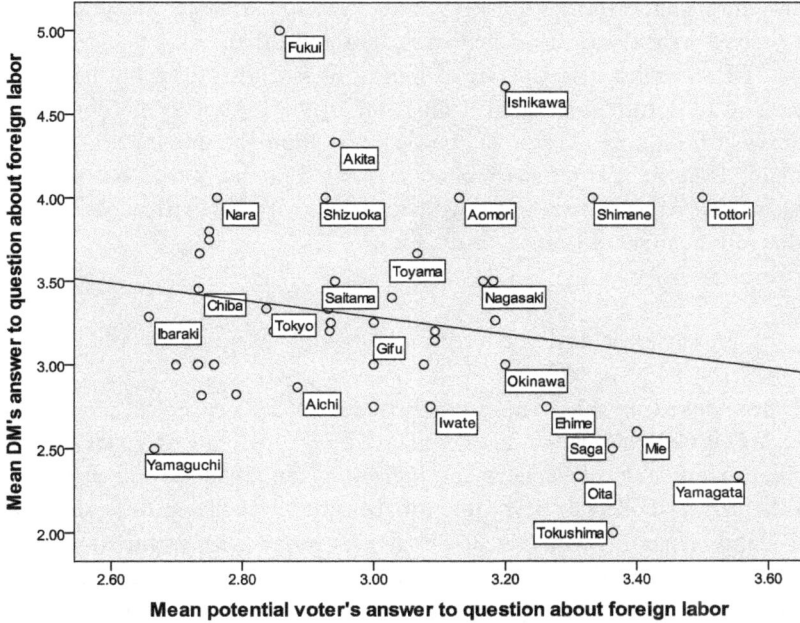

Data from Taniguchi, 2014.

is interesting to note that the relationship between public opinion and Diet-member opinion was weakest when the public was more supportive of immigration than the Diet. This suggests, in a preliminary way, that the public is more willing to punish DMs whom it sees as too supportive of immigration than it is to reward those whom it sees as appropriately supportive of immigration. If that is indeed the case (and more research is needed here to make a more determinative case), then it will continue to be difficult to get large numbers of Diet members to sign on to legislation that would radically expand immigration.

In addition to public opinion, I also looked at the extent to which the demographics and economy of a district might influence a DM's stance on foreign labor. I looked for correlations between a prefecture's mean DM's foreign labor stance and the percentage of trainees in the prefecture (which I used to measure the extent to which that prefecture relies on foreign labor), as well as the mean DM's foreign labor stance and that prefecture's job-seeker's ratio (which I used to measure labor scarcity) for every election between 2009 and 2016.

The results were a series of mostly weak and statistically insignificant relationships that were inconsistent from election to election. This is likely both an indicator of the fact that immigration has not been a major issue in any recent election and the fact that I was not able to locate district level data, and thus that there is variation within prefectures that my analysis did not account for.

Integration and the Future of Japan's Migration Policy

I also looked at the relationship between DMs' answer to a question regarding whether Japan should grant foreign permanent residents the right to vote in local elections and prefectural demographic and economic variables. I looked at this question because it is the only systematic evidence regarding whether and to what extent Diet members believe that foreign residents should be integrated into Japanese society. This issue has been particularly important to the LDP's coalition partner, the CGP, and it is sometimes discussed as a way for Japan to do right by its oldcomer Korean community. That is, since the Japanese state and most of the major organizations in the Korean community have both treated citizenship and ethnicity as identical (and since the Japan state does not even poll citizens about their ethnicity, suggesting that all citizens of Japan also have Japanese ethnicity), some have supported granting members of the oldcomer Korean community the right to vote in local elections so they can participate in their communities while retaining a formal marker of their ethnicity (see chapter 3 and Strausz 2010 for more discussion of this issue).

While these results were mostly weak and statistically insignificant, the strongest correlation that I observed in my analysis was from just before the 2016 House of Councilors election, between percentage of trainees in a prefecture and that prefecture's House of Councilors delegation's mean answer to the question "Should foreign permanent residents be granted the right to vote in Japan?"[9] The results showed that Diet members from prefectures with higher percentages of trainees were more likely to *oppose* granting foreign permanent residents the right to vote in local elections. However, there is no correlation between the total percentage of foreign residents in a prefecture and Diet members' views on granting foreign residents the right to vote in local elections.

In other words, there is some evidence that Diet members whose constituents' only experience with foreign residents is trainees and technical interns, a population whom the state makes no effort to integrate into local communities (assuming that they will leave after their program has completed), oppose efforts to integrate foreigners into local communities in Japan while remaining visibly foreign.

We must be careful not to make too much of this one correlation. However, when we consider this finding along with the reluctance of many in the LDP and the business community to use the word "immigrant," and the reliance of recent successful immigration reforms on expansion of the Trainee and Technical Internship Program, it seems like the loudest reformist voices among Japanese elites are pushing for programs that would look more like Switzerland's guest-worker program—where foreigners are workers but not members—than Germany's—where large numbers of foreigners ended up becoming citizens, thereby changing the nature of what it means to be German in a significant way. Indeed, the December 2018 revision to the Immigration Control and Refugee Recognition Act and subsequent Cabinet Understanding which could lead to the admission of more than three hundred thousand temporary foreign workers (discussed in chapter 4) seem to suggest that the Abe administration is moving Japan toward the Swiss rather than the German model of foreign labor. Abe's insistence that these foreign workers will not be immigrations underscores this point.

Moreover, I suspect that DM support for an influx in foreign laborer is actually higher than it appears when looking at the results of the Taniguchi candidate polls that I discuss above. In an analysis of the results of the 2017 general election, I found a very strong and statistically significant correlation between the number of DMs in a prefecture that take a position on foreign labor and the extent to which they express support for foreign labor (Strausz 2018: 213–14). In other words, as the number of DMs from a prefecture taking a position on foreign labor increases, that prefecture's DMs show favor for foreign labor. That suggests that many of the DMs that are not currently taking a position might actually express support for foreign labor if it were to become a more serious topic of discussion on the national stage.

However, as long as elites continue to discuss immigration reform simply as a way to solve labor shortages, we should not expect Japan to become a country of immigration in the sense discussed in chapter 2. For Japan to become a country of immigration in this sense, a significant number of elites must be persuaded by the population and/or persuade the population that "another Japan is possible" and that inviting foreigners to become formal members of the polity is a fruitful way to build such a Japan.

7

Japanese Immigration in the
Age of Trump

As a part of a 2017 panel discussion at the Brookings Institution
in Washington DC. LDP House of Representatives Diet member
Yasutoshi Nishimura was asked about the rise of income inequality in
Japan, which the questioner suggested has helped create populism in
other advanced industrial countries. In his response, Nishimura argued
that "in England and the United States, globalism has caused a loss of
jobs. On this topic, there are actually two kinds of globalism—trade,
and immigration. However, in Japan's case, there is no unskilled immigration, and regarding trade, when we analyze various data, we can see
that in truth Japan does not lose a great deal of jobs to trade" (2017).
This exchange calls attention to an issue that scholars of immigration
across the advanced industrialized world in the late 2010s have to grapple
with: to what extent will the populist, antiglobalist, anti-immigration
sentiment—exemplified by phenomena including the election of Trump
as the American president and the success of the "Brexit" referendum in
the United Kingdom—alter immigration control policies in the advanced
industrialized world? In this chapter, I suggest that a radical influx of
immigration to Japan will not necessarily lead to the rise of the kind
of anti-immigrant populism that brought us Donald Trump and Brexit.

I begin by considering the similarities and differences between Abe
and Trump's views on immigration. Second, I outline possible futures
for immigration policy in Japan, including some that involve radically

expanded immigration. Third, I look carefully at the relationship between public opinion and immigration policy in advanced industrialized democracies. Fourth, I examine the rise of anti-immigration populism, focusing in particular on Trump and Brexit. And, finally, I return to Japan, considering in particular a way in which Japan could implement an immigration program that might avoid a populist backlash.

Abe and Trump on Immigration

President Trump and Prime Minister Abe have some important similarities. Both aim to challenge norms—the norms against constitutional revision in Abe's case, and the norms against protectionism and in favor of immigration, in Trump's case (Lipscy 2017). Both are concerned about the rise of China, and as Lipscy notes, "Both men came to power promising to make their countries 'great again'" (2017).

Despite these similarities, their views on immigration and nationality have important differences. Kevin Doak's book on nationalism in modern Japan suggests that Abe "invokes a nationalism that locates the people as those who give allegiance to the flag and anthem of their country, not those who share the same blood or descent" (2007: 271). Doak supports this claim with this quote from Abe's 2006 book *Toward a Beautiful Country*:

> [W]hen Japan entered the World Cup qualifying rounds for the first time, the native-born Brazilian [Ruy] Ramos shed tears of disappointment along with the Japanese. Even today, he is greeted with heartfelt applause when he performs in the major Japanese cities. We really have to see that this sense of belonging to the community is found in this consciousness that anyone who fights under the *Hi-no-Maru* [Rising Sun] flag, regardless of his country of origin, is one of us. (2007: 271)

Trump's response to a 2015 speech by President Obama suggests a different set of views on who is "one of us" from this Abe quote. In response to a speech after the San Bernardino shooting where President

Obama said, "Muslim-Americans are our friends, neighbors and sports heroes," Trump tweeted, "Obama said in his speech that Muslims are our sports heroes. What sport is he talking about, and who? Is Obama profiling?" (Eder 2016).[1] From the perspective of Trump's tweet, the idea that people from a minority religion could be "our" heroes is not thinkable. "Our" heroes are people who look (or at least pray) like "we" do.

The above quotes suggest that Abe has a more expansive view of who can qualify as Japanese than Trump's view about who can qualify as an American. However, Abe remains reluctant to advocate immigration to Japan. Glenda Roberts argues: "Under the Abe administration, the 'I' word [immigration] remains taboo." For example, she notes that during a Diet debate over a 2014 proposal to expand the Trainee and Technical Internship Program, Abe said that "we are not adopting a so-called "immigration policy,"' and she suggests that this has been Abe's consistent message on immigration (there are other examples of that sort of rhetoric elsewhere in this volume) (2018: 89). In other words, while Abe may have a civic view of Japanese nationalism, in that he believes that people of any ethnicity can be Japanese if they "fight under the Hi-no-Maru," he is also reluctant to give large numbers of new people the opportunity to participate in such a fight by admitting them as immigrants, rather than as foreign laborers. It is also worth noting that any expansion of immigration to Japan would likely result in a substantial increase in the population of people in Japan without Japanese ethnicity. In short, while Abe advocates a civic nationalism, he also advocates policies which have the effect of limiting challenges to the idea that Japan is an ethnically homogenous nation. To return to language from earlier in the book, Abe is an assimilation optimist, and like other assimilation optimists, he advocates policies that limit the visibility of ethnic minorities.

Possible Futures for Japanese Immigration Policy

What might the future of Japan's immigration policy look like? One possibility is that Japan might continue in the direction that it is going, with some immigration, but not nearly enough to fill the job opening that will become increasingly common as the challenge of Japan's aging society continues. In this future, Japan will have to rely on increasing automation and continued movement of production outside of Japan. However, this seems unlikely, given that Japan will need many more nurses and caregivers to take care of its increasingly elderly population. Elderly people tend to vote in disproportionate numbers, and it is difficult to imagine them voting for politicians who sell them a future where they are cared for by robots instead of people.

Hollifield and Sharpe argue that Japan has reached another "Meiji moment," "with policy innovation and potential transformation of Japanese society" toward "a national immigration policy" (2017: 372). If they are right, what might we expect this new national immigration policy to look like? One possibility is that Japan might decide to admit foreign labor on a large scale but continue to treat those laborers (particularly unskilled laborers) as temporary, rather than permanent. This path seems most likely in the short term as long as Abe's LDP is in control of the government. Indeed, the December 2018 revision to the Immigration Control and Refugee Recognition Act and subsequent Cabinet Understanding are consistent with this vision of the role of foreign laborers in Japan. If subsequent administrations maintain and expand this policy, Japan could end up treating its foreign workers like Switzerland does, where large numbers of laborers without formal higher education rotate in and out at fixed intervals and face a difficult, if not impossible, path to citizenship (or even long-term residency). This is the path most palatable to assimilation optimists.

Finally, Japan might decide to admit large numbers of immigrants, including foreign laborers, but also including large numbers of refugees, the families of foreign laborers, and/or other categories of people who are not admitted primarily for the immediate economic contribution that they might make. In this future, the Japanese state will devote resources, time, and energy into creating and expanding institutions that help immigrants integrate into Japanese society.

In short, it is not inconceivable, even under Prime Minister Abe or a similarly conservative LDP administration, that Japan will decide to radically increase the numbers of foreign residents living in Japan. How might the Japanese public react to this kind of policy change? In order to answer that question, it is first necessary to look at scholarship on the relationship between immigration and public opinion.

Public Opinion and Immigration beyond Freeman

Returning to this book's central claim, I have shown that Japan has few foreign residents when compared with other advanced industrialized countries for two reasons. First, because there is no influential strain of elite thought that suggests that significant numbers of foreign nationals have a legitimate claim to residency and membership. While some elites have more of a civic than an ethnic sense of Japanese national identity, there are not significant numbers of elites—and certainly not in the governing coalition in the Diet—who will articulate a vision of Japanese society that suggests that foreign residents have a major role there. Even when Japan has admitted co-ethnics, those people have been treated primarily as laborers, rather than as Japanese returning to their true homeland. Indeed, as mentioned in chapter 4, during difficult economic times co-ethnics without Japanese citizenship were actually paid to return to their country of origin.

Second, as of now, labor intensive businesses have not succeeded in convincing the Japanese state to admit foreign labor on a large scale. Some labor-intensive businesses began to make those requests as early as the late 1960s, but their requests died off with the oil shock and resulting global recession which suppressed demand and thus the need for laborers. When businesses resumed their requests for foreign labor in the 1980s, the Japanese state, and particularly the Ministry of Justice and its Immigration Bureau, had had more than twenty years to observe the European experience with guest workers and immigrants, and they had concluded that they did not want to repeat what they saw as Europe's mistakes.

Thus, while the 1989 revision of the Immigration Control and Refugee Recognition Act created a number of new visa categories, it did not permit immigration by unskilled laborers, despite the intense labor shortages. Businesses have been creative in their solution to the dilemma posed by this law. They have turned the Trainee and Technical Internship Program (which was sold to the public as an international development program) and the "long-term residency visa" (which businesses used on a scale that shocked the politicians and bureaucrats that wrote the law) into de facto unskilled immigration programs.

This book makes much of Freeman's influential 1995 article, which portrays immigration expansion in liberal democracies as an issue area where businesses get their way behind closed doors, using their concentrated resources to convince the state to permit immigration over the objections of the unorganized public. Freeman's argument has been critiqued from a number of angles. One influential piece critiques Freeman's downplaying the interests and influence of the state itself. Statham and Geddes argue that, in the British case:

> Instead of policies being decisively shaped by the mobilised interests of the "organised public" . . . political elites have considerable autonomy in their actions over immigration. . . . [T]heir dominance over the political environment and the opportunities and incentives it produces . . . decisively shapes the level and contents of pro-migrant and anti-migrant collective action. (2006: 266)

A second critique of Freeman focuses on his argument that public opinion tends to oppose immigration. Contrary to Freeman's theory, Lahav (2004) and Simon and Sikich (2007) note substantial variation among wealthy liberal democracies in public opinion about immigration. Moreover, a recent article suggests that the American public has a more complex view of immigration than Freeman's theory allows. Levy, Wright, and Citrin use a survey experiment to show that, while Americans might express opposition to immigration in the abstract, they are much more likely to support immigration when survey questions specify conditions such as asking about immigrants "with skills employers say they need," "with family members living legally in the U.S." and "fleeing violence or government oppression in their more countries" (and these results hold even when respondents are informed about the actual breakdown by visa category of foreign residents living in the US) (2016: 665–66).

In short, Americans appear somewhat ambivalent about immigration, being more likely to be oppose immigration in the abstract than in reference to specific groups of immigrants. Ellermann (2006) found some evidence that the German public is similarly ambivalent. That is, according to immigration bureaucrats in Germany, the German public supports strict immigration control policies in the abstract but to oppose the application of those policies in particular cases. As one German deportation officer told Ellermann:

> There is a lot of public pressure. . . . The longer that immigrants
> have been here, the bigger the problem gets. All legal recourse
> has been exhausted, . . . administrative proceedings are over.
> And then the church gets involved, or fellow pupils in
> school. . . . There is no legal basis for this. . . . But these
> instances of mobilisation occur on a daily basis. (Ellermann
> 2006: 300–01)

A survey experiment in Japan reveals a similar ambivalence among the
Japanese, as subjects were much more likely to report positive feelings
regarding a specific South Korean or Chinese applicant for Japanese citizenship than they were toward the groups "South Korean workers in
Japan" or "Chinese workers in Japan" (Kobayashi et al. 2014: 13).

In sum, and in contradiction of Freeman's argument, there is
ambivalence and substantial variation between individuals and between
liberal democracies in public opinion on immigration. How can we
explain variation in public opinion about immigration control between
individuals and between countries? A recent review article by Hainmueller and Hopkins points to two different sets of explanations: those that
focus on economic self-interest (particularly the claim that natives fear
immigrants that they see as competing for their own jobs), and those
that focus on "the role of group-related attitudes and symbols in shaping
immigration attitudes" (2014: 226).

Hainmueller and Hopkins call the argument about economic self-
interest "something of a zombie theory" (2014: 241) because they find
little evidence in support of it. They examine two of the most influential
articles that make a version of that argument—Scheve and Slaughter
(2001) and Mayda (2006)—and find two critical weaknesses in those
studies. First, they note that actual scholarship on the wage effects of
immigration is ambiguous in its findings; thus, they argue that "any
consensus about immigration's negative economic impacts among natives
is not shared by the economists who have studied that question" (Hainmueller and Hopkins 2014: 228).

Second, Hainmueller and Hopkins note that the most important
studies making the argument about economic self-interest rely on surveys that do not distinguish between high- and low-skilled immigration (2014: 228). However, Hainmueller and Hiscox's (2010) survey

experiment suggests that both low- and high-skilled workers in the United States prefer high-skilled to low-skilled immigration. Instead, they find that education has a strong and positive relationship with views on all immigration.

The findings of subsequent studies of Japan provide further evidence in support of the argument that group-related attitudes and symbols are a better predictor of immigration attitudes than is economic self-interest. In fact, the findings of Kobayashi and colleagues' (2014) survey experiment run exactly contrary to the predictions of theories of economic self-interest that people tend to oppose immigration from people that they see as potential labor market challengers. Kobayashi and colleagues found that the affluent in Japan are more likely than poor Japanese to oppose granting citizenship to lower-status foreign residents, even though those foreign residents are not likely to challenge affluent natives for jobs. Green (2017) found that the "cultural threat" argument that people fear immigrants that they perceive will challenge their established way of life fits much more clearly with Japanese public opinion data than does the economic threat argument. One interesting finding of Green's analysis is that both individuals who are unemployed and individuals from prefectures with higher unemployment are significantly more likely to support immigration than are employed individuals and individuals from prefectures with lower unemployment (2017: 388).

Immigration and Public Opinion in the Trump Era

Populism is a slippery term, but in the subsequent discussion, I will follow Jan-Werner Müller in identifying three core characteristics of populism. A populist is antielitist and antipluralist, in that they claim that "they, and they alone, represent the people," and populism is "an exclusionary form of identity politics." Müller goes on to explain this last component "populists do not claim 'We are the 99 percent.' What they imply instead is 'We are the 100 percent.' For populists, this equation always works out: any remainder can be dismissed as immoral and not properly a part of the people at all" (2016: 7–8). Who specifically the populists that have burst onto the scene in several Western countries in recent years aim to exclude from the "100 percent" varies somewhat due to national context. However, from the perspective of contemporary populism across the advanced industrialized world, one of the excluded groups seems to be immigrants.

Most scholarship on the determinants of public opinion on immigration was done before the populist successes of 2016. On June 23 of that year, voters in the United Kingdom voted yes on a referendum in support of "Brexit," or the United Kingdom's withdrawal from the EU. That referendum was supported by the relatively small United Kingdom Independence Party (UKIP), led by Nigel Farage. While the two major parties—Labour and Conservative—were divided on the question of Brexit, support of Brexit was a defining issue for UKIP. Throughout the campaign for Brexit, Farage and other UKIP leaders made a number of arguments against continuing to remain in the EU, but it was clear that immigration was one of the main reasons for advocating Brexit. As Farage said in a newspaper column shortly before the referendum: "If we remain inside we will be swept up in a United States of Europe with open borders and which is soon to expand with the addition of more countries as full EU members" (*Independent*, 6/20/2016).

A little over four months after Brexit, on November 8, 2016, the United States elected Donald Trump as president. Like Farage and UKIP, Trump campaigned against immigration. Trump advocated building a wall along the border between the United States and Mexico because, as he stated in the speech in which he announced his candidacy, "When Mexico sends its people, they're not sending their best. They're not sending you. They're not sending you. They're sending people that have lots of problems, and they're bringing those problems with us. They're bringing drugs. They're bringing crime. They're rapists." (*Washington Post* 6/16/2015). In his campaign, Trump also advocated a temporary ban on entry into the United States by all Muslims, and once elected, he banned the issuance of virtually all visas from five majority Muslim countries as well as North Korea and Venezuela.[2] Although his administration successfully argued before the Supreme Court that the ban was fundamentally motivated by concerns about national security and not religious discrimination, Sonia Sotomayor's dissent noted that Trump justified this ban on Twitter by saying, "People, the lawyers and the courts can call it whatever they want, but I am calling it what we need and what it is, a TRAVEL BAN!" (*New York Times* 6/26/2018).

After the success of Brexit and Trump, other anti-immigrant, antiglobalism political forces in the West have not done as well. In December

2016, the candidate from the anti-immigration Freedom Party failed to win the presidency in Austria, and Marine Le Pen lost in a runoff for the French presidency in May 2017. In all, Nate Silver (2017) notes that after the election of Donald Trump, far-right populist parties have underperformed their polls in eight European elections.[3] In short, we must be careful not to overstate the extent to which populist far right parties are taking over politics in Europe and the United States.

However, even if anti-immigration parties have sometimes under-performed their polls, the emergence of these parties as serious contender across Europe is a relatively new phenomenon. Before Farage and Trump, mainstream, successful politicians in the United States and the United Kingdom had not advocated wide-ranging anti-immigration policies or used strong anti-immigration rhetoric in decades. And, while it is a bit early to say definitively, early scholarship on both Brexit and the election of Trump suggest that the most important factor motivating supporters was not economic concerns about losing jobs, but rather concerns about the way in which multiculturalism and immigration are transforming the United Kingdom and the United States.

In a study that they released the month after Brexit, Inglehart and Norris (2016) examine the European Social Survey in thirty-one different countries to develop an explanation of the rise of populism. Ultimately, they suggest that economic explanations for the emergence of populism are much less consistent with the data than are cultural explanations. As Inglehart and Norris argue, "the rise of populist parties reflects, above all, a reaction against a wide range of rapid cultural changes that seem to be eroding the basic values and customs of Western societies. Long-term processes of generational change during the late twentieth century have catalyzed culture wars, for these changes are particularly alarming to the less educated and older groups in these countries" (2016: 30). A study by Matti and Zhou, which focused specifically on Brexit, found that the most important determinants of whether voters in a district voted to support Brexit were demographic variables such as median age, percent female, population density, and education. Districts with more elderly people, fewer women, less population density, and fewer residents with higher education were more likely to support Brexit. Adding variables about unemployment, percent working in the financial industry, the religious and racial makeup of districts, and changes in the religious and racial makeup of a district added little explanatory power to the model.

In short, the authors argue that "the results are indicative of an ageing UK population seeking isolation from the national, racial and religious diversity associated with globalization" (2017: 1132–33).

While peer-reviewed research is just starting to come about regarding why people voted for Trump in the general election, a magazine article by McElwee and McDaniel (2017) suggests that, like Brexit voters and other opponents of immigration, Trump voters appear to have been motivated by racial resentment rather than economic self-interest. McElwee and McDaniel analyzed the National Election Survey, focusing on a variety of questions suggesting that respondents harbor resentment against racial minorities, that respondents support immigration, and that respondents are worried about their personal economic circumstances. They found that those harboring racial resentment and those who oppose immigration were substantially more likely to vote for Trump, while white voters' assessments of their individual economic circumstances did not seem to impact the likelihood that those individuals would vote for Trump. In contrast, white voters feeling more economic anxiety in 2012 were more likely to oppose Romney than where white voters feeling less economic anxiety.

Hooge and Dassonnville tested the theory that Trump voters in 2016 were protest voters who supported Trump because they supported his calls to "drain the swamp" in Washington and distrusted traditional parties. They found that measures of protest voting—including whether voters trusted political institutions (such as Congress) and how voters felt about the presidency—did not explain why people voted for Trump in any of their models. Instead, they found that partisanship remained strong in 2016—Republicans voted for Trump—and that "racial resentment and anti-immigrant sentiments" were both powerful predictor of a Trump vote, even while controlling for partisanship and a variety of other factors (2018: 528).

In sum, a wide variety of public opinion research has long supported the argument that cultural, rather than economic, concerns are the primary drivers of anti-immigrant sentiment. Although it is early to say, this appears to remain when is a central campaign issue, as it was in the populist campaigns in support of Donald Trump and Brexit. Are we likely to see an influential populist campaign in Japan in this model, and if so, what might that mean for the future of immigration policy in Japan?

A Japanese Anti-Immigrant Backlash?

This chapter began with a quote from an LDP House of Representatives Diet member, Yasutoshi Nishimura, who suggested that Japan does not (yet) have a successful populist movement because it has relatively few immigrants. Does this mean that Japan is caught between the major economic and social consequences that will come from *shōshikōreika* and an inevitable populist backlash should Japan decide to address *shōshikōreika* by permitting large-scale immigration?

This kind of backlash, I argue, is not inevitable. Most advanced industrialized countries in the world have large populations of immigrants without major successful populist movements. Even in the United States and the United Kingdom, the election of Trump and Brexit are relatively new developments, developments that have not (as yet) been replicated in other advanced industrialized democracies. Moreover, research on Japanese public opinion suggests that contact with foreign residents increases the likelihood that an individual will support immigration. A number of studies have suggested that, while residents of areas with more foreign residents tend to have more anti-foreigner attitudes, individuals that report more contact with foreign residents tend to have more positive views of foreigners (Green 2017; Nukaga 2006; Nakayoshi 2009; Seebruck 2013).

This suggests that any policy to increase immigration to Japan should include efforts to integrate those immigrants into Japanese society and to encourage those immigrants to live and work in regular contact with Japanese people and Japanese social institutions. Policies that begin with the assumption that foreigners are potential long-term residents (maybe even potential citizens) rather than simply foreign laborers might be helpful in this regard. In order to promote integration of foreign residents into Japanese society, Japan might also consider greatly expanding efforts to teach Japanese all over the world, to make it a more attractive destination for all kinds of immigrants. To that end, Japan might learn from the Confucius Institutes set up by China all over the world to teach Chinese It might also consider reforming its domestic education system to focus on teaching Japanese to speak second and third languages, as opposed to current foreign-language efforts, which largely focus on written, rather than spoken, English.

Moreover, proponents of immigration in Japan—in Japanese politics, civil society, and business—should continue to make a case for immigration to Japan that goes beyond simple economics to argue that immigrants and Japan have the potential to improve each other. This case will have to include a vision of Japanese national identity that allows those without Japanese blood to have a major, positive role in Japan's future.

For those of us who, like myself, believe that that immigration tends to enrich immigrant-receiving countries (in ways including, but going beyond, simply the economic), Brexit and the election of Donald Trump are disturbing. So too is the rise of far-right parties in other European states. For proimmigration liberal democracies to survive in the long term, some of these Brexit and Trump voters must be convinced that immigration policy is made by duly elected representatives with a view toward doing what is best for the population as a whole. The more that people feel excluded from the policy-making process, the more likely they are to turn to an alternative that critiques the elitism of that process. Moreover, and more importantly, civil society groups as well as elites must articulate a vision of national identity in which foreign residents have an essential role, and this vision must persuade a portion of those who voted for Brexit, for Trump, and against proimmigration politicians in liberal democracies all over the world, including Japan.

Appendix

Description of Interview Subjects

1096   House of Councilors Diet member, male, Liberal Democratic Party, December 25, 2009, Tokyo, Japan.

1097   House of Representatives Diet member, male, Liberal Democratic Party, December 24, 2009, Tokyo, Japan.

1098   Ministry of Foreign Affairs bureaucrat, Global Issues Department, male, March 16, 2006, Tokyo, Japan.

1099   House of Representatives Diet member, male, Liberal Democratic Party, December 24, 2009, Tokyo, Japan.

1115   House of Councilors Diet member, female, Liberal Democratic Party, March 14, 2016.

1120   House of Councilors Diet member, male, Liberal Democratic Party, March 9, 2016.

1122   House of Representatives candidate, male, Democratic Party, February 23, 2017, Yokohama, Japan.

1123   House of Representatives Diet member, male, Kōmeitō, May 23, 2016, Tokyo, Japan.

1127   Academic and member of the Ministry of Justice private panel to discuss foreign labor, female, January 20, 2016, Tokyo, Japan.

1128   Businessman and representative of Keizai Dōyūkai, male, June 28, 2016, Tokyo, Japan.

1129   Businessman and representative of Keizai Dōyūkai, male, April 7, 2016, Tokyo, Japan.

1138   President and two representatives of a prefectural chapter of the Japanese Nurses Association (Kango Kyōkai), all females, March 16, 2016 (interviewed in the president's office).

1140   Researcher at an interest group representing Japan's high-technology sector, male, March 22, 2016.

1141   House of Representatives Diet member, female, Liberal Democratic Party, April 19, 2016, Tokyo, Japan.

1145   Administrator dealing with international student-related programs at a public university in Japan, male, May 11, 2016 (interviewed at his university).

1149   Administrator at an English-language international school in Japan, female, February 22, 2016 (interviewed at the school).

1152   Former House of Councilors Diet member, female, Democratic Party of Japan, February 29, 2016, Ibaraki Prefecture, Japan.

1153   Professor who is an expert in the politics of agriculture in Japan, February 17, 2016, Tokyo, Japan.

1156   House of Councilors Diet member, male, Democratic Party, April 20, 2016, Tokyo, Japan.

1170   Representative of a Japanese NGO that advocates for refugees, male, April 19, 2016, Tokyo, Japan.

1172   Representative of a Japanese interest group that represents farmers, male, November 28, 2017, Tokyo, Japan.

1173   House of Councilors Diet member, male, Liberal Democratic Party, March 18, 2016, Tokyo, Japan.

1174   House of Representatives Diet member, male, Liberal Democratic Party, November 28, 2016, Tokyo, Japan.

1190   House of Councilors Diet member, male, Democratic Party, April 26, 2016.

1198   Representative from an immigrants' rights organization, male, May 19, 2016, Tokyo, Japan.

1204   Head of a major immigrants' rights organization (different from subject 1198's organization), male, June 17, 2016.

Notes

Introduction

1. See appendix 1 for descriptions of interviews and interview subjects.

Chapter 1

1. Due to limitations of available data, data for Ireland, France, and Mexico refer to 2012, and data for Canada and Poland refer to 2011. In recent years, a large percentage of migrants within the European Union (EU) come from other EU member nations. In 2016, for example, there were 4.3 million migrants in EU countries, and less than half of that number (2 million people) came from outside of the European Union (Eurostat 2018b).

2. In 2000, Germany changed its citizenship law away from blood-based citizenship. After the law change, a child born to "at least one foreign parent who had been legally resident in Germany for at least eight years" would be treated as a dual national of his or her parent's country and Germany until the age of twenty-three, when he or she can choose a nationality. Martin suggests that this policy "move[d] the country from one of the most restrictive paths to naturalization to one of the most liberal in allowing dual nationality" (Martin 2014: 236).

Chapter 2

1. Almost six months later, Japan announced that it would be admitting 150 foreign exchange students as Syrian refugees (Asahi Shimbun 5/19/2016), and that number was later increased to 300 (Asahi Shimbun 2/3/2017). This program is discussed in chapter 5.

2. Similarly, Messina argues that states continue to permit immigration

flows with a view toward maximizing their own interests and despite public opposition to immigration. He suggests that "the political costs of post–WWII immigration to the states of Western Europe have not been extremely onerous" (2007: 239), while the benefits (for European countries) have included addressing both labor shortages and declining populations. Regarding the costs of immigration, Messina's book was written before the referendum in the United Kingdom to exit the EU and before the election of Donald Trump as president of the United States. Both of these events are discussed in the conclusion.

3. Whaling is the most famous exception to this general tendency (Strausz 2014).

4. Japan does make generous financial contributions to the refugee regime. See chapter 5.

5. Fitzgerald, Lebang, and Teets use ordinary least squared regression to estimate a "gravity-based empirical model of migration flows" (2014: 414) based on the work of Hatton and Williamson (2003).

6. See Schmidle (2015) for a discussion of one particular refugee's struggle to reach Sweden.

7. Cholewinski (1994) makes a similar argument about the role of European institutions in pushing states toward family reunification.

8. I am grateful to Greg Noble for this insight.

9. See Scheiner et al. 2013 for a review of this literature, as well as an interesting argument about why interest groups sometimes lobby politicians and other times lobby bureaucrats.

10. After the fall of the Iron Curtain, there were similar concerns in the former West Germany about the impact of the "new eastern Länder" on the country as a whole: "[M]any West Germans grumbled that their comfortable, affluent society was, for the first time in many years, more at risk of recession, inflation, and increased taxes than they had initially been led to believe by the ever-ebullient 'unification Chancellor,' Helmut Kohl" (Fulbrook 1996: 100).

11. One of the anonymous reviewers of this manuscript raised both of these objections.

12. I call Germany a "country of immigration" during even the postwar years when German elites took care to avoid that label, because even when Germany was not calling itself a country of immigration, it was admitting large numbers of foreign residents though its generous asylum politics, discussed above, in combination with its guest-worker policy.

13. Fitzgerald, Curtis, and Corlis review the literature that fails to find a relationship between immigration and crime (2012: 478). They go on to show that, particularly among those interested in politics, German citizens who worry about crime also worry about immigration.

14. Elsewhere, I have called these two groups "conservative optimists" and "conservative pessimists" (Strausz 2010). Here I use "assimilation optimists" and "assimilation pessimists" because these phrases highlight the fact that these groups differ in their optimism about the degree to which foreign residents can and should be assimilated into Japanese society. There are many in Japan who support promoting multiculturalism instead of assimilation. However, support for multiculturalism is not an "influential strain of elite thought," as defined earlier in this chapter.

Chapter 3

1. On this last point, see Rao (2017: 74–76).

2. There was a much smaller population of Chinese and Taiwanese "colonial subjects" in Japan in 1945. At the end of the war, this population numbered between one hundred thousand and two hundred thousand, but by the middle of 1946, only around thirty thousand of that population remained (Chung 2010: 73).

3. In 1952, 94 percent of Koreans in Japan were from South Korea (Chung 2010: 78, note 7).

4. Chōsen-Sōren did not form until 1955. Between 1945 and 1955, there had been two other major Communist organizations formed in Japan's Korean community. For a discussion of these groups, see Yamawaki (2001) and Chung (2010: 77–79). For an excellent ethnography of the North Korean community in Japan that pays particular attention to North Korean schools in Japan, see Ryang (1997).

5. I was not able to find prefectural population data on North Korean oldcomers, but since 98 percent of North Koreans in Japan are oldcomers, the prefectural population of North Koreans is a good approximation.

6. Dower cites a member of the Japanese government's constitutional revision group who suggests that "kokumin" was chosen for people because it did not "convey a sense of the people in exclusion and opposition to the Emperor" (Dower 1999: 382).

7. Periodic fingerprinting was legally required of all foreign residents of Japan at the time, even of those who, like most Koreans, were born in Japan.

8. The fingerprinting requirement was later reinstated for most foreign visitors to Japan, but Koreans and Chinese who can trace their ancestors' time in Japan to 1945 or before are among those excluded from the new requirement.

9. The Ministry of Foreign Affairs made a similar argument before domestic audiences. In 1980, the Domestic Public Relations Division published

a Japanese-language pamphlet that aimed to explain the new treaties to "all Japanese people." The pamphlet argues that the treaties' provisions forbidding discrimination against people because of their national or social origins fall under the Japanese constitution's prohibition against discrimination based on one's social status or family origin (Ministry of Foreign Affairs (Japan) 1980: 8).

10. This is a reference to Japan's hosting of its first G7 meeting in Tokyo in June 1979.

11. 483,185 of 638,806.

12. All three of these public corporations have since privatized.

13. The debate between assimilation optimists and assimilation pessimists is primarily a debate among Japanese conservatives. I focus on a debate that occurred among conservatives in Japan because conservatives controlled the Japanese state for much of the period about which I write. Japanese progressives also disagree about the appropriateness of immigration to Japan, but among progressives, the disagreement is about the relative importance of labor unions verses cosmopolitan values.

14. Taikin Tei is the romanization of the Japanese pronunciation of his name. However, Tei is a naturalized Japanese citizen of Korean ethnicity, and the romanization of the Korean pronunciation of his name is Daekyun Chung.

15. In fairness, it might have been challenging for him to avoid acknowledging this because this statement is drawn from a debate with DPJ DM Shinkun Haku, a naturalized citizen of Japan with Korean ethnicity.

16. These three paths are not mutually exclusive. It is possible that Japan could go down more than one of these paths at the same time.

Chapter 4

1. There is much more discussion of this community in chapter 3. Additionally, see Chung (2010) for an excellent discussion of the politics of this Korean community in Japan.

2. As table 4.2 shows, 39.5 percent of foreign students in Japan come from China. Liu-Farrer suggests that, while there is a long history of Chinese coming to Japan both for economic opportunity and to study, "the magnitude of the contemporary trend of student migration between these two countries is unprecedented. What is new is the merging of these two types of migration [student migration and labor migration] and the blurred boundary between students and laborers" (2011: 141).

3. Hennings and Mintz argue that, partially because the Ministry of Justice does not keep track of the work status of foreign students, Japan undercounts foreign workers (2018: 104).

4. As an anonymous reviewer pointed out, there may be another factor accounting for the relatively high percentage of Japan's labor force employed in agriculture: Japan agricultural cooperatives historically gave individuals living in rural areas an incentive to declare themselves at least part-time farmers in order to get access to the various economic benefits that those cooperatives control. (See MacLachlan and Shimizu 2016 for more on this.) However, this OECD comparative data is the best comparative data that I was able to find on this issue.

5. In 2004, the Trafficking in Persons Report called Japan a tier 2 country that was on the watch list for movement to tier 3 if problems with human trafficking (including the entertainer visa, which was specifically named in the report) were not addressed. The report defines tier 3 countries as those "whose governments do not fully comply with the minimum standards and are not making significant efforts to do so," and the report notes that the "U.S. Government may withhold non-humanitarian, non-trade-related assistance" from tier 3 countries.

6. The admission of nurses and caregivers associated with the Vietnam EPA was negotiated in 2011, two years after the EPA went into force, in accordance with a provision in the agreement that permitted "future negotiation" regarding nurse and caregiver admission. The Japan-India EPA, which went into force in 2011, has a similar "future negotiation" provision (Naiki 2015: 352–53).

Chapter 5

1. I do not have the data to independently assess this claim. One scholar, however, has argued that because of Japan's low refugee acceptance rate, "Japan is not complying with international norms of refugee protection" (Wolman 2015: 2).

2. This kind of argument is common among those supporting limiting refugee admissions outside of Japan also.

3. Japan's tendency of granting humanitarian status much more frequently than asylum is relatively unusual. Between 2008 and 2017, Japan granted humanitarian status 8.04 times for every time that it granted asylum. In contrast, the mean EU country granted humanitarian status .24 times for every time that it granted asylum (Eurostat 2018a).

4. Miyashita similarly argues that Japan makes its foreign policy in response to American pressure because of the power asymmetry between Japan and the United States (2003: 8).

5. Akashi argues that a combination of changing domestic public opinion and international pressure led to Japan's decision to allow refugee resettlement. However, as will be discussed below, Japanese public opinion was not particularly pro-refugee at the time the Japanese government made their decision.

6. Asahi Shimbun did not report on this group of refugees, and instead called two boys that landed in Kitakyushu on May 12 the first group of boat people to arrive in Japan (5/12/1975). A government report confirms that the Chiba nine were the first refugees to reach Japan, but suggests that they landed on May 12, not May 11 (Cabinet Secretariat 1980: 7).

7. Although Japan had begun to admit Indochinese refugees as residents in April, as of December 14, it had not granted residency status to any applicants (Asahi Shimbun12/15/1978: 2).

8. Because they are not authored by people with the potential to change policy, editorials and opinion pieces are not examples of "influential strains of elite thought," in the sense discussed in chapter 2. I include this discussion of editorials and opinion pieces in Japan's newspapers to illustrate the way that concern about Japan's international image had permeated discourse about Indochinese refugees. However, I did not find evidence that these articles had a direct causal impact on Japan's refugee policy (i.e., when DMs and bureaucrats referred to the media, they generally focused on news articles rather than opinion pieces and editorials).

Chapter 6

1. Keidanren first took this position in 2000, and Nikkeiren in 2001 (Komai 2007: 23). The two groups merged in 2002.

2. Although this DM was correct to note that mainstream labor unions in Japan have been opposed to foreign labor, there are labor unions that represent foreign workers in Japan, including trainees and technical interns, as well as undocumented workers, including members of the Zentōitsu Workers Union. Kremers (2014) shows how these groups were influential in reforming the Trainee and Technical Internship Program in 2009, and Shipper (2008) shows how these groups have effectively advocated for the interests of foreign workers at the local level in Japan.

3. In an earlier book, Sakanaka (2005) advocated immigration in even greater numbers, calling for Japan to admit 20 million immigrants.

4. Of course, this reading of Japanese history does not acknowledge the oppression of Japanese Christians in the first half of the seventeenth century or the way that Japanese people were obligated to participate in State Shinto regardless of their religious beliefs in prewar and wartime Japan.

5. In the following discussion, I consider those "agreeing" or "somewhat agreeing" as agreeing, and those "disagreeing" or "somewhat disagreeing" as disagreeing.

6. While pro–foreign labor Caucus members were less likely to win reelection than were Caucus members that were less supportive of foreign labor, I do not have evidence to support a more forceful version of this sentence, such as the claim that "the electorate punished representatives who were too strongly proimmigration."

7. The precise role of public opinion in immigration policy making is Japan is difficult to study because the terrific Taniguchi data cited above does not include public opinion on foreign labor before 2009. Thus, we are not able to see what, precisely, the Japanese public believed about immigration in the years leading up to the 1989 revision of the Immigration Control and Refugee Recognition Act. However, given that, at the time of this writing, immigration has never been one of the major position issues discussed in a postwar Japanese election, it seems implausible to argue that public opinion has been a primary driver of immigration policy making.

8. In 2009, Pearson's r was .239 (one-tailed significance level .059), in 2012, Pearson's r was .245 (one-tailed significance level .048), and in 2014, Pearson's r was −.192 (one-tailed significance level .093).

9. The Pearson's r was .344, with a one-tailed statistically significance of .009. The correlations in all other elections were positive, but 2016 was the only election when the results were strong and statistically significant.

Chapter 7

1. This was a particularly bizarre tweet from Trump as famed Muslim boxer Muhammad Ali had presented Trump with the Muhammad Ali award in 2007 (Eder 2016).

2. Candidate Trump changed his specific proposal regarding immigration from the Muslim world several times. His initial statement of the policy suggested that even Muslim citizens of the United States would not be permitted to return should they leave the country, but future statements removed that particular aspect of the policy.

3. Silver looked at the Austrian presidential election (December 4, 2016), the Dutch general election (March 15, 2017), the Bulgarian Parliamentary election (March 26, 2016), the Finnish municipal election (April 9, 2017), the French presidential first round (April 23, 2017) and run off (May 7, 2017), the UK general election (June 8, 2017), and the French legislative election (June 11, 2017).

References

Akashi, Junichi. 2010. *Nyūkoku Kanri Seisaku: "1990 Nen Taisei" no Seiritsu to Tenkai* [Japan's Immigration Control Policy: Foundations and Transitions]. Tokyo: Nakanishina.

Akashi, Junichi, and Naoki Ogawa. 2008. "Imin 1,000 Man Nin 'Taminzoku Kokka' e: Tabuu ni Chōsen Suru Jimintō Giren [Toward a Multiethnic Country with 10 Million Immigrants: An LDP Dietmember Caucus Challenging a Taboo]." *Ekonomisuto*, 68–73.

Asao, Kei'ichiro, Kōhei Ōtsuka, Kōji Hosono, Motohisa Furukawa, Kōji Matsui, and Takeaki Matsumoto. 2003. "1000 Man Nin Imin Ukeire Kōsō: Nihon wo 'Akogare no Kuni' ni Shitai [A Plan to Admit Ten Million Immigrants: Let's Make Japan 'A Country to Long For']." *Voice*, 142–49.

Barnett, Laura. 2002. "Global Governance and the Evolution of the International Refugee Regime." *International Journal of Refugee Law* 14 (2/3): 238–62.

Barnett, Michael N., and Martha Finnemore. 2004. *Rules for the World: International Organizations in Global Politics*. Ithaca, N.Y.: Cornell University Press.

Bartram, David. 2000. "Japan and Labor Migration: Theoretical and Methodological Implications of Negative Cases." *International Migration Review* 43 (1): 5–32.

Bartram, David V. 1998. "Foreign Workers in Israel: History and Theory." *International Migration Review* 32 (2): 303–25.

Bedford, Richard, and Paul Spoonley. 2014. "Competing for Talent: Diffusion of an Innovation in New Zealand's Immigration Policy." *International Migration Review* 48 (3): 891–911.

Bonjour, Saskia. 2011. "The Power and Morals of Policy Makers: Reassessing the Control Gap Debate." *International Migration Review* 45 (1): 89–122.

Breunig, Christian, and Adam Luedtke. 2008. "What Motivates the Gatekeepers? Explaining Governing Party Preferences on Immigration." *Governance* 21 (1): 123–46.

Cabinet Office (Japan). 1980. "Gaikō ni Kansuru Yoron Chōsa [A Public Opinion Poll on Foreign Policy]." http://survey.gov-online.go.jp/s55/S55-05-55-04.

———. 1982. "Indoshina Nanmin Mondai ni Kansuru Yoron Chōsa [A Public Opinion Poll on Indochinese Refugees]." http://survey.gov-online.go.jp/s57/S57-06-57-04.html.

Cabinet Secretariat. 1980. *Indoshina Nanmin no Genjō to Kokunai Engo* [The Present Condition of Indochinese Refugees and Domestic Relief]. Tokyo: Indoshina Nanmin Taisaku Renraku Chōsei Kaigi Jimukyoku [Liaison and Coordination Council for Indochinese Refugees and Displaced Persons].

———. 1987, 1990–94. *Indoshina Nanmin no Genjō to Kokunai Engo* [The Present Condition of Indochinese Refugees and Domestic Relief]. Tokyo: Indoshina Nanmin Taisaku Renraku Chōsei Kaigi Jimukyoku [Cabinet Secretariat, Liaison and Coordination Council for Indochinese Refugees and Displaced Persons].

Calder, Kent E. 1988. "Japanese Foreign Economic Policy: Explaining the Reactive State." *World Politics* 40 (4): 518–41.

Chan, Jennifer. 2008. *Another Japan Is Possible: New Social Movements and Global Citizenship Education.* Stanford, Calif.: Stanford University Press.

Chapman, David. 2004. "The Third Way and Beyond: Zainichi Korean Identity and the Politics of Belonging." Japanese Studies 24 (1): 29–44.

———. 2008. *Zainichi Korean Identity and Ethnicity.* Routledge contemporary Japan series 17. London: Routledge.

Chiavacci, David. 2012. "Japan in the 'Global War for Talent': Changing Concepts of Valuable Foreign Workers and Their Consequences." *ASIEN* 124:27–47.

Chiswick, Barry R., and W. Miller. 2011. "The 'Negative' Assimilation of Immigrants: A Special Case." *ILR Review* 64 (3): 502–25.

Cholewinski, Ryszard. 1994. "The Protection of the Right of Economic Migrants to Family Reunion in Europe." *The International and Comparative Law Quarterly* 43 (3): 568–98.

Chung, Erin Aeran. 2003. "Noncitizens, Voice, and Identity: The Politics of Citizenship in Japan's Korean Community." First Annual Summer Institute on International Migration Conference, University of California, San Diego.

———. 2010. *Immigration and Citizenship in Japan.* Cambridge: Cambridge University Press.

Clark, Gregory. 1970. "Wanted—Cheap Labour." *Far Eastern Economic Review,* 42–43.

Cohen, Linda, Mathew D. McCubbins, and Frances McCall Rosenbluth. 1995. "The Politics of Nuclear Power in Japan and the United States." In *Structure and Policy in Japan and the United States,* edited by Peter F. Cowhey and Mathew D. McCubbins, 177–202. Cambridge: Cambridge University Press.

Curtis, Gerald L. 1988. *The Japanese Way of Politics*. New York: Columbia University Press.

Doak, Kevin Michael. 2007. *A History of Nationalism in Modern Japan: Placing the People*. Leiden: Brill.

Dobson, Hugo. 2004. *Japan and the G7/8: 1975 to 2002*. London: Routledge.

Douglass, Mike. 2000. "The Singularities of International Migration of Women to Japan: Past, Present and Future." In *Japan and Global Migration: Foreign Workers and the Advent of a Multicultural Society*, edited by Mike Douglass and Glenda S. Roberts. London: Routledge.

Douglass, Mike, and Glenda S. Roberts. 2000. "Japan in the Age of Global Migration." In *Japan and Global Migration: Foreign Workers and the Advent of a Multicultural Society*, edited by Mike Douglass and Glenda S. Roberts. London: Routledge.

Dower, John W. 1999. *Embracing Defeat: Japan in the Wake of World War II*. New York: Norton.

Eddy, Melissa. 2015. "German Leaders Seek to Ease Tensions over Migrant Crisis." *New York Times*, August 26.

Eder, Steve. 2016. "Donald Trump Reflects on His Relationship with Muhammad Ali." *New York Times*. June 4.

Ellermann, Antje. 2006. "Street-level Democracy: How Immigration Bureaucrats Manage Public Opposition." *West European Politics* 29 (2): 293–309.

———. 2013. "When Can Liberal States Avoid Unwanted Immigration? Self-Limited Sovereignty and Guest Worker Recruitment in Switzerland and Germany." *World Politics* 65 (3): 491–538.

Eurostat. 2018a. "Asylum and Managed Migration." http://ec.europa.eu/eurostat/web/asylum-and-managed-migration/data/main-tables.

———. 2018b. "Migration and Migrant Population Statistics." http://ec.europa.eu/eurostat/statistics-explained/index.php/Migration_and_migrant_population_statistics#Migration_flows:_2_million_non-EU_immigrants.

Ferrer, Ana M., Garnett Picot, and William Craig Riddell. 2014. "New Directions in Immigration Policy: Canada's Evolving Approach to the Selection of Economic Immigrants." *International Migration Review* 48 (3): 846–67.

Fitzgerald, Jennifer, David Lebang, and Jessica C. Teets. 2014. "Defying the Law of Gravity: The Political Economy of International Migration." *World Politics* 66 (3): 406–45.

Fitzgerald, Jennifer, K. Amber Curtis, and Catherine L. Corliss. 2012. "Anxious Publics: Worries about Crime and Immigration." *Comparative Political Studies* 45 (4): 477–506.

Flowers, Petrice R. 2009. *Refugees, Women, and Weapons: International Norm Adoption and Compliance in Japan*. Stanford, Calif.: Stanford University Press.

Freeman, Gary P. 1995. "Modes of Immigration Politics in Liberal Democratic States." *International Migration Review* 29 (4): 881–902.

Fulbrook, Mary. 1996. "Germany for the Germans? Citizenship and Nationality in a Divided Nation." In *Citizenship, Nationality and Migration in Europe*, 98–115. New York: Routledge.

Gordon, Andrew. 2009. *The Wages of Affluence: Labor and Management in Postwar Japan*. Cambridge: Harvard University Press.

Government of Japan. 1980. Reported in "Consideration of Reports Submitted by State Parties under Article 40 of the Covenant," Human Rights Committee, International Covenant on Civil and Political Rights, October 24, UN Document number CCPR/C/10/Add.1.

———. 1987. Reported in "Consideration of Reports Submitted by State Parties under Article 40 of the Covenant," Human Rights Committee, International Covenant on Civil and Political Rights, December 24, 1987, UN Document number CCPR/C/42/Add.4.

Green, David. 2017. "Immigrant Perception in Japan: A Multilevel Analysis of Public Opinion." *Asian Survey* 57 (2): 368–94.

Greenhill, Kelly M. 2010. *Weapons of Mass Migration: Forced Displacement, Coercion, and Foreign Policy*. Ithaca, N.Y.: Cornell University Press.

Guiraudon, Virginie, and Gallya Lahav. 2000. "A Reappraisal of the State Sovereignty Debate: The Case of Migration Control." *Comparative Political Studies* 33 (2): 163–95.

Gurowitz, Amy. 1999. "Mobilizing International Norms: Domestic Actors, Immigrants, and the Japanese State." *World Politics* 51 (3): 413–45.

Hainmueller, Jens, and Daniel J. Hopkins. 2014. "Public Attitudes toward Immigration." *Annual Review of Political Science* 17:225–49.

Hainmueller, Jens, and Michael J. Hiscox. 2010. "Attitudes toward Highly Skilled and Low-Skilled Immigration: Evidence from a Survey Experiment." *American Political Science Review* 104 (1): 61–84.

Hamano, Sylvia Brown. 1999. "Incomplete Revolutions and Not So Alien Transplants: The Japanese Constitution and Human Rights." *University of Pennsylvania Journal of Constitutional Law* 1 (3): 415–91.

Hatton, Timothy J., and Jeffrey G. Williamson. 2003. "Demographic and Economic Pressure on Emigration out of Africa." *The Scandinavian Journal of Economics* 105 (3): 465–86.

Hellman, Donald C. 1990. "Japanese Politics and Foreign Policy: Elitist Democracy within an American Greenhouse." In *The Political Economy of Japan:*

The Changing International Context, edited by Takeshi Inoguchi and Daniel I. Okimoto. Stanford, Calif.: Stanford University Press.

Hennings, Matthias, and Scott Mintz. 2018. "Toward a Comprehensive Estimate of the Number of Foreign Workers in Japan." *Social Science Japan Journal* 21 (1): 103–15.

House of Councilors (HoC). 1979 (March 26). Budget Committee.

———. 1982 (March 24). Budget Committee.

———. 1982 (December 10). Plenary Session.

———. 1989 (November 27). Budget Committee.

———. 1989a (November 30). Budget Committee.

———. 1989b (November 30). Justice Committee.

———. 2005 (April 6). Committee on the Declining Birthrate and an Aging Population.

———. 2006 (December 4). Budget Committee.

———. 2006 (March 13). Budget Committee.

———. 2008 (April 23). Committee on the Declining Birthrate and an Aging Population.

Hollifield, James F. 2000. "The Politics of International Migration: How Can We Bring the State Back In?" In *Migration Theory: Talking Across Disciplines*, edited by Caroline B. Brettell and James F. Hollifield, New York: Routledge.

Hollifield, James F., and Michael Orlando Sharpe. 2017. "Japan as an 'Emerging Migration State.'" *International Relations of the Asia-Pacific* 17 (3): 371–400.

Honma, Hiroshi. 1990. *Nanmin Mondai to wa Nani ka?* [What Is the Refugee Issue?] Tokyo: Iwanami Shoten.

Hooghe, Marc, and Ruth Dassonneville. 2018. "Explaining the Trump Vote: The Effect of Racist Resentment and Anti-Immigrant Sentiments." *PS: Political Science & Politics* 51:1–7.

House of Representatives (HoR). 1975 (June 25). Justice Committee.

———. 1977 (February 14). Budget Committee.

———. 1977 (October 26). Foreign Affairs Committee.

———. 1978 (April 25). Justice Committee.

———. 1978 (May 10). Foreign Affairs Committee.

———. 1978 (December 20). Foreign Affairs Committee.

———. 1979 (September 6). Plenary Session.

———. 1980 (March 5). Budget Committee.

———. 1981 (May 27). Combined Meeting of the Justice, Foreign Affairs, and Society and Labor Committees.

———. 1990 (April 24). Committee on Society and Labor.

———. 1990 (April 26). Second Budget Subcommittee.

———. 2004 (November 16). Special Committee for the Establishment of Political Ethics and the Reform of the Public Officials Election Law.

———. 2004 (November 18). Public Hearing on Constitutional Revision.

———. 2005 (February 2). Constitution Research Committee.

———. 2006 (March 16). Special Committee to Examine the Constitution.

———. 2006 (May 19). Foreign Affairs Committee.

———. 2008 (January 21). Plenary Session.

———. 2014 (April 8). Justice Committee.

———. 2016 (February 25). Third Budget Subcommittee.

Hymans, Jacques E. C. 2015. "After Fukushima: Veto Players and Japanese Nuclear Power." In *Japan: The Precarious Future*, edited by Frank Baldwin and Anne Allison, 110–38. New York: New York University Press.

Hyodo, Nisohachi. 2009. "Imin Ukeire ha Kyōki no Sata [Admission of Immigrants Is an Act of Madness]." *Seiron* 9 (438): 46–47.

Iguchi, Yasushi. 2012. "What Role Do Low-Skilled Migrants Play in the Japanese Labor Markets?" *American Behavioral Scientist* 56 (8): 1029–57.

Inglehart, Ronald F. and Pippa Norris. 2016. "Trump, Brexit, and the Rise of Populism: Economic Have-Nots and Cultural Backlash." Faculty Research Working Paper Series. Harvard University. August. https://research.hks.harvard.edu/publications/workingpapers/Index.aspx.

Ishii, Akira, Ken'ei Shu, Yoshihide Soeya, and Shōkō Rin, eds. 2003. *Kiroku to Kōshō: Nicchū Kokkō Seijōka/Nicchū Heiwa Yūkō Jōyaku Teiketsu Kōshō* [Documents and Investigation: Negotiations of the Japan/China Diplomatic Normalization and the Japan/China Treaty of Peace and Friendship]. Tokyo: Iwanami Shoten.

Iwasawa, Yuji. 1998. *International Law, Human Rights, and Japanese Law: The Impact of International Law on Japanese Law.* Oxford: Oxford University Press.

Japan International Training Cooperation Organization (JITCO). 2018. "Ginōjishū Kenshū ni Kansuru JITCO Gyōmu Tōkei [JITCO-Managed Statistics about the Trainee and Technical Internship Program]." http://www.jitco.or.jp/about/statistics.html.

Johnson, Chalmers. 1982. *MITI and the Japanese Miracle: The Growth of Industrial Policy, 1925–1975.* Stanford, Calif.: Stanford University Press.

Joppke, Christian. 1998. "Why Liberal States Accept Unwanted Immigration." *World Politics* 50 (2): 266–93.

———. 1999. *Immigration and the Nation-State: The United States, Germany, and Great Britain.* Oxford: Oxford University Press.

Kamibayashi, Chieko. 2015. *Gaikokujin Rōdōsha Ukeire to Nihon Shakai: Ginō Jishūseido no Tenkai to Jirema* [Accepting Foreign Workers into Japanese

Society: The Dilemmas of a Temporary Immigrants Program]. Tokyo: Tokyo University Press.

Kashiwazaki, Chikako. 1998. "Nationality and Citizenship in Japan: Stability and Change in Comparative Perspective." PhD Dissertation, Sociology, Brown University.

Keefer, Philip, and David Stasavage. 2003. "The Limits of Delegation: Veto Players, Central Bank Independence and the Credibility of Monetary Policy." *American Political Science Review* 97 (3): 407–23.

Kim, Chan-Jeong. 1997. *Zainichi Korian Hyakunenshi* [One Hundred Years of History of Koreans in Japan]. Tokyo: Sango Kan.

Kneebone, Susan, and Felicity Rawlings-Sanaei. 2007. "Introduction: Regionalism as a Response to a Global Challenge." In *New Regionalism and Asylum Seekers: Challenges Ahead*, edited by Susan Kneebone and Felicity Rawlings-Sanaei. New York: Berghahn Books.

Kobayashi, Tetsuro, Christian Collet, Shanto Iyengar, and Kyu S. Hahn. 2014. "Who Deserves Citizenship? An Experimental Study of Japanese Attitudes toward Immigrant Workers." *Social Science Japan Journal* 18 (1): 3–22.

Komai, Hiroshi. 2007. "Gurōbaruka Jidai no Imin Seisaku [Immigration Policy in a Japan that Is Globalizing]." In *Kokusaika no Naka no Imin Seisaku no Kadai: Guroobaruka Suru Nihon to Imin Mondai* [Issues in Immigration Policy Amid Internationalization: Immigration Problems and a Japan that is Globalizing], edited by Hiroshi Komai. Tokyo: Akashi.

Koseki, Shoichi. 1989. *Shinkenpo no Tanjō* [The Birth of the New Constitution]. Tokyo: Chūō Kōronsha.

Kremers, Daniel. 2014. "Transnational Migrant Advocacy from Japan: Tipping the Scales in the Policy-Making Process." *Pacific Affairs* 87 (4): 715–41.

Kume, Ikuo. 1998. *Disparaged Success: Labor Politics in Postwar Japan*. Ithaca, N.Y.: Cornell University Press.

Lahav, Gallya. 2004. "Public Opinion toward Immigration in the European Union: Does It Matter?" *Comparative Political Studies* 37 (10): 1151–83.

LDP Foreign Human Resource Dietmembers Caucus. 2008. "Jinzai Kaikoku! Nihongata Imin Seisaku no Teigen [National Opening to Human Resources! An Opinion on a Japanese-Style Immigration Policy]." June 12.

Leitner, Helga. 1995. "International Migration and the Politics of Admission and Exclusion in Postwar Europe." *Political Geography* 14 (3): 259–78.

Levy, Morris, Matthew Wright, and Jack Citrin. 2016. "Mass Opinion and Immigration Policy in the United States: Re-Assessing Clientelist and Elitist Perspectives." *Perspectives on Politics* 14 (3): 660–80.

Lipscy, Phillip Y. 2017. "Trump and Abe Are Natural Allies." *The Diplomat*. February 9. https://thediplomat.com/2017/02/trump-and-abe-are-natural-allies/.

Liu-Farrer, Gracia. 2011. *Labour Migration from China to Japan: International Students, Transnational Migrants*. Abingdon, Oxon: Routledge.

Maclachlan, Patricia L., and Kay Shimizu. 2016. "Japanese Farmers in Flux: The Domestic Sources of Agricultural Reform." *Asian Survey* 56 (3): 442–65.

ManpowerGroup. 2018. "2016/2017 Talent Shortage Survey." https://www.manpowergroup.com/talent-shortage-explorer/#.Wyvsl1VKjIU.

Martin, Philip L. 2014. "Germany: Managing Migration in the Twenty-First Century." In *Controlling Immigration: A Global Perspective*, edited by James F. Hollifield, Philip L. Martin, and Pia M. Orrenius. Stanford, Calif.: Stanford University Press.

Matti, Joshua, and Yang Zhou. 2017. "The Political Economy of Brexit: Explaining the Vote." *Applied Economic Letters* 24 (6): 1131–34.

Mayda, Anna Maria. 2006. "Who Is against Immigration? A Cross-Country Investigation of Individual Attitudes toward Immigrants." *The Review of Economics and Statistics* 88 (3): 510–30.

McElwee, Sean, and Jason McDaniel. 2017. "Economic Anxiety Didn't Make People Vote Trump, Racism Did." *The Nation*, May 8.

McLean v. Justice Minister. 1978. Decision of the Supreme Court, Grand Bench. Translated by Douglas Payne. In L. Beer and H. Itoh. 1996. *The Constitutional Case Law of Japan: 1970–1990*. Seattle: University of Washington Press.

Mednicoff, David. 2012. "The Legal Regulation of Migrant Workers: Politics and Identity in Qatar and the United Arab Emirates." In *Migrant Labor in the Persian Gulf*, edited by Mehran Kamrava and Zahra Babar. New York: Columbia University Press.

Messina, Anthony M. 2007. *The Logics and Politics of Post–WWII Migration to Western Europe*. New York: Cambridge University Press.

Milly, Deborah J. 2014. *New Policies for New Residents: Immigrants, Advocacy, and Governance in Japan and Beyond*. Ithaca: Cornell University Press.

Mindan. 1997. *Zuhyō De Miru Kankoku Mindan 50 Nen No Ayumi* [A Walk through Fifty Years of Mindan's History in Graphs]. Tokyo: Gogatsu Shōbō.

———. n.d. "Nendo Betsu Jinkō Suii [Annual Population Change]." http://www.edrdg.org/cgi-bin/wwwjdic/wwwjdic?1E (accessed on October 5, 2016).

Ministry of Foreign Affairs (Japan). 1965. *Nihon ni Okeru Ippan Gaikokujin no Kokunaihōjō no Chii* [The Status of General Foreigners in Domestic Law]. Tokyo: Gaimushō Jōyakukyoku Hōkika [Ministry of Foreign Affairs, Treaty Bureau, Legal Section].

———. 1980. Kokusai Jinken Kiyaku [International Human Rights Agreements]. Bureau of Information and Culture, Domestic Public Relations Division.

————. 1981. Indoshina Nanmin Mondai to Nihon [The Indochinese Refugee Problem and Japan]. Tokyo: Jōhō Bunkakyoku [Ministry of Foreign Affairs Information and Culture Division].

Ministry of Health, Labor, and Welfare (Japan). 2018. "Ippan Shokugyō Shōkai Jōkyō [An Introduction to the State of the General Labor Market]. http:// www.mhlw.go.jp/toukei/list/114-1.html.

————. n.d. "Indoshina, Firipin, Oyobi Betonamu Kara no Gaikokujin Kangoshi/Kaigofukushishi Kōhosha no Ukeire ni Tsuite [About the Admission of Nurses and Caregivers from Indonesia, the Philippines, and Vietnam]. http://www.mhlw.go.jp/stf/seisakunitsuite/bunya/koyou_roudou/koyou/ gaikokujin/other22/index.html (accessed on September 28, 2016).

Ministry of Internal Affairs and Communications (Japan). 2016–18. "Jinkō Suikei no Kekka no Gaiyō [An Overview of the Results of Population Estimates]." http://www.stat.go.jp/data/jinsui/2.htm#monthly.

Ministry of Justice (Japan). 1959. *Shutsunyūkoku Kanri to Sono Jittai* [Regulation of Immigration and Emigration and the Actual Conditions]. Tokyo: Ōkurashō Insatsukyoku [the Printing Office of the Ministry of Finance].

————. 1964. *Shutsunyūkoku Kanri to Sono Jittai* [Regulation of Immigration and Emigration and the Actual Conditions]. Tokyo: Ōkurashō Insatsukyoku [the Printing Office of the Ministry of Finance].

————. 1971. *Shutsunyūkoku Kanri to Sono Jittai* [Regulation of Immigration and Emigration and the Actual Conditions]. Tokyo: Ōkurashō Insatsukyoku [the Printing Office of the Ministry of Finance].

————. 1976. *Shutsunyūkoku Kanri: Sono Genjō to Kadai* [Regulation of Immigration and Emigration: The Present Situation and Issues]. Tokyo: Ōkurashō Insatsukyoku [the Printing Office of the Ministry of Finance].

————. various years. "Honpō ni Okeru Fuhō Zairyūshasū ni Tsuite [Regarding the Number of Unlawful Residents in This Country]." http://www. moj.go.jp.

————. n.d. "Zairyū Shinsa Tetsuduki Q&A [Procedures for Screening of Residence]." http://www.immi-moj.go.jp/tetuduki/zairyuu/qa.html (accessed on September 23, 2016).

————. 2006–18. "Zairyū Gaikokujin Tōkei (Kyū Tōroku Gaikokujin Tōkei) Tōkeihyō [Statistical Tables of Foreign Residents of Japan (Formerly Registered Foreigners in Japan)]." http://www.moj.go.jp/housei/toukei/ toukei_ichiran_touroku.html.

————. 2006a. "Guidelines for Permission for Permanent Residence." http:// www.moj.go.jp/content/000099622.pdf.

————. 2014. "Ginōjisshū Seido ni Kansuru Kiso Shiryō [Basic Resources about the Trainee and Technical Internship System]." http://www.moj.go.jp/content/ 001128653.pdf.

———. 2015. "The Immigration Control Act Was Amended." http://www.immi-moj.go.jp/english/nyukan2015/index.html.

———. 2018a. "Puresu Ririisu [Press Releases]." http://www.moj.go.jp/press_index.html.

———. 2018b. "Tōkei ni Kansuru Puresu Ririisu [Press Releases About Statistics]." http://www.moj.go.jp/nyuukokukanri/kouhou/nyuukokukanri01_0 0013.html.

Miyashita, Akitoshi. 2003. *Limits to Power: Asymmetric Dependence and Japanese Foreign Aid Policy*. Lanham, Md.: Lexington Books.

Momochi, Akira. 2009. "Kaisei no Kokuseki Hō ga Nihon wo Yōkai Saseru [Reform of Citizenship Law Will Dissolve Japan]." *Seiron*: 118–27.

Morris-Suzuki, Tessa. 2006. "Invisible Immigrants: Undocumented Migration and Border Controls in Early Postwar Japan." *Journal of Japanese Studies* 32 (1): 119–53.

———. 2010. *Borderline Japan: Frontier Controls, Foreigners and the Nation in the Postwar Era*. New York: Cambridge University Press.

Mukae, Ryuji. 2001. *Japan's Refugee Policy: To Be of the World*. Fucecchio, Italy: European Press Academic Pub.

Müller, Jan-Werner. 2016. *What Is Populism?* Philadelphia: University of Pennsylvania Press. Bluefire EBook file.

Murata, Sayaka. 2018 [2016]. *Convenience Store Woman*. Translated by Ginny Tapley Takemori. New York: Grove.

Nagayoshi, Kikuko. 2009. "Whose Size Counts? Multilevel Analysis of Japanese Anti-Immigrant Attitudes." *JGSS Research Series* 9 (2009): 157–74. http://jgss.daishodai.ac.jp/english/research/monographs/jgssm9/jgssm9_10.pdf.

Nefesh B'Nefesh. 2018. "The Aliyah Process." http://www.nbn.org.il/aliyahpedia-home/aliyah-process/.

Nukaga, Misako. 2006. "Xenophobia and the Effects of Education: Determinants of Japanese Attitudes toward Acceptance of Foreigners." *JGSS Research Series* 5: 191–202. http://jgss.daishodai.ac.jp/english/research/monographs/jgssm5/jgssm5_15.pdf.

Naiki, Yoshiko. 2015. "Labour Migration under the Japan-Philippines and Japan-Indonesia Economic Partnership Agreements." In *Palgrave Handbook on International Labour Migration*, edited by Marion Panizzon, Gottfried Zurcher, and Elisa Fornale. London: Palgrave Macmillan.

Nishimura, Yasutoshi. 2017. Remarks on "Continuity and Change in U.S.-Japan Economic Relations" at an event hosted by the Brookings Institution, May 2. https://www.brookings.edu/events/continuity-and-change-in-u-s-japan-economic-relations/.

OECD. 2016. Annual Labor Force Statistics Database. http://www.oecd.org/std.

———. 2018a. Foreign-born population (indicator). doi: 10.1787/5a368e1b-en.

———. 2018b. Gross domestic product (GDP) (indicator). doi: 10.1787/dc2f7 aec-en.

———. 2018c. Population (indicator). doi: 10.1787/d434f82b-en.

Ogawa, Reiko. 2012. "Globalization of Care and the Context of Reception of Southeast Asian Care Workers in Japan." *Southeast Asian Studies* 49 (3): 570–93.

Oguma, Eiji. 2002. *A Genealogy of "Japanese" Self-Images*. Translated by David Askew. English. Melbourne: Trans Pacific.

Oishi, Nana. 2012. "The Limits of Immigration Policies: The Challenges of Highly Skilled Migration in Japan." *American Behavioral Scientist* 56 (8): 1080–1100.

Ōnuma, Yasuaki. 1993 [1978]. "Shutsunyōkoku Kanri Hōsei no Seiritsu Katei: 1952 Nen Taisei no Zenshi [The Process of Establishing the Legal System of Immigration Regulation: the History of the 1952 System]." In *Tan'itsu Minzoku Shakai no Shinwa o Koete: Zainichi Kankoku, Chōsenjin to Shutsunyōkoku Kanri Taisei* [Transcending the Myth of a Monoethnic Society: Koreans in Japan and the Regulation of Immigration], edited by Yasuaki Ōnuma, 15–114. Tokyo: Tōshindō.

Pyle, Kenneth B. 2007. *Japan Rising: The Resurgence of Japanese Power and Purpose*. New York: Public Affairs.

Rao, Anand. 2017. "To Dodge or Bite the Bullet: Immigration Politics in Japan." *Japan Studies Association Journal* 15 (1): 66–82.

Roberts, Glenda S. 2012. "Vocalizing the 'I' Word: Proposals and Initiatives on Immigration to Japan from the LDP and Beyond." ASIEN (124): 48–68.

———. 2018. "An Immigration Policy by Any Other Name: Semantics of Immigration to Japan." *Social Science Japan Journal* 21 (1): 89–102.

Ryang, Sonia. 1997. *North Koreans in Japan: Language, Ideology, and Identity*. Boulder, CO: Westview.

Sakanaka, Hidenori. 1999 [1975]. "Zainichi Chōsenjin no Taigū [The Treatment of Koreans in Japan]." In *Zainichi Kankoku/Chōsenjin Seisakuron no Tenkai* [The Expansion of a Policy Dialogue about Resident Koreans]. Tokyo: Nihon Kajo Shuppan Kabushiki Gaisha.

———. 2005. *Nyūkan Senki: 'Zainichi' Sabetsu, 'Nikkeijijn' Mondai, Gaikokujin Hanzai to, Nihon no Kin-Mirai* [An Immigration Bureau War Diary: Discrimination against 'Foreigners in Japan,' the problem of 'People of Japanese Descent,' Foreign Crime, and Japan's Near Future]. Tokyo: Kōdansha.

———. 2009. *Towards a Japanese-style Immigration Nation*. Tokyo: Japan Immigration Policy Institute.

Scheiner, Ethan. 2006. *Democracy without Competition in Japan: Opposition Failure in a One-Party Dominant State*. Cambridge: Cambridge University Press.

Scheiner, Ethan, Robert Pekkanen, Michio Muramatsu, and Ellis Krauss. 2013. "When Do Interest Groups Contact Bureaucrats Rather than Politicians? Evidence on Fire Alarms and Smoke Detectors from Japan." *Japanese Journal of Political Science* 14 (3): 283–304.

Scheve, Kenneth F., and Matthew J. Slaughter. 2001. "Labor Market Competition and Individual Preferences over Immigration Policy." *The Review of Economics and Statistics* 83 (1): 133–45.

Schmidle, Nicholas. 2015. "Ten Borders: One Refugee's Epic Escape from Syria." *The New Yorker*, October 26.

Schoppa, Leonard. 1997. *Bargaining with Japan: What American Pressure Can and Cannot Do.* New York: Columbia University Press.

Schoppa, Leonard J. 2006. *Race for the Exits: The Unraveling of Japan's System of Social Protection.* Ithaca, N.Y.: Cornell University Press.

Seebruck, Ryan. 2013. "Technology and Tolerance in Japan: Internet Use and Positive Attitudes and Behaviors toward Foreigners." *Social Science Japan Journal* 16 (2): 279–300.

Seigo, Hirowatari. 1997. "Foreign Workers and Immigration Policy." In *The Political Economy of Japanese Society*, edited by Junji Banno. Oxford: Oxford University Press.

Seol, Donh-Hoon, and John D. Skrentny. 2009. "Why Is There So Little Migrant Settlement in East Asia?" *International Migration Review* 43 (3): 578–620.

Shipper, Apichai W. 2008. *Fighting for Foreigners: Immigration and Its Impact on Japanese Democracy.* Ithaca: Cornell University Press.

Silver, Nate. 2017. "Donald Trump Is Making Europe Liberal Again." *FiveThirty Eight.* June 14. https://fivethirtyeight.com/features/donald-trump-is-making-europe-liberal-again/.

Simon, Rita J., and Keri W. Sikich. 2007. "Public Attitudes toward Immigrants and Immigration Policies across Seven Nations" *International Migration Review* 41 (4): 956–62.

Statham, Paul, and Andrew Geddes. 2006. "Elites and the 'Organised Public': Who Drives British Immigration Politics and in Which Direction?" *West European Politics* 29 (2): 248–69.

Strausz, Michael. 2006–2007. "Minorities and Protest in Japan: The Politics of the Fingerprinting Refusal Movement." *Pacific Affairs* 79 (4): 641–56.

———. 2010. "Japanese Conservatism and the Integration of Foreign Residents." *Japanese Journal of Political Science* 11 (2): 245–64.

———. 2014. "Executives, Legislatures, and Whales: The Birth of Japan's Scientific Whaling Regime." *International Relations of the Asia-Pacific* 14 (3): 455–78.

———. 2018. "Does the LDP Want to Build a Wall Too? Immigration and the 2017 Election in Japan." In *Japan Decides 2017: The Japanese General*

Election, edited by Robert J. Pekkanen, Steven R. Reed, Ethan Scheiner, and Daniel M. Smith. Cham, Switzerland: Palgrave Macmillan.

Takahashi, Kōichi 2002. "Nanmin Mondai ni Taisuru Nihon no Toriskumi [Japanese Efforts toward the Refugee Problem]." *Kokusai Mondai* 513:46–59.

Takao, Yasuo. 2003. "Foreigners' Rights in Japan: Beneficiaries to Participants." *Asian Survey* 43 (3): 527–52.

Takeda, Isami. 1998. "Japan's Response to Refugees and Political Asylum Seekers." In *Temporary Workers or Future Citizens? Japanese and U.S. Migration Policies*, edited by Myron Weiner and Tadashi Hanami, New York: New York University Press.

Takenaka, Ayumi, Makiko Nakamuro, and Kenji Ishida. 2016. "Negative Assimilation: How Immigrants Experience Economic Mobility in Japan." *International Migration Review* 50 (2): 506–33.

Takizawa, Saburo. 2015. "The Japanese Pilot Resettlement Program: Identifying Constraints to Domestic Intergration of Refugees from Burma." In *Urban Refugees: Challenges in Protection, Services and Policy*, edited by Koichi Koizumi and Gerhard Hoffstaedter, 206–40. New York: Routledge.

Tanaka, Hiroshi. 1995. *Zainichi Gaikokujin—Hô no Kabe, Kokoro no Dobu* [Foreigners in Japan—The Walls of Law, the Gutter of the Heart]. Tokyo: Iwanami Shinsho.

Taniguchi, Masaki. 2009, 2010, 2012, 2014, 2016. "The UTokyo-Asahi Survey," conducted by Masaki Taniguchi of the Graduate Schools for Law and Politics, the University of Tokyo and the Asahi Shimbun. http://www.masaki.j.u-tokyo.ac.jp/utas/utasindex.html.

Tatsumi, Nobuo. 1966. *Zainichi Kankokujin no Hōteki Chii Kyôtei to Shutsunyūkoku Kanri Tokubetsu Hō Kaisetsu* [A Commentary on the Agreement on the Legal Status of South Koreans in Japan and the Special Law on Immigration and Emigration]. Hōmusho Nyūkoku Kanrikyoku [Ministry of Justice Immigration Bureau].

UNHCR. 2018. Population Statistics. http://popstats.unhcr.org/en/time_series.

United Nations Population Division. 2017. World Population Prospects 2017. https://esa.un.org/unpd/wpp/Download/Standard/Population/.

Upham, Frank K. 1987. *Law and Social Change in Postwar Japan*. Cambridge, MA: Harvard University Press.

Urano, Naoki. 2018. "Hōmushō ga Zairyū Kanri Kyōka e: Gaikokujin Rōdōsha Ukeire Kakudai [Ministry of Justice Moves toward Strengthening Residency Status: Expansion of Admission of Foreign Labor]." *Asahi Shimbun*, June 15.

United States Government Printing Office (USGPO). 1980. *Public Papers of the Presidents of the United States: Jimmy Carter: 1979, Book 2*. Washington, D.C.: United States Government Printing Office.

Vogt, Gabriele. 2018. *Population Aging and International Health-Caregiver Migration to Japan*. Cham, Switzerland: Springer.

Wade, Robert. 1990. *Governing the Market: Economic Theory and the Role of Government in East Asian Industrialization*. Princeton, N.J.: Princeton University Press.

Wilson, James Q. 1980. *The Politics of Regulation*. New York: Basic Books.

Wolman, Andrew. 2015. "Japan and International Refugee Protection Norms: Explaining Non-Compliance." *Asian and Pacific Migration Journal* 24 (4): 1–23.

Yamawaki, Keizō. 2000. "Foreign Workers in Japan: A Historical Perspective." In *Japan and Global Migration: Foreign Workers and the Advent of a Multicultural Society*, edited by Mike Douglass and Glenda S. Roberts. London: Routledge.

———. 2001. "Sengo Nihon no Gaikokujin Seisaku to Zainichi Korian no Shakai Undō—1970 Nendai wo Chūshinni [Foreigner Policy in Postwar Japan and Social Movements among Koreans in Japan—Focus on the 1970s]." In Kokusaika to Aidentiti [Internationalization and Identity], edited by Takamichi Kajita. Kyoto: Minerva Shobō.

Zairyū Gaikokujin Tōkei [Statistics on the Foreigners Registered in Japan]. 1964. Tokyo: Hōmushō [Ministry of Justice].

———. 1970. Tokyo: Hōmushō [Ministry of Justice].

———. 1975. Tokyo: Hōmushō [Ministry of Justice].

———. 1985. Tokyo: Hōmushō Nyūkoku Kanrikyoku [Ministry of Justice, Bureau of Immigration].

———. 1998. Tokyo: Hōmushō [Ministry of Justice].

———. 1999. Tokyo: Nyūkan Kyōkai [Japan Immigration Association].

———. 2002. Tokyo: Nyūkan Kyōkai [Japan Immigration Association].

Index

1990 System, 72–75

Abe, Shinzo
  as assimilation optimist, 145
  on constitutional revision, 22
  on foreign labor, 88–89, 132, 141
  on immigration, 9, 144–45, 146
  Trainee and Technical Internship Program expansion announced by, 84
  on voting rights for foreign residents, 56–57
Afghanistan
  political refugees from, 115
agricultural labor
  from Indochina, 105
  in Japan, 25, 68–69, 90, 165n4 (chap. 4)
  under the Trainee and Technical Internship Program, 82, 83–84
Akimoto, Tsukashi
  on voting rights for foreign residents, 57–58

Akutsu, Yukihiko
  on voting rights for foreign residents, 56
Asahi Shimbun
  on Japan's Indochinese refugee policy, 110, 166n6
Asao, Kei'ichiro
  on immigration to Japan, 122–23, 124
Asao, Mihara
  on Japan's Indochinese refugee policy, 106
Asō, Tarō, 56
  on voting rights for foreign residents, 56, 57
assimilation
  alternatives evaluated, 58–59, 91–92, 94
  Clean Government Party (CGP) and, 54
  elites on, 49–53
  Hidenori Sakanaka on, 43–46
  See also naturalization
assimilation optimism
  as conservative debate in Japan, 164n13

assimilation optimism *(continued)*
  in current Japanese political
    environment, 122, 146
  defined, 27, 49, 58, 163n14
  Hidenori Sakanaka on, 44–46
  oldcomer Koreans and, 53
  Shinzo Abe and, 145
  writers on, 51–53
assimilation pessimism
  as conservative debate in Japan,
    164n13
  defined, 27, 49, 58, 163n14
  Masazumi Gotōda and, 57
  oldcomer Koreans and, 53
  writers on, 49–51
asylum
  in the European Union (EU),
    9, 12
  in Germany, 20, 162n12
  in Japan, xii, 12, 27, 93–98,
    102, 117, 118, 165n3
  in the United States, 119
  See also refugees
Australia
  immigration policy in, 14, 23,
    75, 112
Austria
  far-right populism in, 152

birthrate
  in Japan, xii, 7, 10
Brexit, 143, 151, 154–55
  voters' attitudes toward, 152–
    53
British Nationality Act (1948), 20
bureaucracy of Japan
  bloat of, 122
  on development, 18

  on immigration policy, 22–23,
    27–28, 48, 86, 90, 127, 147
  legislation and, 48, 147
  on *nikkeijin*, 73
  power of, 18, 27–28
  on refugee policy, 84, 101,
    109, 110–11, 113, 114, 115,
    116–17
  social change and, 39
  See also specific ministries
Bureau of Immigration. *See under*
  Ministry of Justice

Cambodia
  refugees from, 98–117, 118
Canada
  immigration policy in, 14, 23,
    75, 125
  refugees and, 112, 113, 116
Carter, Jimmy
  on Japan's Indochinese refugee
    policy, 104–5, 105, 106
Caucus for the Promotion of
  Foreign Human Resources.
  See under Liberal Democratic
  Party (LDP)
China, 144
  Confucius Institutes of, 154
  immigrants to Japan from,
    88, 149, 163n2, 163n8, 164n2
  immigration policy of, 57
  refugees from, 116
Chōsen-Sōren, 33–34, 56, 163n4
Christians in Japan, 166n4
citizenship policy, 18–19
  of France, 42
  of Germany, 20, 161n2 (chap. 1)
  of Israel, 3, 20, 23–24

of Japan, 3, 26–27, 29, 33–34, 35–36 42, 47, 49–50, 57, 124, 130, 140, 146, 149, 150
of South Korean, 20
of West Germany, 2, 42
See also dual citizenship
civil society in Japan, 15, 155
Clean Government Party (CGP)
on assimilation, 54
immigration policy of, xi, 75, 91, 135
on voting rights for foreign residents, 31, 53–55, 56–57, 58, 140
crime
correlation between immigration and, 26, 71, 151, 162n13
Czechoslovakia
political refugees from, 115

Democratic Party (DP), 123
immigration policy of, 11, 86–87, 118
Democratic Party of Japan (DPJ)
immigration policy of, 121, 123–24, 135
refugee policy of, 117
on voting rights for foreign residents, 55–56
developmental state ideology of Japan, 17–18
Diet
on immigration to Japan 134–35, 141–42
voting rights for foreigner residents debated in, 53–58
dual citizenship in Japan, 11, 42

Dubai
guest worker program of, as model for Japan, 91

East Germany
concerns about, in West Germany, 162n10
Economic Partnership Agreements (EPAs), 78–81, 130, 165n6
effects of, 90
education policy
Koreans and, 48
elites
on assimilation, 49–53
immigration policy and, 21–22, 26–27, 147
entertainers
visas for, 77–78, 90, 165n5 (chap. 4)
ethnic homogeneity of Japan
as component of Japanese identity, 27, 29, 30, 32, 43, 44, 59, 98, 101, 145
immigrants as challenge to, 46, 48, 100, 112–13, 114
Jimmy Carter on, 106
origins of belief in, 29
European Union (EU)
family reunification policy in, 13, 14
far-right in, 151–52, 155
immigration policy in, 13, 14, 26, 57, 74, 90–91, 147
migration in, 161n1 (chap. 1)
public opinion toward immigration in, 162n2
refugees and asylum in, 9, 12, 94, 97, 165n3

European Union (EU) *(continued)*
  United Kingdom departure
    from *(see* Brexit)

Farage, Nigel, 151, 152
Fingerprinting of immigrants to
  Japan, 39, 163nn7–8
foreign exchange student
  programs, 70–71, 161n1
  (chap. 2)
foreign labor *(gaikokujin rōdosha)*
  in Japan, 62–67
  immigrant *(imin)* compared to,
    1–2
  See also guest worker policies;
    undocumented labor
France
  citizenship policy in, 42
  elites and immigration policy
    of, 21
  guest worker policies in, 24,
    74, 75
  immigration policy in, 23
  industrial labor in, 68
  Japan's immigration policy
    compared to, 17
  refugees in, 112, 113, 116
Fukuda, Takeo, 108
  on Indochinese refugees, 102–3,
    104
Fukuda, Yasuo, 55
  on voting rights for foreign
    residents, 56, 57
Fukushima, Yutaka, 55
Fuyushiba, Tetsuzō, 56
  as assimilation pessimist, 57
  on voting rights for foreign
    residents, 54–55, 57

General Association for Korean
  Residents in Japan. *See*
  Chōsen-Sōren
Germany
  citizenship policy of, 20, 161n2
    (chap. 1)
  as "country of immigration,"
    162n12
  elderly in, 7
  elites and immigration policy
    of, 21
  guest worker policies in, 16,
    68, 75, 90, 91, 141
  immigration policy in, 23
  Japan's immigration policy
    compared to, 17
  public opinion about
    immigration in, 148–49
  refugee policy of, 9, 19–20, 118
  See also East Germany; West
    Germany
Gotōda, Masazumi
  on voting rights for foreign
    residents, 57, 58
guest worker policies
  in Dubai, 91
  in France, 24, 74, 75
  in Germany, 16, 68, 75, 90,
    91, 141
  in Hong Kong, 91
  in Israel, 26
  in Singapore, 91
  in South Korea, 91
  in Sweden, 24
  in Switzerland, 16, 141
  in Taiwan, 91
  in West Germany, 2, 24–25,
    74, 91

Haku, Shinkun, 164n15
on voting rights for foreign
residents, 55, 56
Hatoyama, Iichirō
on Vietnamese refugees, 103–4
health insurance in Japan
for foreigners, 47, 67–68
highly skilled immigrants
Japan as unattractive destination
for, 11
Japan's efforts to attract, 12, 72,
122
point system for, 75–77
Holbrooke, Richard
on Japan's Indochinese refugee
policy, 104
Hong Kong
guest worker program of, as
model for Japan, 91
Japan's refugee policy compared
to refugee policy of, 109
human trafficking, 165n5 (chap.
4)
entertainment visas possibly
used for, 78
Trainee and Technical
Internship Program possibly
used for, 129
Hungary
immigration policy in, 24
Hyodo, Nisohachi
on assimilation, 50–51

immigrant (*imin*)
foreign laborer (*gaikokujin
rōdosha*) compared to, 1–2
Immigration Control and Refugee
Recognition Act, 67

1989 reform of, 62, 72, 81, 90,
147 (*see also* 1990 System)
1990 reform of, 63, 67, 125
2018 reform of, 88–89, 141, 146
entertainers' visas under, 77–78
points system of, 75–77
Immigration Policy Institute, 126
income inequality in Japan, 143
India
Economic Partnership
Agreement with Japan of,
165n6
Indochina
refugees from, 98–117, 118
Indonesia
Economic Partnership
Agreement with Japan of, 78
nurses from, 50, 78
nurses' wages in, 9, 80
industrial labor in Japan
shortage of, 25, 90–91
under the Trainee and Technical
Internship Program, 82–83
institutional explanations
for Japanese immigration
control policies, 12–14
interest groups in Japan
on immigration, 80–81, 122,
126
influence and power of, 13,
15–16, 21, 24
See also specific interest groups
International Conference on
Indochinese Refugees (1979),
105–6, 109
International Covenant for Civil
and Political Rights (ICCPR),
39, 40, 42

International Covenant on
   Economic, Social, and
   Cultural Rights (ICESCR),
   39, 42
international role
   immigration policy and, 19–20,
   27
investment immigrants (*tōshi
   imin*), 129
Israel
   citizenship policy of, 3, 20,
   23–24
   guest worker policies of, 26
   immigration policy in, 23–24
   Japan's refugee policy compared
   to refugee policy of, 109
   "law-of-return" policy of, 3, 20,
   23–24
   refugee policy of, 118
Italy
   elderly in, 7
Iwakura Mission (1871–1873), 42
Iwasaki, Kei'ichi
   on 2003 *Voice* article, 123

Japan
   agricultural labor in, 25,
   68–69, 90, 165n4 (chap. 4)
   asylum in, xii, 12, 27, 93–98,
   102, 117, 118, 165n3
   birthrate in, xii, 7, 10
   bureaucracy of
     bloat of, 122
     on development, 18
     legislation and, 48, 147
     on *nikkeijin*, 73
     on immigration policy,
      22–23, 27–28, 48, 86, 90,
      127, 147

     power of, 18, 27–28
     on refugee policy, 84, 101,
      109, 110–11, 113, 114,
      115, 116–17
     social change and, 39
   citizenship policy of, 3, 26–27,
     29, 33–34, 35–36 42, 47,
     49–50, 57, 124, 130, 140,
     146, 149, 150
   civil society in, 15, 155
   developmental state ideology of,
     17–18
   Diet of
     on immigration to Japan
      134–35, 141–42
     voting rights for foreigner
      residents debated in, 53–58
   education policy of, 48
   elites of
     on assimilation, 49–53
     immigration policy and,
      21–22, 26–27, 147
   ethnic homogeneity of
     as component of Japanese
      identity, 27, 29, 30, 32,
      43, 44, 59, 98, 101, 145
     immigrants as challenge to,
      46, 48, 100, 112–13, 114
     Jimmy Carter on, 106
     origins of belief in, 29
   foreign exchange student
     program in, 70–71, 161n1
     (chap. 2)
   foreign labor in contemporary,
     62–67
   health insurance for foreigners
     in, 47, 67–68
   immigrants and foreign laborers
     compared in, 1–2

immigration policy of, 24
possible futures of, 145–46,
   154–55
income inequality in, 143
industrial labor in
   shortage of, 25, 90–91
   under the Trainee and
      Technical Internship
      Program, 82–83
interest groups in
   on immigration, 80–81, 122,
      126
   influence and power of, 13,
      15–16, 21, 24
international role of
   immigration policy and,
      19–20, 27
labor shortage in, xi, 5–10,
   61–92
life expectancy in, xii, 7, 10
low-skilled labor in, 67, 73–75
majoritarianism in, 14
"mixed-nation" theory for, 30,
   31–32, 42, 58
   assimilation optimists and, 49
   Koreans and, 33
multiculturalism in, 163n14
national identity of
   debates over, 27, 147, 155
   ethnic homogeneity and, xi–
      xii, 3–4, 30, 32, 101, 119
   formal national citizenship
      and, 34
naturalization policy in, 11
   Akira Momochi on, 50
   Heidenori Sakanaka on, 45–46
   statistics of, 33
   Taikin Tei on, 52–53
negative assimilation in, 11

nuclear power policy in, 14
as one-ethnicity country
   (tan'itsuminzoku), 27
populism in, 143
public discourse of
   on immigration policy
      generally, 135–40, 149–50,
      154
   on Indochinese refugee
      policy, 106–7, 107–8,
      110
   on refugee resettlement,
      165n5 (chap. 5)
refugees in, xii, 9, 10, 27,
   93–119
religious pluralism of, 130–31,
   166n4
separatist idea in
   defined, 32
   intellectual challenges to,
      43–44, 48
   legal challenges to, 38–43
   political implications of,
      35–38
undocumented immigrants in,
   65–67, 70, 71, 72
visas to, 62–65, 73, 77–78,
   88–89
wages in
   foreigners' repatriation of,
      80–81
   immigrants and effects on,
      149
   labor shortage's effect on, xi,
      8, 26
   negative assimilation and, 11
   of nurses, 9, 80
   point system and, 84
xenophobia in, 17, 135

Japan Association of Corporate
  Executives (Keizai Dōyūkai)
  on skilled labor, 76–77
  on unskilled labor, 81
Japan Business Federation
  (Keidanren)
  on immigration to Japan, 68,
  122
Japanese Nursing Association
  on foreign nurses in Japan,
  80–81
Japanese Socialist Party (JSP), 21,
  22
  on low-skilled immigrants, 75
Japan Federation of Employer's
  Associations (Nikkeiren)
  on immigration to Japan, 122
Japan Monopoly Corporation
  Korean employment by, 46–47
Japan National Railway
  Korean employment by, 46–47
Japan Nursing Federation (JNF)
  on foreign nurses in Japan, 16

Kagei, Umao
  on Japan's Indochinese refugee
  policy, 111
Kamibayashi, Cheiko
  on foreign nurses in Japan, 81
Kamishima, Jirō
  on Japan's ethnic homogeneity,
  29
Kato, Tsunetaro
  on foreign labor, 70
Kim Dae-jung
  on voting rights of Koreans in
  Japan, 54

Kodama Chemical
  foreign labor at, 70
Kokuba, Kōnosuke
  on guest worker programs, 91
Kōno, Yōhei
  on Japan's Indochinese refugee
  policy, 108
Korea
  fingerprinting of Japanese
  residents from, 39
  immigrants to Japan from,
  30–31, 32–35, 62–63, 140
  Japanese annexation and
  occupation of (1910–1945),
  30, 32
  residentialization (*teichakuka*)
  of immigrants to Japan of,
  43–46
  treatment of residents in Japan
  from, after the Sakanaka
  thesis, 46–49
  voting rights for residents in
  Japan from, debated, 54–55
  See also North Korea; South
  Korea
Korean Residents Union of Japan.
  See Mindan

labor shortage in Japan, xi, 5–10,
  61–92
labor unions in Japan
  for foreign workers, 166n2
  immigration policy and, 16,
  124
Laos
  refugees from, 59, 98–117, 118
Lee Myung-bak, 55

Legal Training and Research Institute
Korean attendance at, 47
Le Pen, Marine, 152
Liaison and Coordination Council for Indochinese and Displaced Persons (Liaison Council), 110, 111–12
on Japan's Indochinese refugee policy, 114, 116
Liberal Democratic Party (LDP)
Caucus for the Promotion of Foreign Human Resources of, 125–32, 135, 167n7
implementation of proposals by, 132–34
clientelism in, 14
on constructional revision, 22
foreign labor policy of, 86–87, 91
immigration policy of, 11, 74–75, 121, 124–32, 135, 141, 146
on voting rights for foreign residents, 54, 56–58
life expectancy in Japan, xii, 7, 10
low-skilled labor in Japan, 67, 73–75

Magami, Yasunari
on Japan's Indochinese refugee policy, 109
majoritarianism in Japan, 14
Matano, Kagechicka, 75
on 1990 System, 72–73
on low-skilled immigrants, 74

Matsubara, Hitoshi
on voting rights for foreign residents, 56
media of Japan, 103, 128
on immigration policy, 41–42, 84, 108
mixed-nation theory and, 32
See also specific media outlets
Meiji period (1868–1912), 42
immigration opening in modern-day Japan compared to, 29, 146
vision of Japanese origins during, 31
Meiji Seisaku
foreign labor at, 70
Merkel, Angela
on refugees, 9, 19
Mexico
immigrants from, Donald Trump on, 151
immigration policy in, 24
Japanese laborers in, xi
Mindan, 33–34, 56
Ministry of Construction (Japan)
on Koreans in public housing, 47
Ministry of Economy, Trade, and Industry (Japan)
on Korean employment, 47
Ministry of Foreign Affairs (Japan)
on Japan's immigration policy, 40–41, 42, 43, 73
on Japan's Indochinese refugee policy, 104, 109, 117
on unskilled labor, 81

Ministry of Health and Welfare
(Japan)
on foreigners' access to health
insurance, 66–67
on Koreans' welfare eligibility, 47
on refugees' access to pensions,
43
Ministry of Home Affairs (Japan)
on Korean employment, 47
Ministry of Justice (Japan), 126
on asylum, 96–97, 98, 117
Bureau of Immigration, on
Koreans, 46
on citizenship policy, 42
on entertainer visas, 78
on foreign students, 64–65
on foreign trainee program, 72,
84, 85
on high skilled labor, 76, 129
on immigration, 36–38, 147
on Japan's Indochinese refugee
policy, 111
on low-skilled labor, 73
on permanent residents, 62
on undocumented foreign
residents, 65–66, 67
on unskilled labor, 81
Ministry of Labor (Japan)
on low-skilled labor, 73, 75
on trainees, 70
on unskilled labor, 81
Ministry of Posts and Telegraphs
(Japan)
on Korean employment, 47
Mise, Hitoshi
on Japan's Indochinese refugee
policy, 109

"mixed-nation" theory, 30, 31–32,
42, 58
assimilation optimists and, 49
Koreans and, 33
Momochi, Akira
on assimilation, 49–50
multiculturalism in Japan,
163n14
Murazumi, Hiro
on Japan's Indochinese refugee
policy, 114
Myanmar
refugees from, 117, 118

Nagata, Yoshio
on low-skilled immigrants, 75
Nagawa, Hidenao
on immigration to Japan, 125,
126
Nakagawa, Masaharu
on immigration to Japan, 124
Nakagawa, Yoshimi
on Japan's Indochinese refugee
policy, 108
Nakasone, Yasuhiro
foreign exchange student
programs and, 70–71
on Japan's ethnic homogeneity,
101
on Japan's Indochinese refugee
policy, 109, 115–16
national identity in Japan
debates over, 27, 147, 155
ethnic homogeneity and, xi–xii,
3–4, 30, 32, 101, 119
formal national citizenship and,
34

naturalization in Japan, 11
  Akira Momochi on, 50
  Heidenori Sakanaka on, 45–46
  statistics of, 33
  Taikin Tei on, 52–53
  See also assimilation; citizenship
    policy
negative assimilation, 11
Netherlands
  family reunification policy in,
    14, 17
New Zealand
  immigration policy in, 14, 23
Nihon Keizai Shimbun
  on immigration policy, 41
  on Japan's Indochinese refugee
    policy, 109, 110
nikkeijin, 3, 27, 73
  visas for, 88
Nippon Telephone and Telegraph
  (NTT)
  Korean employment by, 46
Nishida, Yuzuru
  on guest worker programs, 91
Nishime, Junji
  on Japan's Indochinese refugee
    policy, 105–6
Nishimura, Yasutoshi
  on income inequality and
    populism in Japan, 143,
    154
Noboru, Masuyama
  on separatist idea, 32
North Korea, 59, 151
  immigrants to Japan from, 34,
    37, 38, 47, 163n5
  Japanese in, 129, 130

  refugee policy in, 20
  See also Chōsen-Sōren; Korea
nuclear families
  in Japanese immigration policy,
    117
nuclear power in Japan, 14
nurses and caregivers, 146, 165n6
  Caucus for the Promotion of
    Foreign Human Resources
    program for, 129–30
  Economic Partnership
    Agreements for, 75, 78–81, 90
  Japanese Nursing association
    and, 15–16
  Ministry of Home Affairs on, 47
  Nisohachi Hyodo on, 50–51
  wages in Japan of, 9

Ohira, Masayoshi, 104
  on Japan's Indochinese refugee
    policy, 105, 109
Ōtaka, Hirome
  on Japan's Indochinese refugee
    policy, 115
Ozawa, Ichirō, 55

Pak, Chŏng-sŏk, 39
Philippines
  Economic Partnership
    Agreement with Japan of, 78
  entertainers from, 77
  nurses from, 50
  nurses' wages in, 9, 80bb
point system
  of Immigration Control and
    Refugee Recognition Act,
    75–77, 90

Poland
  immigration policy in, 24
  political refugees from, 115
populism
  defined, 150
  immigrants and, 151
  in Japan, 143
  rise of, explanations for, 152–53
prostitution, 78
public discourse in Japan
  on immigration policy
    generally, 135–40, 149–50,
      154
    on Indochinese refugee policy,
      106–7, 107–8, 110
    on refugee resettlement, 165n5
      (chap. 5)

Qatar
  immigration policy in, 23

Refugee Convention. See UN
    Convention Relating to the
    Status of Refugees
refugees, 93–119
  in European Union, 9, 94
  in Japan, xii, 9, 10, 27
  in United States, 3
religious pluralism in Japan,
    130–31, 166n4
Renhō, 55
residentialization (teichakuka)
  of Koreans in Japan, 43–46
Revised Parliamentary Electoral
    Law (1948), 35, 36
Roh Moo-hyun
  on voting rights of Koreans in
    Japan, 54

Saitō, Tetsuo, 55
Sakaiya, Taichi
  on immigration to Japan, 122
Sakanaka, Heidenori
  on assimilation optimism, 44–46
  on immigration to Japan,
    125–26, 166n3
Sakurai, Kijun
  on low-skilled immigrants, 74
Sankei Shimbun, 123
Sano, Ayako
  on assimilation, 51
Sato, Eisaku
  on foreign labor, 69–70
Satō, Shigeki
  on Japanese multiculturalism,
    55, 57
separatist idea
  defined, 32
  intellectual challenges to, 43–44,
    48
  legal challenges to, 38–43
  political implications of, 35–38
service labor
  under the Trainee and Technical
    Internship Program, 84
Setoyama, Michio
  on Japan's Indochinese refugee
    policy, 110
shared ethnic heritage
  immigration policy and, 20
Shirahama, Kazuyoshi
  on low-skilled immigrants, 75
shōshikōreika, 59, 122, 126, 154
  Caucus for the Promotion of
    Foreign Human Resources
    and, 127, 129
  defined, xii

Singapore
  guest worker program of, as
    model for Japan, 91
Slovenia
  immigration policy in, 24
Sonoda, Sunao, 42, 106
  on Japan's Indochinese refugee
    policy, 108, 109, 112
Sotomayor, Sonia, 151
South America
  Japanese-heritage peoples in (see
    nikkeijin)
South Korea
  guest worker program of, as
    model for Japan, 91
  immigrants to Japan from, 34,
    36–37, 163n3
  immigration policy in, 24
  refugee policy in, 20
  See also Korea, Mindan
Soviet Bloc
  refugees from, 3
Suga, Yoshihide
  on Japan's labor shortage, 89–90
Su-gil Yoon, 107
Supreme Command of the Allied
    Powers (SCAP)
  Japanese immigration policy
    and, 35–36
Supreme Court (Japan)
  on citizenship, 49
  on foreigners at the Legal
    Training and Research
    Institute, 47
  on refugees and asylum, 107
  on rights of foreigners, 38
  on voting rights for foreign
    residents, 53

Supreme Court (United States)
  on Donald Trump's immigration
    policy, 151
Suzuki, Shun'ichi
  on low-skilled immigrants, 75
Sweden
  guest worker policies in, 24
  refugees and, 112
Switzerland
  guest worker policies in, 16,
    141
  immigration policy in, 23, 146
  refugees in, 112
Syria
  refugees from, 9, 11, 12,
    97–98, 118, 161n2 (chap. 2)

Taisho period (1912–1926)
  vision of Japanese origins
    during, 31
Taiwan, 70
  guest worker program of, as
    model for Japan, 91
  immigrants to Japan from, 34,
    36, 37, 163n2
  refugees in, 109
Takayoshi, Taniguchi
  on voting rights for foreign
    residents, 55
Tatsumi, Nobuo
  on South Koreans in Japan,
    36–37, 44–45
Tei, Taikin, 164n14
  on assimilation, 51–53
teichakuka. See residentialization
  (*teichakuka*)
Tiananmen Square massacre
  (1989), 116

Toda, Katsunori
on *nikkeijin* settlement in
Japan, 73
Tokyo Shimbun, 123
tōshi imin. *See* investment
immigrants (*tōshi imin*)
Trainee and Technical Internship
Program, 81–88
2009 reform of, 15, 141, 166n2
2014 proposed expansion of,
145
Caucus for the Promotion of
Foreign Human Resources
program compared to, 129
criticism of, 129
effects of, 90, 147
as low-skilled labor source, 73
Trump, Donald, 152
on immigration, 144–45, 151,
167n2
refugee policy of, 118–19
voters for, rationale of, 153

UN Convention Relating to the
Status of Refugees, 43, 47,
48
refugees defined in, 114–16,
116–17
Indochinese and, 113
Japanese attitude toward, 100
undocumented immigrants in
Japan, 65–67, 70, 71, 72
unions. *See* labor unions in Japan
United Arab Emirates
immigration policy in, 23
United Kingdom
immigration policy in, 20, 21,
23, 75

industrial labor in, 68
Japan's immigration policy
compared to, 17, 41, 110,
143
populism in, 154
withdrawal from EU by (*see*
Brexit)
United Kingdom Independence
Party (UKIP), 151
United States
immigration policy in, 23
on Japan's Indochinese refugee
policy, 100, 104
populism in, 154
public opinion about
immigration in, 148, 152
refugees in, 3, 19, 118–19

Vietnam
Economic Partnership
Agreement with Japan of, 78,
165n6
nurses' wages in, 9
refugees from, 59, 98–117, 118
Vietnam War, 38
refugees from, 98–117, 118
visas to Japan, 62–65, 73, 77–78,
88–89
Voice (magazine)
pro-immigration article in
(2003), 122–24, 126
voting rights for foreign residents
debated in Diet, 53–58,
140–41

wages, 68
foreigners' repatriation of,
80–81

immigrants and effects on, 149
labor shortage's effect on in
   Japan, xi, 8, 26
negative assimilation and, 11
of nurses, 9, 80
point system and, 84
Waldheim, Kurt, 103–4
Watanabe, Rō
on Japan's Indochinese refugee
   policy, 113
West Germany
agricultural labor in, 25, 68
citizenship policy in, 42
concerns about East Germany
   in, 162n10
guest worker policies in, 2,
   24–25, 74, 91
immigration policy in, 41

industrial labor in, 68
See also Germany
World War II
Japanese identity after, 32
Korean community in Japan
   after, 33

xenophobia in Japan, 17, 135

Yamamoto, Takashi, 55
Yomiuri Shimbun, 104, 123
on Japan's immigration policy,
   29
on Japan's Indochinese refugee
   policy, 109–10, 111, 112–13
on nurse and caregivers, 84
Yoshida Doctrine, 100
Yoshii, Hidekatsu, 55

www.ingramcontent.com/pod-product-compliance
Lightning Source LLC
Chambersburg PA
CBHW030330270326
41926CB00010B/1572